# STAYING ATTACHED

## Systemic Thinking and Practice Series

*Charlotte Burck and Gwyn Daniel (Series Editors)*

This influential series was co-founded in 1989 by series editors David Campbell and Ros Draper to promote innovative applications of sys temic theory to psychotherapy, teaching, supervision, and organisational consultation. In 2011, Charlotte Burck and Gwyn Daniel became series editors, and aim to present new theoretical developments and pioneering practice, to make links with other theoretical approaches, and to promote the relevance of systemic theory to contemporary social and psychological questions.

### Other titles in the Series include

# STAYING ATTACHED

## Fathers and Children in Troubled Times

*Gill Gorell Barnes*

**KARNAC**

First published in 2018 by
Karnac Books Ltd
118 Finchley Road, London NW3 5HT

British Library Cataloguing in Publication Data

A C.I.P. for this book is available from the British Library

ISBN 978 1 78220 594 4


Edited, designed and produced by The Studio Publishing Services Ltd
www.publishingservicesuk.co.uk
email: studio@publishingservicesuk.co.uk


Printed in Great Britain by TJ International Ltd, Padstow, Cornwall


www.karnacbooks.com

# CONTENTS

# ACKNOWLEDGEMENTS

In addition to thanking my editors, Gwyn Daniel and Charlotte Burck, without whose friendship and encouragement the book would still be in one hundred and forty folders, I would like to thank the following people who helped me get started and keep going: Susan Fyvel for her patient reading and incisive comments, Rose Martin and Elizabeth Kyriakides for their work on the text, and Alan Cooklin for many discussions, his input on families and mental illness over the past fifteen years, and his assistance in making a complex text more simple.

*This book is dedicated to my father Jack and my son Chris;*
*and to the fathers of the future, the grandsons in the family:*
*Sam, Tom C-S, Dan, Joe, Nick, Tom C, Finbar, Milo, and Felix*

# ABOUT THE AUTHOR

**Gill Gorell Barnes**, MA MSc, has been working with children and families since the 1960s, first as a psychiatric social worker and subsequently as family and couples therapist, in both the Child and Family Department at the Tavistock Clinic and at the Institute of Family Therapy, which she co-founded with colleagues in the 1970s. As Training Director, she subsequently co-founded the Master's Degree in Systemic Family Therapy with Birkbeck College, London. The nature of her work has always reflected the changing nature of family life, including divorce, step-family living, single parent family living, and the growth of gay and lesbian family lifestyles.

Gill has written three books on working with families in social change, with a focus on multi-cultural family lives, and co-authored another five, as well as over fifty scholarly articles and chapters relating to working with families.

Gill has taught internationally since 1980, and specialises in keeping her teaching grounded in clinical practice. Her three research studies, on step-family living, on children's experience of going through divorce and post-divorce living, and her current writing about fathers are all related to clinical practice as well as to research.

In her civic work, Gill has been a Trustee of the Medical Foundation for Victims of Torture (now renamed Freedom from Torture) for twelve years, and was Trustee or chair of the Post Adoption Centre for ten years. She sits on a grant-giving charitable foundation, which keeps her in touch with current social issues relating to poverty and mental health in the UK today.

# SERIES EDITORS' FOREWORD

## Charlotte Burck and Gwyn Daniel

Fatherhood has always presented challenges of definition, since it mainly tends to be theoretically elaborated in relation to constructions of motherhood. As ideas about gender, about mothering, and about family have evolved and radically changed, so fathering has been brought into focus, which, in turn, has posed questions and dilemmas for both men and women. For this reason among others, this exciting book by Gill Gorell Barnes is extremely welcome. Here, she places fathers, with all their complexities, at the centre of her thinking and practice, thereby redressing their marginalisation by clinicians working with children and families and by family relationship theorists.

In this rich and comprehensive book, Gill invites us to share her extensive experience of working with fathers and their families over many years. First, she lays out the history and context of contemporary fatherhood in the UK before going on to explore the many meanings and issues of fathering in the families with which she has worked, as well as sharing her experience of her own father. As her title implies, Gill has particularly focused on, and is acutely sensitive to, the many dilemmas facing men and their families when they are living separately, needing to find ways of "doing family" across more than one household. She considers different contemporary family structures and multiple variations of relationship between fathers and children. She works with a range of social fatherhoods: fathers going through relationship transitions, non-live-in fathers, fathering in the context of acrimonious divorce, and fathers re-entering their children's lives after long absences.

The book is bursting with lively descriptions of family therapy at its best. The reader will find riveting accounts of Gill's skilled and nuanced clinical work. Her work is embedded in a framework that incorporates cultural and societal influences and draws upon a wide range of family therapy influences. She is a systemic therapist, accomplished at eliciting and holding complexities and moving between levels in her work. Her unique way of interweaving the pragmatic and concrete details of family life with meaning-making and emotional matters is illuminating and inspiring.

Gill demonstrates a fluidity in her therapeutic practice with an ability to move between different therapeutic positions to find creative ways of enabling different conversations between family members. At times, she explicitly elaborates systemic thinking with fathers and other members of their family. She sometimes incorporates "child developmental talk" which she and fathers together can consider with regard to their wish to connect more fruitfully with their children and which can free them from a polarised position in which they often seem trapped. Her tracking with fathers of micro interactions in their relationships with their children enables a focus on strengthening their abilities to tune into their children, bypassing their emphasis on rights and entitlements that has often left them disconnected. This is particularly helpful for many fathers brought up within patriarchal frameworks who struggle with changes in expectations and whose attempts to replicate patriarchal ideas can contribute to oppositional and troubled relationships with mothers and their children. Crucial here is Gill's validation of the men she works with as fathers with serious intent. Her ability to engage with their wishes for better relationships acts as a powerful driver in the therapy.

Gill breaks new and exciting ground in the ways that she invites children into increasingly bold questioning of their fathers, holding them to account for developing their relationships, while simultaneously supporting both children and fathers. There are lovely examples of Gill's conversations with individual children, bringing forth their moral positioning and puzzling over questions such as "What are

Dads for?" This direct work also challenges traditional ways of locating fathering as dependent on mothers. Gill tangles with the dilemmas of mothers who have given up on the need for fathers and ways that have informed children's own views of their fathers. She works with fathers to be tenacious in demonstrating that they do have something different to offer, instead of being consumed with rage about these "unfair" influences. This goes alongside her sessions with children that unpack the fragments of stories and small episodes that have sometimes constructed a "bad" father identity. This is therapeutic work that has frequently been interwoven with families' entanglement with lengthy court processes.

Gill addresses the additional complexities involved for families who are living separately when mothers or fathers experience depression and mental illness. Helping parents to step into each other's roles when needed and the particular ways in which fathers can be helped to manage this process has been a particular interest in Gill's clinical work and is elaborated in fascinating detail here.

We believe this book will become a landmark for clinicians working with families. Clinicians will find it a powerful provocation to "think fathers" in their work. The wide-ranging challenges facing fathers and children living separately when relationships have become fraught are considered alongside the many challenges for therapists working in this context. Therapists should discover ways to hold on to their confidence to persist with this often difficult work. The book provides many relevant ideas and stimulates important reflections for clinicians. Gill Gorell Barnes' book should ensure a place for fathers in family therapy that is long overdue.

## PREFACE

## Sebastian Kraemer

This is a monumental text. It encompasses half a century of practice, always—wherever located—a public service. It is inconceivable that Gill could do anything less. Neither could she work with clients in any context without being therapeutic. This is an effect that can also be shared by longstanding colleagues like me. If you have not met Gill in person, you will find her here. "I'd like to see Daddy. I'd like to talk to Daddy," says the child. "Shall we ring him now?" says Gill.

As a social worker in a 1960s children's department, Gill learnt to see families from the child's point of view. It was less than twenty years since the 1948 Children Act had encouraged social workers "to view children as individual human beings with both shared and individualised needs, rather than an indistinct mass". Yet, this enlightened view was soon to be swept aside by Seebohm reforms that diluted practice knowledge of children into a too-ambitious focus on families, now to be supported by generic social workers. Rather than abandon one position for the other, Gill combined both in what became her singular style of working therapeutically with parents and children, where her early experience is still evident decades later: "much of what we have to do with fathers requires a practical and educative stance in addition to a 'therapeutic' stance".

In her consultations with fathers, Gill locates the man emotionally suspended between his own childhood and his child. "Anxious, jealous and over possessive fathers may narrate stories of being locked in the 'coalhole'; having their heads put under the cold tap, made to eat out of the dog's bowl on the floor," She offers father a "culture-free science", showing him that "a child's brain is influenced by the environment into which he is growing". He learns that his child's brain has to be respected as much as his own, still reeling from the terror of the coalhole. He finds out from Gill that what a father does and says to his child when he is in a rage with the child's mother can affect the child for life, just as he was affected.

"Working with estranged fathers, I have found that talking in detail about their interactions with their children when they were very small, and taking an intensely child focused approach to their 'remembering' about their own childhoods, allows for rapid cognitive and emotional processing under the intensified lens of wishing to regain their relationships as parents to their children. Men who are so often reported as 'reluctant to engage' are very keen to engage in these circumstances".

Thus, the man learns something about the experiences of childhood, while retrieving a "memory of quarrelling voices" from his own. Instead of a reflex rebuke that "he's just a little devil", father now notices that his child "gets upset when the wife and I shout at each other".

This work, a distillation of decades of national leadership, scholarship, and practice in family therapy, is systemic social work of the highest order. It is informed by an attachment theory that has developed in parallel with Gill's own life, which she now shares with the reader. "Following a good principle of female sociology to work from the bottom up" she recalls her growing up:

> my network consisted of a fulltime working mother, a working father whose work life I often shared, a live in Irish "nanny/companion", a Greek grandmother and aunt whom I visited more than once a week, and an English granny with whom I spent much of my early years' school holidays. In spite of multiple kin care, I have no doubt that my mother "held me in mind", but each of them also held aspects of my "mind" in their minds, and in my professional thinking this wider knowledge is often not sufficiently taken into account either in

psychoanalytic thinking or in attachment theorising, or, indeed, in many developments of a systemic approach.

All theories fall under the critical gaze of this lifelong practitioner, holding the light of lived experience to them. Gill brings to her task a unique mix of a permissive childhood where all things seemed possible, a privileged education, immersion in the cultural revolutions of the 1960s and 1970s, a leading role in the first generation of British family therapists as trainer, conference presenter, and writer, and decades of intimate therapeutic contact with families in conflict. These families find themselves in the presence of someone fearless and eminent, yet without a trace of arrogance. With her clients, Gill is plain-speaking and practical; accepting what she finds yet determined to help change it so that children and parents can get on better—and more safely—with one another. Quite a presence.

> I have stepped into the remit on several occasions where a father had been accused of child neglect, sometimes supervising childcare at home where neglect was a contested issue, teaching a father how to keep children safe while cooking their tea, or making sure they were able to give a child a wash-down safely, without being accused of inappropriate touching, in addition to thinking about wider safety issues in the home or the street.

Besides coaching the father, Gill puts herself in the place of the besieged child caught between feuding parents. Mother says, "He's trying to label me mentally ill again. I haven't got mental illness." Father says, "You see and hear one thing, I recollect another." Gill writes, "this interview showed me how this couple had the capacity to drive each other into a state from which there is no returning to a middle collaborative position. I commented on this, and on the confusing effect of our conversation on my own mind". Here, she is suggesting that their daughter refuses to take part in family life precisely because she does not want to be in this disturbing place between the parents, which Gill is occupying now. How often mental illness is invoked, yet family consultations reveal the breakdown that is between parents, rather than in one or the other. By temporarily experiencing and reporting on it, Gill shows them, there and then, what they do to their child.

Here you can see the product of years of experience with children in families, but also of having worked in places where there are child psychotherapists as colleagues:

> He showed me a puppet he had made with strong legs for walking "a long way". I said he had a lot to deal with in his young life and had needed his strong legs, and I congratulated him on all he had done and been through. He said, "Sometimes I am like a young man and sometimes I like to be a baby as well".

I think another source of Gill's intuitive understanding of unconscious family process could be more openly acknowledged. What is it about fathers that makes them so important to children? It is not always an attachment, but it must be an idea. Children know how they were made. Whatever the facts and present circumstances, in the child's mind there is a sexual relationship that is both fundamental to her existence but from which, at the same time, she is excluded (Kraemer, 2017). A psychoanalytical formulation is entirely consistent with systemic, developmental, anthropological, and sociological discourses, and is recognisable in this simple and poetic observation: "One continued experience I have had in much of the clinical work described in this book is that the father is not held in mother's mind in any ways that can be of value to the child".

*Staying Attached: Fathers and Children in Troubled Times* is, in many respects, a report from a war zone. Gill describes being screamed at by a persecuted father who could not allow her to express a view at odds with his own. Her courage in keeping her head under that kind of fire is evident. The capacity to tolerate being the bad object is fundamental to the analytic process. Therapeutic neutrality means holding on to your own mind while straining to acknowledge the value of another's. As Gill says, this comes first from "wider knowledge" in one's own development. Working as a nine-year-old in her father's Soho café, "I was taught to greet all around me with respect and make and serve coffee as well as I could. This gave me a security in the world which has never left me".

# Speaking up for fathers

This book is a tribute to the many committed and involved fathers I have worked with over the past forty years, fathers who have contributed to my thinking about what it takes to go on being a dad when the going gets tough. The caring by these fathers, in the context of mothers suffering from long-term physical illness or major mental illness, was outside the "normal" parameters of what was expected of men as fathers in the decades that followed the Second World War, so that they were challenging norms of what was laid down as expected male behaviour at that time. My father was the starting point for stories of unorthodox masculinity in my own life. Additionally, the book focuses on fathers whose relationships with their children were in trouble, in the context of working with them in child and family mental health settings as well as alongside the family court, where they were struggling to maintain or regain relationships with their children. It could often be seen that fathers were not keeping up with mothers' wishes and expectations of them and, in some situations, had become marginalised and were in danger of disappearing from their children's lives. Why was this happening and how had they arrived in these complex, troubled, oppositional situations? Solicitors, often stuck for a way forward, were looking for some therapeutic intervention on behalf of their clients into family systems that had reorganised without them and often against them. While a new job description for father-hood was clearly needed for many of these men, there was little discussion about this and such an idea was very slow to develop in any public forum. In relation to this work, I have asked many ques-tions about father's visions of their own role in their children's lives and included ideas and accounts of how fathers, over my lifetime, have now largely become repositioned in public and private thinking about family life.

Throughout the book, I have paid attention to some of the impacts of extreme emotional distress which co-exist on a continuum with many forms of mental disturbance, and which can affect both moth-ers and fathers. Stress-related illnesses have an impact on fathers, and have been part of my clinical concern, whether with couples or with fathers living alone, as well as in relation to making decisions around the lives of children. In the family court context, I also worked with the families of mothers who no longer saw their children, in each case for reasons attributed to their own mental illness, which had domi-nated their children's early lives. In these cases, fathers had become primary carers very soon after birth. The book pays particular atten-tion to mental health difficulties, and ongoing mental illness, which is often unaddressed as a component in the lives of families in main-stream social family research. It also remains largely neglected in family therapy theory and training. The ways in which mental ill-health can complicate the lives of all members of a family, so that the ideal relationship a father might wish to have with his children has to be re-positioned in the light of changing rhythms of mental distur-bance, is revisited as a subject in different chapters.

Many men present with extreme forms of behaviour that can include failure to connect to others' feelings, often a lack of awareness about themselves, and sometimes accompanied by violent responses towards others. What can move someone between extreme emotional distress, on the one hand, and mental illness, on the other, how these two states of being are defined and categorised for any one individ-ual, and how this affects the work we do in particular contexts of chil-dren and families, is a question that always remains open to scrutiny. In general, fathers who manifest high levels of poorly regulated emo-tion, leading to attitudes perceived by others as irrational, are unlikely to be seen as being in need of therapeutic services unless they can attract a defined diagnosis of a major mental illness (McLean et al., 2002). States of intense distress and "mental illness", defined and undefined, are, in principle, thought of throughout the book as being on a continuum, and are further discussed in the chapters that follow.

## Gender equality in parenting practices: doing "male" and "female" in the post-war decades

Although, in North European societies, we now have, as part of mainstream social narratives about the family, models of fatherhood which subscribe to gender equality in relation to responsibility for children, the way fatherhoods are, in reality, played out shows widely differing performances. These differences are practised both within and between diverse cultural groups, and include a wide range of fatherhoods lived and carried out away from the child's daily home with her mother. Following the Second World War, the shared ideologies of cohesive family life and ways of "doing male and female" in families in the UK were more commonly defined by work structures and associated "accepted" definitions of class than is now the case. There might never have been a single framework for marriage and family life to which women subscribed, but researched descriptions of family life showed more homogeneity than would be the case now, and little was researched or written-outside the context of war itself-about children's relationships with fathers who did not live with them. Following two World Wars, ideologies constructed around recreating a secure society in the UK, as described and defined by sociologists and journalists of the time, are discussed briefly in Chapter One. New arrangements of gender and sexuality, and associated practices around responsibility for children, continue to change the shape and definition of what might be recognised and socially allowed as "family", which is touched on throughout the book.

## Fathers on the margins of family lives: 1975–2015

Since 1945, family configurations and roles within families have been in continual change. Some fathers described in this book (from 1975 onwards) have never lived with the mothers of their children, while some have co-habited but ceased to live in the family home, separating early in the lives of their infants or toddlers. Some have married and divorced and are struggling to develop new ways of maintaining meaningful relationships with their children in the context of ongoing hostility. Many of these men were experiencing competition or conflict with other men who were "social" fathers to their children, whether live-in partnerships, or married "step fathers", to whom mothers had subsequently given preference in the role of father. In these diverse contexts, many conflicts of interest between mothers and fathers can be generated, not only about how the bringing up of children is to take place, but also over whether a father can have a serious place in his child's life at all. Further complexity was stirred up by many fathers who continued to have assumptions about "patriarchal" rights, beliefs that usually belie the reality of the way the families they are part of actually think about family life. The positions to which men might become relegated by their families, which have become primarily constructed around women and children and outside which fathers have to struggle to redefine their own relevance and importance in their children's lives, has been my particular interest, working alongside solicitors and the family courts since the 1990s.

### Fathers' invisibility within the professional "gaze": why are fathers left out of personal and professional thinking? Findings from research

Fathers are often the less visible members of family households, and may frequently live separately from their children. As an "entity", their needs have been, and remain, relatively neglected by the mental health and therapeutic services. Walters (2011) in her book on working with fathers in the child and family mental health service described this as both extraordinary and sad, given the rapid changes in the roles of fathers in the previous twenty years. Many fathers, both in and out of families, struggle with prolonged, and sometimes severe, states of mental illness or depression for which there is, in reality, no service provision (and themselves often generate unsympathetic discussion from professionals). A study of views about fathers in social work offices found that they were mainly given a negative press and that there were few discourses around fathers which were positive (Scourfield, 2006). Fathers often do not fit current diagnostic priorities and the type of services available rarely meet their social and emotional needs. Furthermore, qualitative research has shown that fathers have been seen to be neglected by professionals working with families, including within the field of systemic family therapy (Smith, 2011). At the same time, contemporary research from studies of families that focus on parenting programmes has shown that including fathers in thinking about family, and working with them alongside mothers and children, whether or not they live in the same households, increases both the likely long-term involvement of these fathers with their children and increases the support they give to the mothers (Matta & Knudson-Martin, 2006).

Other work additionally found that the competence of "high risk" fathers with their children increased, in direct relationship to their capacity to work closely within the framework offered by the child's mother (Ngu & Florsheim, 2011). Where a mother is demoralised or depressed following a child's birth, including fathers in the thinking about the children can also increase a mother's involvement in positive ways (Vik & Hafting, 2009). Yet, a recent overview of many thousands of family interventions worldwide has found that fathers are still largely ignored by parenting programmes (Panter Brick and Leckman, 2013). Family intervention programmes rarely evaluate their own impact on *both* parents: impacts such as co-parenting quality, overall family functioning, depression, or stress within either parent. This omission is likely to be partly due to the ongoing shifts and influences between often rapidly changing cultures that do not fit easily into pre-planned research formulations. However, in my view, the omission might also reflect a wider social difficulty in thinking about whether there is a distinctive role that fathers have in family life, and a lack of commitment at higher organisational levels to create changes in working patterns and working hours, both for fathers who are clients and fathers who are professionals.

## *Working with fathers in the UK over fifty years*

What is my own interest in fathers and their special place in the lives of children? During my clinical work with fathers over half a century, I have seen many changes in the expectations held of them between different generations and within diverse family groups of different cultures and ethnicities. My direct work with fathers has been mainly limited to the multi-cultural contexts of the UK, although I have also worked with families in Greece, in Singapore and Hong Kong, mainland China, and in Russia. In my early family therapy days (1968–1972) working at Woodberry Down Child Guidance Clinic (as it was then known) in Hackney, under the clinical directorship of Robin Skynner, there was an emphasis on whole family work and the inclusion of fathers wherever possible in all families seen in the clinical service (Gorell Barnes, 2011). While the families in our geographical catchment area were predominantly white working-class and Caribbean families who had only recently arrived in the UK, the area also included a small number of Nigerian families, who were mainly in the UK to study. The range of ways of "doing father" in the Nigerian families included fathers who were absent from their children's lives for many months at a time, moving between Nigeria and the UK, yet who, it seemed, did not lose their own idea of fatherhood, or their identity as fathers, and neither were they devalued by mothers and children. Caribbean fathers, on the other hand, were often seen by their mothers, partners, and sisters to have a more tenuous identity as fathers, and were frequently less valued as part of the ongoing child-rearing structure (Arnold, 2012). Caribbean parents, at that time, suffered from the lack in this country of grandparental and other kinship networks that would normally have cared for the children. However, the older generation had generally stayed in the Caribbean to care for the children "back home" while the parental generation came to this country both as economic providers and ambassadors for possible new lives.

Further family variations also included the cultural mix which constituted part of my own background: European families from Greece and Cyprus, as well as Turkey, who bordered "cultures" of Western and Eastern Europe and whose "cultural difference" was harder to take conscious account of in my work because it was so familiar to me in life (Gorell Barnes, 2002). Earlier, in the 1960s, I had worked in Islington Children's Department, the precursor of modern children's services, doing family work of all kinds, with a similar mix of families from different ethnicities. This work included assessing and supervising foster placements, adoption assessment, supervising day care "child minding" placements, and providing support to fathers of all cultures when a mother was ill or admitted to hospital and other relatives were not available. Like Jennifer Walters, whose book *Working with Fathers* was published shortly before I started work on this one, I have "repeatedly been struck by men's love for their children and their desire to participate in family life" (Walters, 2011, p. 83). My own early experience with my father, described in Chapter One, was an inner guide to believing in the potential nurturing capacity of men when a context for the legitimised expression of nurture became socially available. I use the word "legitimised" deliberately, as I believe there have been many social distortions in the development of men's emotionality, some of which are discussed in the chapters that follow.

## *Fathers at the centre and fathers on the margins: personal research studies*

My own professional interest in developing the subject of working with disenfranchised fathers developed further in the context of two earlier research and clinical studies: the first looking at the experiences of young people who grew up in step-families (Gorell Barnes et al., 1998), and learning from their narratives about both fathers and stepfathers in the 1970s and 1980s. The second study was carried out in the context of a project on children and parents going through separation and divorce in the child and family department of the Tavistock Clinic in the 1990s (Dowling & Gorell Barnes, 1999). Subsequently, a colleague, Mary Bratley, and I interviewed twenty fathers who were the primary carers for their children (Gorell Barnes & Bratley, 2000, unpublished). The study was not finished due to unexpected illness and death in the families of both researchers. However, I have drawn on some of those interviews to illustrate fathers' enjoyment of bringing up their children in spite of complex and adverse circumstances which led to major adaptations in their own lives. Their narratives of the daily experiences of managing lives as primary carers for their children, sometimes in the context of a former partner who had, and continued to have, a major mental illness, offered varied thoughts and multiple options on how "family life" (offering nurture to, and taking responsibility for, children) can be maintained. I have continued to work intensively with fathers following marital or partnership separation and re-marriage problems, in addition to fathers living through family changes as a result of mental illnesses in partners or children (involving some 120 fathers altogether).

## Key contemporary studies

The book draws mainly on my clinical and court work experience, with a background of key contemporary studies from the large social science literature on fathers and families. To cite all this work would not be possible, but there are special thanks to *Intimate Fatherhood* (Dermott, 2008), *Researching Intimacy in Families* (Gabb, 2010), and from the socio-legal angle, *Fragmenting Fatherhood* (Collier & Sheldon, 2008). In addition, I have referenced studies from the past decade focusing on men, challenging stereotypes in gendered roles, *Do Men Mother?* (Doucet, 2006), and the work on *Contemporary Fathering* (Featherstone, 2009). The dedicated research by Michael Lamb is a necessary companion to writing anything on fathers and will be referenced in later chapters. Earlier work from the 1980s (*Re-assessing Fatherhood*, Lewis & O'Brien, 1987) and 1990s (*Children in Families*, Brannen & O'Brien, 1996; "Fathers and fatherhood in Britain", Burghes et al., 1997) took the form of research studies and reflections to which I have often turned, and which influenced my clinical thinking throughout that period and onwards.

## Interdisciplinary influences on clinical work over time: multiple contributions to a systemic approach

My own clinical work has drawn widely on four main fields outside the schools of systemic therapy itself. Each of these has contributed to the ongoing construction of a personal systemic framework.

1.  Social research into families and the effect of social policy on families; the intersection of the public and the private.
2.  Child development research in different social contexts,
3.  Psychodynamic relational understanding extended through twenty-five years working at the Tavistock Clinic, given a complementary framework of attachment theory by John Bowlby, whose

attachment research from the 1970s onwards influenced my thinking. In my own mind, the added lens of being a working woman, as well as a different cultural lens from Dr Bowlby regarding the value of wider kin care for any single child, brought additional questions to the focus of the mother–child attachment frame.

4.    An earlier and continuing influence which brought together the three areas above within a wider systemic framework was ethology (or the patterning of relationship structures within animal as well as human living systems). This started as a child when I read Konrad Lorenz's early studies (1952) and continued in the 1970s through the reading not only of Gregory Bateson, but of his nephew P. P. G. Bateson (1976) and colleague Robert Hinde (1979). My later friendship with Patricia Minuchin, a developmental psychologist, brought together through her own writing and connections further reading of attachment theory within the wider frame of ethology (Hinde & Stevenson Hinde, 1988; Minuchin, 1988).

Recently, neurobiology has further contributed to my understanding of particular developmental difficulties and how these can intersect with relational complexities in family struggles, and has again drawn attention back to wider social contexts and the impact these can have on individuals and the internal effects of social stress. The book draws on these diverse but intersecting frames and puts them together within a systemic approach that addresses them at the levels of individual and family. This makes sense for clinical work with fathers finding and maintaining relationships with children in difficult circumstances

## *Idiosyncratic threads that help fathers hang into therapeutic work*

Although what follows is not a manual or detailed guide to practice, I have tried to draw out aspects of my work with fathers which I believe have made it more possible for them to pick their way through tangles of troubled family relationships, regain threads of connection, and, when they persevere, scaffold more secure relationships with their children. These include the following.

1.  A recognition of their often passionate feelings about children, frequently a depth of emotion not formerly discovered through previous partner relationship experience.
2,  Drawing on an approach that is educative about child development and child care.
3.  Describing openly a systemic framework that takes into account and discusses mutual influence in family relationships.
4.  Collaborative conversations, thinking with fathers about their own life experiences and the intergenerational influences on these, as well as the larger social discourses that have a bearing on their views about, and practices of, fatherhood.
5.  Using a sense of humour as part of communal reflection on life's mistakes, life dilemmas and pitfalls, and the ways that we try to overcome them. Often, the work with a particular father and family has been long term, sometimes more than two years, through provision made by both County Court and High Court judges for family conflict cases of exceptional complexity. My thirty-five years of independent practice has allowed for consultations with fathers over long periods, sometimes ten years or more. These three settings of the National Health Service (NHS), of family courts, and independent practice have allowed me the richness of working across boundaries of class and ethnicity. I have always been vigilant about the nuances of cultural difference, though sometimes making wrong assumptions that have got me into trouble. I have been able to work with fathers from a diverse range of social and employment settings, from penal institutions to lawyers, businessmen, and entrepreneurs to fathers dependent on welfare, government and NHS employees, doctors and clergy, as well as a range of therapeutic practitioners and healers.

Unlike social research, which focuses on what specific groups of fathers have *achieved*, this book addresses some of the relational struggles that co-exist with the potential for both the achievement and the failure of good relations with children for men of different classes and cultures, within wider contexts of their families. It considers how

professionals can help with processes of mediating emotional difficulties between fathers, partners, and their children. This can take the
form of modifying their "wished for" and sometimes unrealistic
fantasies about relationships between fathers and children towards
more solid emotional territory, embedding them in realities which are
smaller than the fantasies, but which can grow and develop their own
momentum. It draws on "local knowledges" (Geertz, 1983) developed
on a case-by-case basis with fathers, whose own subjective experience
I might have shared over periods of between two and ten years. I also
take aggregated knowledge into account, reflecting settings in which
performances of "father" have been required by others: by mothers,
by children, by ex-wives, by kinship networks, and by the courts. In
these different settings, I try to look at those specificities of the meaning of "father" that is being "sought" in any particular family, and by
the different individuals within it.

## Following the decline of patriarchy, how does a father think about his role?

Once the securities of "patriarchy" were dislodged during the second
half of the past century, which is discussed in Chapters One and
Three, a puzzle for many fathers became how to position themselves
within a family. This involved different dilemmas in different cultures.
There is no single father role to which all fathers should aspire. A
successful father, as defined in terms of his children's development, is
one who finds the right fit between the demands and prescriptions of
his own social and cultural context and his own interpretation of these
in terms of love and responsibility within which his children can
thrive. In our family practice, the urgent need to redress the balance
between men and women in the direction of women's empowerment
might have led to some lacunae in our own thinking as professionals
about concurrent developing dilemmas for fathers around "how to be
a father". Most women taking on feminist ideas in the 1960s and 1970s
believed men should be responsible for their own thinking. This
necessary neglect by women ignored the "perturbations" urgently
needed in men's thinking at that time to allow for more rapid and
positive changes to occur, if fathers were to "keep up" in relation to
changing ideas about fatherhood, contemporary to each decade.

Current research shows that families can thrive well with and without fathers, which further complicates thinking for men about "father and family". However, fathers themselves might not thrive without their families, particularly when they are excluded from the lives of their children, and this recognition entered the field at a later date, when research on men's health in response to post divorce living began to emerge (Hetherington, 1989). Not to think "about" fathers and their changing positions in families, as well as "thinking with" them, seems to me now to be unsystemic. That is with the reflective capacity of hindsight, rather than the anger of an earlier time, and the associated vigour for women of "getting on with it". For a professional as well as for a family, it can become a habit not to think about the possible effects of ignoring one part of the "circuits of relationship" in which a child grows. Following the increased social freedom to divorce, as well as to create families without marriage at all, there was a failure to think about the changing relational processes resulting from break-away and the development of new systems. Thinking about family continued along former paths, in too many habitual ways. Habit, as Bateson delineated it, is a major economy of conscious thought, but might be an economy carried out at a price (Bateson, 1973c). When fathering becomes "tokenised", and acts of "performing fatherhood" are disconnected from the changing emotional and intellectual matrix of the child's mind, it becomes difficult for the child to think about "family as a whole" and a father's part in it. Separated fathers suffer from this.

Throughout this book, I do not think about the "performance of fatherhood" as a universal constant in pattern, shape, and practices throughout any child's life. It is the recognition and witnessing of the changing nature of what a family requires of a father within the life-time of one or two generations, which long-term clinical work can offer, that fleshes out sociological analysis of fatherhood. What fathering entails can vary in detail within the life of one man; it is a constant work in progress. A person's understanding of their own intimate life, and the sets of relationships within which their own execution of the role of father has been constructed, can dramatically change from year to year, and even from week to week.

# CHAPTER ONE

# The changing social context for fathering in the United Kingdom in my lifetime: the family and fathers remembered following the Second World War

## Men, women, work, family, and babies

Following the end of the Second World War, family life had to reorganise around the inclusion of fathers returning from the world of combat. Contemporary studies of the family did not include any difficulties this reinstatement had involved, and also ignored variations in gendered family practices—ways that men and women might have behaved within the privacy of the family that were different from roles publically assigned for "mother" and for "father". Idiosyncratic contradictions that might have been tolerated and even enjoyed in family life in the 1950s were not reported, so that how fathers "behaved" in families is recorded under broad research agreements on how family life was put together: the domain of sociology *vs.* the idiosyncratic and anecdotal interpretations of how this was actually have lived (more the domain of diaries, biography, comedy, popular songs, and seaside postcard jokes (Orwell, 1941)). The larger institutionalised construction of family, with a preferred frame of two parents, is our official version of family life (Mogey, 1956; Young & Wilmot, 1957).

The 1950s and the 1960s marked the rise of "maternal" pre-eminence (Bowlby, 1951). Women were urged to prioritise looking after their babies over working outside the home. This emphasis on childcare was in part to compensate for the retreat of women from the marketplace, encouraged in order to allow men back into the labour forces at the necessary level after the war. Anecdotally referenced by Grace Robertson, who herself went on to become a world-famous photographer, was the gratitude and guilt women felt towards the men who had fought and won a terrible war and

> not wanting to steal their work . . . you couldn't avoid the men who had been hurt in the war: they were everywhere, blind or scarred, on crutches or in wheelchairs. This made women less voluble on the subject of equality than they might otherwise have been . . . I could no more have thought of feminism in the face of what I could see in the streets than I could have flown to the moon. It would have been indecent as far as I was concerned. (Robertson, quoted in Cooke, 2013, p. xix)

The primary role consigned to women, to have babies, also marked the significance given to re-populating a society decimated by war through bombing and loss of civilians as well as loss of fighting men: "the chief means of fulfilment in life is to be a member of and reproduce a family" (Oakley, 2014). During the Second World War, men had been distanced from the daily experience of their families and in the immediate post-war period of re-entry and accommodation into family life their role as breadwinner was privileged. A father's role was socially defined as "the economic provider and the emotional support of mother" (Bowlby, 1953, p 15).

## Creating homes for families: public policy and private life

Standards of living for families as a whole improved in the context of massive rebuilding programmes following the bombing and destruction of civilian life in some of the major cities in the UK (Imperial War Museum London Blitz Archives), creating new possibilities for family living. The population of Britain at every social level had been shocked to discover the quality of life many families had suffered in pre-war housing, and there was a national wish to give families of all social classes the opportunity for a better quality of life. A further emphasis on the importance of motherhood as an activity arose from public recognition of the deprivations experienced by children during the war, both within their homes through bombing and as a result of evacuation, an attempt to avoid the effects of bombing on children. Evacuation itself had opened up wider public awareness of the poverty and associated poor nutrition and health standards within which many children were raised, creating a public momentum for social change. There was a "spirit of hope" pushing forward the legislations of the Welfare State—health, housing, and benefits all being proposed as part of a better quality of life. The importance of the well-being and connectedness of people throughout the country was a new social recognition, and became a post-war principle of shared belief embodied in the early post-war construction of the Welfare State "a place where young people, besieged for six years of war could finally feel they had a future. You could fairly feel the rush of air as they raced forward to greet it" (Dundy, quoted in Cooke, 2013, p. xv). In the early 1950s, rationing ended, economic policy showed growth, and there were higher wages. Numbers of babies could be controlled through increased use of birth control (but within marriage only; at that time, contraception was provided only if a woman produced a marriage certificate). These were all factors contributing to pleasanter homes, husbands more at home, shared activities such as radio listening and, subsequently, watching television, more participation in family life, a move towards the modern "involved" dad and, though not yet realised, the father as co-parent.

## Fathers in family life following the Second World War: glimpses of gender and role

Lamb (2013), the foremost researcher on fathers' roles in family life, confirms that social scientists of the 1940s and 1950s did not study fathers. In the aftermath of war, little was recorded about how meaningful emotional and psychological relationships were formed by and with fathers. Unusual performances of "father" in daily life, therefore, falls to those of us who remember these from our own lives to supplement what research studies describe. A vignette of my own family variations follows below. Fathering, like mothering, involves the repetitive enactment of patterns of daily care and the distribution of these among family members depending on their age, gender, and competence: feeding the family, doing the laundry, paying the bills, management of children's lives, problem-solving, boundary-keeping, regulation of emotions, homework assistance, stress management, demonstration of affection and aggression at expected and unexpected times. Patterns of family "chores" as well as emotional and relational life for fathers in families are unlikely to have been organised in any single manner.

Women sociologists of the time dismissed the "romanticised" stereotyped picture emerging (from the male sociologists of the 1950s) of the large, three-generation, gender-divided, working-class family. Oakley noted how Gavron, the first woman and feminist sociologist to address similar terrain in the UK, considered men's and women's particular experience in her analysis. Gavron's accounts of family life differed from other pictures painted of fathers by showing how small numbers of men were actively entering the domain of hands-on fathering (over five per cent doing "anything or everything" and a further twenty-seven per cent doing most things except nappies (Gavron, 1966, cited in Oakley, 2014). The Newson studies (conducted by a married couple, thus including perspectives from both genders) concurred that men were playing a larger part in family life, with thirty per cent of fathers of one-year-old's putting their children to bed and over eighty per cent playing with them regularly. Their study shows differences related to social class, with more involvement from fathers higher up the class scales of their time. Their population was not in London, but in Nottingham, and social, gender, and family norms were likely to have been differently constructed relating to the labour practices of their population (Newson & Newson, 1963). The research field of sociology, and, therefore, the subjects studied, was itself tightly controlled by men, including a patriarchal stance held at the London School of Economics. This is likely to have affected what could be investigated and recorded in relation to changing patterns in family life and controlled research into gender and change itself (Gavron, 2015; Oakley 2014).

Female strength was acknowledged in the reporting of family life in the UK, but not complemented by knowledge of men's changing behaviours in the family. In the 1960s and the decades that followed, rates of maternal employment amplified, with the growth of industries that were machine or technology led and offered new, as well as part-time, employment for women. So also did the growth of commerce and administration, catering, and the service industries, providing further work for women compatible with family life. The expansion of teaching, nursing, and social services also provided opportunities for women, like myself, to train and work in professions approved by the contemporary male "gaze" as non-threatening. Attitudes were changing between generations. The increase in the employment of married women naturally had an effect on married relationships, as many wives were now released from complete financial dependence on their husbands. Therefore, they became freer to think for themselves, exchange ideas with other women in the workplace, and express different opinions at home (Gorell Barnes, 1990). The high wages that school leavers were able to obtain gave sons and daughters more financial independence from their parents, and the establishment of the Welfare State—in particular the National Health Service—now offered services for those events in life for which parents were once the only source of help and advice. The "family" moved towards becoming a collective of thinking individuals, in many cases with attendant anxieties about role, power, and new gendered freedoms. By the 1990s, fifty-nine per cent of mothers were working; a decade later, seventy per cent of married mothers were working, the hours depending on the age of their children (Brannen et al., 1997).

## Family patterns and men's social experience

The social and emotional positions through which boys work towards becoming fathers have always been diverse, affected by wartime or peacetime, by ethnicity, culture, class, family composition, and by idiosyncratic experience. Shared male cultural experience runs in parallel with individual development: schools, religious venues, playgrounds, sports changing rooms, "hanging out" spaces such as teenage bedrooms, music venues, clubs and gangs, coffee bars, workplace canteens, as well as pubs. Shared "cultural" input from radio and, after the 1950s, television is now overtaken by social media and multiple cultural choices. Until 1963, there was also the powerful collective experience for men of doing National Service—two years in one of the armed forces or work associated with defence. War, and men as fighters of war and "protectors of women and children", remained a powerful aspect of respected masculinity into the mid-1960s and continued to influence ideas about fatherhood. The job of becoming a father, and developing any parity as a parent, remained secondary to what was required of men in life outside the home, an ideology also subscribed to by many women. This further contributed to the elevated positions of "authority" often accorded to men across a wide number of social domains. The research ideology and premises about how family life should be conducted also remained within this framework, promoting the peacetime ideal of cohesion, rather than looking at differences in family life.

In addition, how might a father's beliefs about his role in his child's life have been affected by contemporary wider economic systems? Fatherhood roles in the 1950s and 1960s were strongly related to the requirements of production, and the expectations held of men in the workplace, which "excluded men from the home as effectively as they held women to it" (Lummis, 1982). A father's beliefs about father-hood were primarily linked to current traditions related to labour. The structures of many industries and their particular disciplines in differ-ent parts of the UK were strongly associated with how family life was run.

### How do men develop their ideas about fathering from their families as well as society?

Walters (2011), in her research, found that where fathers had experi-enced closeness to their own fathers, they were more likely to be participatory with their own children. However, clinical work, as well as non-clinical interviews with fathers, suggest that when a father has had a bad fathering experience himself, good enough care from other relatives can mitigate the effects of this and he could strive to achieve a better relationship with his own children than his father had with him. He might also feel freer to try out better practices. As Sam, who is bringing up his daughter as primary parent said,

> "My dad was virtually never home . . . barely at home, used to beat us frequently. What can I say about my dad, I think my dad was awful. My dad was awful, you know, but you still love him don't you . . . he

was just . . . I think my dad taught me the dangers of excessive masculinisation very early. I just looked at it even as a kid. This is weird . . . this is not right . . ." (Gorell Barnes & Bratley, 2000)

Quality of fathering alone might be less significant in influencing a father's determination to become a hands-on parent than wider family experience of being nurtured by mothers, sisters, elder brothers, uncles, and grandfathers. Recent websites (e.g., Fatherhood Institute, 2012) now offer forums where men can explore questions about what makes a "good enough" father with other fathers and offer practical advice and models of practice (Cabrera et al., 2000), However, this was unavailable to the fathers discussed later in this book, who relied mainly on male relatives and friendship groups as well as their "mum" to instigate better fathering.

### Social discourses and individual narratives: male and female power—multiple intersections

Men still continue to hold the larger political and economic power in the UK, still dominating the institutions of government, judicial, and military systems and the world of international business. However, the population of men and women is now moving to women in the majority (51% in the UK in 2015), and there has been an increase in women gaining larger percentages of the intake into professional trainings in the old as well as the new universities. The former organisation of gender balance within larger social systems has the potential to be in rapid disequilibrium in the next half century, in spite of male resurgences of power in different parts of the world. Many schools, particularly public schools, have formerly contributed to rigidified ideas of masculinity and fatherhood through their attitudes to growing boys. They have traditionally reinforced distance from femininity, and paradoxically created idealisation of it, dependence on it, and disrespect for it (Burck & Daniel, 1995). This has had the power to shape and restrict men's tenderness and their capacity for intimacy, and to form emotional connections with others close to them. With the increase of co-education in all sectors of education within the UK, girls' influence will have more ongoing impact on these former arrangements of power and intimacy in the future, despite the chauvinist backlash that many girls are experiencing in schools and on line. Men's capacity for intimacy will change. The patterns that still affect the majority of men over fifty who are currently fathers are now largely in flux for those under forty.

While recognising the reality of men's power, I have chosen, for diverse reasons, to take a position in my work with fathers estranged from their children that also considers men's emotional disadvantage. This is often shaped by the same social and economic processes that gave them power in more public domains. When power is moved from one domain to another, from public to private, to contexts constructed around intimacy and caring, some men might not understand the basic principles of the systemic change involved and find themselves on the margins of family life. How can we usefully harness the complementary power of women on men's behalf? While changes in fatherhood have inevitably been linked to changes in motherhood, the wider changes and growth in women's power in the world outside the home demand further and more rapid changes of men within the domain of family life—changes for which they have often been unprepared, and have sometimes been unwilling to make.

## What is a father for, and who decides? Changing social discourses

The expectations of a father within the home have changed over the past fifty years from being the "mother's part-time helper" of the 1960s to becoming the "co-parent" of the twenty-first century. However, there remain many fathers who have themselves not been raised to share household and childcare tasks in a responsible manner. They are often taken by surprise at the powerful impact of the emotional tasks involved in day-to-day child rearing. Changes in the collective social consciousness about gender, power, and men's roles in the UK and Europe in the past twenty years have left many contemporary fathers behind in an assortment of troubled contexts. They are often ill equipped to respond to the wider de-construction of old style patriarchy, but choose to fall back on its rhetoric when challenged to perform differently in family life. The introduction of greater shared paternity leave in 2015 (Paternity Leave Policy, 2015) offered further opportunity to change this frame; but there are many reasons, primarily led by the economics and pressures of workplaces, which have militated against change (Jacobs, 2016). Becoming a real dad is less likely to be regarded as an optional "add on" in a father's life now, and more likely to be a requirement from mothers and from children demanding involvement and responsibility.

## Gay fathers

With the legal recognition of same-sex marriage coming into force in March 2014, the primary structural family feature of "institutionalised patriarchy"—father as head of the heterosexual and legally privileged form of family—became invalid. While heterosexual family life remains the predominant form of family, it is no longer exclusive in law. This can further free fathers to "invent" fatherhood forms and expand definitions of family in multiple ways, as gay fatherhood has shown. Inevitably, as male partners are having their own children, there will also be dramatic changes in the range of motherhoods. Some aspects of this are touched on further in Chapter Eight.

## Fatherhood following breakup: children as players in the definitions of what a father should be

Following partnership breakup, changes in fatherhood also need to develop congruence with children's wishes. An influence that men often do not face until they have to do so is the power their own children carry to shape the way they will perform fatherhood. This scrutiny and questioning by children has meant that many fathers can no longer expect that formerly held assumptions about the nature and status of being a father can be taken for granted. Following a separation from a mother which he has initiated himself, a man's children will be especially unlikely to subscribe to any ideas he might have about "rights" or respect "due to him as a father". This will be particularly true if the children have no understanding of why he left and of his chosen way of life away from them and their mothers. Even where a father is secure in the knowledge of his own biological parenthood, other men are often preferred as social father by a mother. Social fathers will often form an equally strong attachment to the child if they are actively involved in co-parenting with the children's mother. The more we go into the texture of what a father is "for", the more we recognise how strategically mothers might re-position themselves on behalf of children and family life. This can involve choosing partners whom they regard as more suitable for social fatherhood, relying on their own family and friends, or preferring to "go it alone" rather than sustain the uncertainty of relationship with former "unsatisfactory" partners.

## Non-traditional fatherhood

I have always been interested in the use of the term "non-traditional fatherhoods", presuming, as it did, that there was a "traditional" fatherhood against which other models of "doing father" were to be measured. As noted above, the parental features specific to fathering (other than relations of power and control) were given little attention by early post-war family research. Lamb himself became responsible for much of the research documenting child development in contexts then named "non-traditional" because they did not reflect the demographic characteristics of the traditional families on which contemporary social scientists had largely focused (Lamb, 1999, 2013). One large, under-researched group which itself was "traditional", but not studied, includes the fathers reared in fatherless families following the First World War. This includes my own father. In the 1990s, Lamb published numerous studies on changes in fatherhood in the contexts of changing patterns of marriage, co-habitation, and partnership separation (Lamb, 1999; Lewis & Lamb, 2005). The chapters that follow illustrate aspects of these changes. As clinical practitioners, we are always, in addition, potential pioneers in small-scale research. We enquire about the idiosyncratic way that each family has constructed itself, and record these differences to broaden our historical knowledge of diversity in family forms and behaviours. We are likely to see variations of family that are more diverse than research frameworks are often able to encompass, including hidden "femininities" emerging in the private discourses of men, shown in family life but undeclared to social researchers.

## *My own experience of non-traditional fatherhood: putting it together in a personal frame (1943–1960)*

As my own experience of being "fathered" was non-traditional for the time, I developed most of my personal notions of mother and father outside the contemporary mainstream of the patriarchal culture of the time, and have never carried that particular internal model or the emotional dynamic of a male-dominated family framework. My mother was the economic provider, model of authority, and the powerful and emotionally "violent" one, and my father was the figure of safety and secure attachment. Patriarchy as a lived experience of my own did not become a significant part of my consciousness until the 1960s, when I married a man who worked within the business world of contemporary "institutionalised masculinity". I then found myself relegated to the fringe of "woman's work" within the gaze and intellectual framework of his "city" peer group.

While growing up, I was more aware of class, culture, and ethnicity as different lenses through which to view the world and locate ideas than I was of the lens of gender—my own versions of multiple descriptions lodged within the former at the expense of the latter. The wider family I grew up in was a matriarchal family on both sides, the grandfathers having died earlier: one (English) in the service of country in the First World War, and the other (Cretan Greek) in the service of business, losing his venture in the 1920s crash. Thus, the women on both sides (my mother's mother and sister and my father's mother), as the holders of family stories, provided a series of robust female discourses which limited my perceptions of patriarchy as an adverse social influence. Throughout my childhood, fatherhood was narrated predominantly within a southern European frame of strong women as the power behind the throne, ("take power but never openly subvert your man while doing so"). In the case of my English granny, father was remembered and honoured, but never discussed at all.

Fatherhood as a childhood experience of my own was also dominated by the two World Wars: during the first (1914–1918) my father lost his own father and during the second (1939–1945) he had to choose what being a man in wartime Britain meant for him. How to perform fatherhood, and how to be a man in and out of the family, required my father to find a new invention for himself. While there is obviously a level at which this is true for every father, he had grown up without a father himself, and with a clever twin sister and mother as his intimate household companions. I never learnt about what he was expected to do in the way of household tasks as a child, except by the delegation of what he taught me to do in turn. He taught me how to wash and hang up his drip-dry shirts when I was eight (a role I believe he wanted to avoid for himself, as I knew my granny, his mother, had always done all the washing) and how to cook a Sunday lunch by the time I was nine—cooking being a way in which I believe he had allowed himself to identify with some of her skills. The life stories that could organise a role called masculine in his childhood family were absent from the telling, although the articulation of values, mainly subversive to the predominant culture of the time, were handed down in two widely divergent ways. On the one side was a love of music hall and of seaside "end of the pier" humour that specialised in meanings about otherness (not exactly smutty, but always with double meanings). On the other side was a commitment to pacifism and Fabian Socialism, striving for a better world for all, ideals strongly handed down in gender-free and non-specific ways.

During the Second World War, when masculinity outside the home was largely determined by a capacity to fight for country, he chose, and hung on fiercely to, pacifism. This was perhaps the main legacy from his mother's narrative about his father, who was killed in the final year of the First World War and whom he never saw. He went through the contemporary assessments of authenticity of pacifism, was found to be sincere in his views by the legal tribunals and was, therefore, required to carry out civilian war work. He subsequently spent the war years working for the Pacifist Service Unit. When the Second World War ended, he did not pick up any of the threads of the institutional masculinities available at the time in which he might have found employment. He avoided hierarchical structures with a dominant male at the top. Instead, he opened a café in Soho, which formed a second childhood base during my school holidays (and at weekends) from the age of seven onwards.

In considering how the domains of home, wife, and café mutually influenced one another in the development of his fathering of me, I saw my father as the nurturing, feeding parent and my mother as the economic provider (since the café project barely covered its own maintenance costs). I learnt that it is hard to maintain one without the other and that it was important to do both. However, it was only later in life that I realised how powerfully contemporary gendered social roles were being subverted in my family at that time. I never had the experience, so powerful among many female colleagues and friends, of a mother who sacrificed herself to domesticity to support her husband's career (see Oakley, 2014). There was little debate about the unusual nature of what had been created, and what had been avoided, by constructing this second intimate familial context of café as companion and rival to the project of home life, although there were endless arguments about the café not making money and my father not having a "proper job".

My father merged levels of intimacy into a single context. We (the café and the customers) were all family. The café was my validation as much as I was part of the café—the context in which I could have my own life witnessed as well as observe and accommodate others. A multi-layered description of aspects of life with my father would include intimacy, nurturance, pacifism, equality, and freedom from gender and class definitions. This could be found in his choice of lifestyle (as well as the lifestyle of many of his customers). Through the experience of life in the café in Soho, I also learnt most of the tenets of respect for people that inform my way of seeing the world. A Fabian Socialist framework, with some complex Marxist reworking on the subject of sex and the capitalist machine, taught me that we were each performing our part and that prostitution is as valuable as making coffee. I was, therefore, taught to greet all around me with respect and to make and serve coffee as well as I could. This gave me a security in the world that has never left me; I operated on assumptions of basic respect and trust, as well as recognition of the value of different skills. At the same time, it left me vulnerable through lack of a developed ability to make certain distinctions. In the intimacy of the café culture, there was an absence of discussion of difference and social discriminations as the rest of the world (my school friends, my mother, and, later, the world into which I married) understood them. I had to learn to perceive, though not necessarily respect, these social and classed nuances as I travelled through life. In a world where, through the eyes of my father, everything except the abuse of power (epitomised by the Nazi atrocities of the war era) was to be respected for its potential intrinsic goodness and necessary function, it was difficult for me to distinguish "bad". This has remained hazardous for me throughout my working life and, while of immense benefit in getting on with and enjoying humanity, has led me most often to seek consultation about how I distinguish between changeable, or possibly unchangeable, "badness" in the various contexts I have worked in (Gorell Barnes, 1990, 2002).

## Gender studies and gay and lesbian studies

Readings about performance of gender in family life and wider social contexts clarify how language itself contributes to maintaining unnecessary dualism and gender stereotypes in social and family groups. Similarly, readings in gay and lesbian writing about family over the past ten years has led to further clarifications in my own mind about my long-term interest in the diversities of fatherhood and my lifelong mistrust of totalising assertions about the "role of father" (Lewis et al., 1976; Parsons et al., 1955; Skynner, 1968). Our everyday language contributes to the discourses about being a father and shapes fathers' ideas about themselves. Gay men and women have overtly challenged and written about traditional role assumptions in their own family lives over the past twenty years, which throws reflections on to other forms of contemporary family life as well as historically illuminating the shadows of my own (Portch, 2011, pp. 3–8 Reynolds, 2010). My father was bisexual and sustained a hidden gay lifestyle in a period of post-war living when to be gay was to be criminalised. Being "allowed" to be legally gay did not take place until after his death and to be caught in homosexual acts could lead to imprisonment and often did. In my family life, and among the network of my parents' friends, this was joked about—possibly as a way of distancing themselves from the reality that they faced. My mother was working in the film industry where, as a woman, she was breaking through a number of gender barriers in the male dominated studio and production industry. This meant that, for long periods of time, "the film came first", with studio hours that were often twelve hours a day. In my later childhood, she also worked away from home in other countries, and so my father operated as the nominal, if erratic, "responsible parent". My reliable other companion of mind and of humour at that time was my Irish "nanny Kathleen", who was the person who was there after school, with whom I listened to *Workers Playtime, Life with the Lyons, Take It from Here, The Goon Show,* and other BBC comedy staples of life.

We both deferred to the magic phone call my father would make at 7.45 p.m., which was the time to "stop reading and go to bed". He rarely came home, but he usually made the phone call. He then conducted his gay life in the Turkish Baths—a place which retained impermeable layers of mystery for me, in that nothing, of course, was explained.

*Grannies as caring kin*

Nothing, therefore, was run traditionally in the family household. The discordance between these arrangements and those highlighted by the sociological studies of the families of that time confirm how unusual it was for a woman to be the source of economic strength in England in the 1940s and 1950s. My father's mother became my additional base during school holidays in my pre-adolescent years. She represented the stability of a single-person female household and lived within the framework of a very small war widow's pension in the small bungalow in Margate where my father had grown up. Under her calm English exterior, a Fabian political stance was quietly imbued in me, along with knowledge of how to make white sauce, the daily reading of the *News Chronicle* and the enjoyment of "end of the pier" entertainments. Too young to train for a profession, she had worked as a clerk before the First World War. The *Sex Disqualification Removal Act,* which allowed women's entry to the professions, was not passed until 1919, by which time she was the lone widowed mother of twins. The rigid divisions between what constituted male activity and what was considered appropriate for females were further deconstructed by the processes of the war itself (Adie, 2013). None the less she did not gain full women's franchise (the vote) until 1928, by which time she had lived ten years of managing as a lone mother. She represented a class of women who were widowed and did not remarry—strong and able. In a country that had lost over a million of the young men who might have become fathers, and those whose sons were growing up without fathers, this female power was respected. Undoubtedly, they drew on mother's brothers, cousins, and available others in their community and school network as male models for their sons, but it was not a "golden era" of two-parent families as is sometimes romanticised by politicians.

*Sex, birth control, babies, and rights over children: the slow*
*decline of patriarchy and the emergence of nurturing fathers*

Following the ending of the Second World War, changes in attitude towards marriage and divorce continued to alter decade by decade as did attitudes to sexual relationships outside marriage. Marriage initially became more popular and people married younger, but simultaneously an increasingly permissive attitude towards sex outside marriage, which had developed in the earlier context of war, loss and death, continued to develop more openly when those threats had diminished. However, the significant change in attitudes to sexual freedom came with the arrival of safer contraception in the form of "The Pill" in the mid-1960s. For women whose religious beliefs did not proscribe the use of contraception, this drastically changed their options regarding their sexual activity Increasingly, women in the UK did not feel they had to wait for marriage and "save themselves" for marital legitimisation of their sexuality, however much their parents continued to champion these time-honoured ideas. During the 1970s, much of the mystique around marriage disappeared as freedom to have safe sexual partnerships developed outside marriage, and marriage became more connected to the idea of family than to sexuality on its own. Subsequently, the internet and social media, by creating the possibility for multiple conversations and contexts for legitimising different performances of sexuality, has transformed women's as well as men's freedoms to "do sex" on their own terms. The context for different conversations is now pervasive (BBC, 2015). The development of sexual and economic freedoms for women began to affect men and, in turn, the many possible performances of fatherhood.

Being able to regulate fertility more safely also created other freedoms for women. It provided opportunities and time to think without the constant anxiety about not becoming pregnant and about the hazards of surviving the economic and daily physical pressures of a household with many children. Both outside and inside marriage, this new assurance opened up multiple opportunities to critique male assumptions and male discourses. Women were freed, as Goldner later wrote, to become preoccupied with establishing themselves as actors in the public, not just the domestic, arena (Goldner, 1991). The combination of greater earning possibilities, control of fertility, and a new capacity to think about who defines relationships and how the rules are made, contributed to a huge increase in women seeking separation when the "fault-free" divorce law was enacted by Parliament in 1969. This legislation, in addition, elaborated earlier changes that had given mothers preference over fathers in the rights over the care of children (*Guardianship of Infants Act*, 1925). The welfare of the infant was now to be the consideration of paramount importance in deciding where a child should live. Mothers were able, therefore, to be even less fearful about the potential loss of their children if they chose to separate. This significant shift in legal emphasis towards women as primary guardians further led away from the prevalent model of family that, in the early 1960s, could still be depicted as a cohesive social institution that was father-led.

However, in spite of the advent of women's greater sexual freedom in the later 1960s, the power base in families continued for many years to be seen and experienced by women as resting primarily with men. This was largely due to their greater earning capacity, but was also because contemporary families were still operating by earlier internalised models of male and female role and power in family life. Sexism remained prevalent in the national ruling educational and financial institutions of the time and it carried over into much of family life (Gorell Barnes, 1990). None the less, the increase in higher education for women and the increasing pace of debate about male and female power, as well as the growth of collective female voices challenging the legitimacy of male assumptions in almost all previously taken for granted social domains, inevitably began to restructure assumptions about family itself and about fathers and mothers and their required performances in family life. Fletcher's 1962 gender-determined definition of "family" defines the following functions: regulating sexual behaviour, providing a legitimate base for the procreation and rearing of children, providing sustenance and care for its dependant members, acting as an agent of socialisation, of education and the transmission of culture, giving status to its members, both in terms of role and relationship.

Forty years on, Hill and colleagues (2003) offered a set of principles in a different language, suggesting that the key elements of family can be seen as "defining attachment processes and offering affect regulation, interpersonal understanding and the provision of comfort within intimate relationships" (p. 205). This way of thinking about family is much less dependent on gender and role but, instead, uses descriptions that are more related to domains of nurture and responsibility (Bugental, 2000).

### Psychoanalytic framing of fatherhood: what are the "essential" characteristics of "father"?

As family-systems thinking developed in the UK in the early 1970s, the predominant influence, other than sociology, was psychoanalytic thinking. The collected volume on the psychoanalytic study of the father (Trowell & Etchegoyen, 2002) reflects some contemporary thinking about the role of fathers in the second half of the twentieth century. Fonagy and Target were pioneers in pointing out that while mothers' and fathers' roles are not identical in terms of the child's psychic organisation, their roles were not as clearly separated and defined as some psychoanalytic writers assumed. They proposed the view that generalities about fathers are of less value in theory than considering a particular father within the context of a relationship with a particular mother (Target & Fonagy, 2002). However, strong positions on a definition of "the father's job" were put forward by other (male) writers. For them, mothers were central to the formation of the child's psychological wellbeing, and fathers were primarily positioned in relation to acting as a bridge to the world outside the family. Fakhry Davids, for example, proposed that, in both biological and psychological spheres, the mother "psychoanalytically the first object is the essential parent, and the father necessarily has a secondary place" (2002 p. 75).

While advances in assisted fertilisation in the twenty-first century mean that none of the bodily functions, either male or female, need to be held in fixed positions for reproduction, and may even be transferred from other carers of different biological roles, the question of how psychological roles will change remains open for exploration in these multiple changing contexts. In families co-created with other bodies in a number of different ways (for example, sperm or egg donation, in addition to surrogacy, carrying a child for a heterosexual or a gay couple), the notion proposed by Hrdy (2009, p. 25) that "infants with several attachment figures grow up better able to integrate multiple mental perspectives" will be a key model for co-constructed families to practise, as well as for attachment researchers to hold in mind.

## *Bringing fathers in or leaving fathers out: how does a mother's mind affect a father's position?*

Fakhry Davids also outlines a belief, vital to the continuation of the function of "fatherhood" as formerly constructed, that "an internal father can arise even when the child has no direct experience of a father figure within the family", additionally proposing that the child who does not have a father will find "fathers" in the outside world. Theoretically (the analyst) deals with this (absence) by postulating that the "presence of father in the mother's mind is sufficient to compensate for his physical absence" (2002, p. 87).

Alternatively, Kraemer (2017) has put it thus: "in his mind no child is without a father and in the absence of a given story he will invent one" (p. 115).

One continued experience I have had in much of the clinical work described in this book is that the father might not be held in a mother's mind in any ways that can be of value to the child. This experience is replicated across court work, work with mothers who have never lived with the fathers of their children, and with those situations where children have been conceived without a specific father in the mind of the mother (other than as sperm donor for her eggs). Many fathers recognise the possibility of another man succeeding them, choosing to be with their children whether they live with the children's mother or not, before someone else does their work. Sometimes, however, mothers reject the terms on which a father offers a presence, denying that their child has a need for a second parent. Frosh located some of the dilemmas for fathers in positioning themselves in the context of contemporary cultural and social developments, suggesting

> not only is it hard to become the nurturing pre-oedipal father created de novo from the absence of any received ideology of fathering but it is difficult to sustain any sense of being a proscriptive father enforcing social values. (Frosh, 1997, p. 49).

## *Families should be father led: sociology, and some early family therapy lenses on fathers' role, authority, and power*

The diversity of what is publicly recognised as "father" from the institutionalised and idealised model so prevalent when I began practice in the 1960s is discussed in the chapters which follow. "Father as boss" was prescribed by sociologists such as Talcott Parsons (Parsons et al., 1955) and taught by some influential male family therapists of the 1960s and 1970s. (Skynner, 1968, 1976 in the UK; Minuchin, 1974 in the USA). Both Skynner and Minuchin had themselves had analytic training and despite coming from widely different cultural backgrounds (Minuchin Argentinian Jewish and Skynner from Cornwall in South West England), both firmly positioned the father as "head of the family". In doing this they were not necessarily men of the decade within which they were teaching, but were more of their own father's time, and had not accommodated wider social and gender changes in their outlook. Concomitantly, if unintentionally, they underplayed recognition of, and questioning around, male control and spousal and family violence, which so easily accompanied family life whose successful functioning was modelled on a "dominant' male" . As Goldner (1991) described in a later critique of structural approaches to family work in the 1970s, the notion that motherhood and fatherhood were socially constructed notions and not "biological givens" barely entered the thinking, let alone the discourse, of family therapists at that time. Fatherhood as authority was justified within a contemporary "recommended" performance of masculinity "for the good of the family". The dangers of this preference could be seen within some contemporary recordings of family sessions, which often did not integrate or value the different and divergent thinking expressed during interviews by women and mothers. Their views and opinions in family sessions were normally placed second to those of men, or could not be "heard" unless expressed again by a man. This was not the whole story in relation to fatherhood and family therapy in the 1970s, but, in retrospect, it was a surprisingly powerful force at a time when women's thinking had progressed more widely in other social domains.

*Pattern and mutual influence: the development*
*of systemic approaches to family work within*
*a psychodynamic frame in the 1970s*

In the earliest days of family therapy in the UK, systems theory was eagerly welcomed by some therapeutic practitioners as a way to free the prevailing field of ideas from psychoanalysis, with its assumptions about position and role in the family, and its dominant discourse about the inner workings of the individual mind. Systems thinking developed around the concept of mutual influence and of the interrelationship of "parts" within a given framework; proposing that problems could most usefully be thought about in context, as part of a network of mutually influencing interrelated events within a defined boundary. Different clinicians championed different aspects of a systemic approach as being of most importance, some focusing on hierarchy and some on information and feedback (Gorell Barnes, 1985).[1]

For me, systemic thinking allowed an integration of social and psychological factors as an overall framework for considering family difficulties, with each family managing aspects of both in different proportions at different times. These included developmental strengths and difficulties within individuals, and the ways family patterns influenced and, in turn, were shaped by these over time. Later, genetics and epigenetics (factors concerned with the transitions of genetic specificities) could be additionally brought into systemic thinking. A widely shared approach to family disturbance centred around error-controlled systems and "runaways", resulting from the increased stress created by divergence from the system's central properties, and much clinical practice included studying such processes in families. (This is discussed in more detail in Chapter Twelve.) However, other early thinkers preferred propositions drawn from anthropology, biology, and ethology. These looked for the more general principles that could be used to explain those aspects of biological processes that led to increasing complexity of organisation within living, as distinct from mechanical systems (von Bertalanffy, 1950). Within these alternative stances for considering the processes of living in families, social influences which related to increasing gender struggles in family life and ways in which these were diverging from gendered "norms", as discussed above, was given little attention.

Pattern recognition forms a key dimension of understanding life in a family. This fundamental aspect of living together over time was described early in systemic theory as a key issue in human problem solving:

> that elusive sense for patterns which we humans inherit from our genes . . . involves all the mechanisms of representations of knowledge,

'nested contexts, skeleton conceptualisation, and mapping: the replicated ways in which ideas slip or become fuzzy; as well as the ways in
which shared descriptions, metadescriptions, symbols and different
dimensions of description are shared'. (Hofstadter, 1979, p. 674)

This poetic attempt to capture and define the core of idiosyncrasy in
family functioning that constitutes a particular family has been an
ongoing quest in family therapy theorising. Dunn, whose professional
research lifetime has paralleled my clinical work lifetime, came to
name this as the "core coherence" in families in her epidemiological
studies of the development of children within varying family contexts.
She described them as patterns of finely tuned anticipation and
response known to, and constitutive of, core aspects of "family" which
she unpacked through research projects into children and family life
(Dunn, 2004). Hill and colleagues (2003, 2014) have conceptualised
these patterns within different domains of family function and behaviours around love and attachment, and authority and discipline,
making it more possible for therapists to observe and consider where
conflicts are arising in family communications between misclassified
sequences and domains.

### The failure to recognise patterns: dilemmas for estranged fathers

The concept of shared patterns in family life and the failure to recognise these is particularly problematic for fathers living separately from,
or estranged from, their children. Following parental separation, the
development of differing living patterns with their "loops" and
"tangled hierarchies", as well as "stories" about these, develop rapidly.
Either partner might increasingly fail to understand the new patterns
and rules (epistemologies) of the other parent (see Chapters Five and
Six). Whereas in separating couples there is often an attempt to re-
establish the system as it was before (usually by fathers), mothers more
often aim to establish new patterns of behaviour, new structures, and
the development of new problem-solving abilities within these.

### A new focus on fathers in clinical practice

In the 1980s, more focused attention began to be given to differences
in family structure through the study of reconstituted families and

their differences from first time intact marriages and, therefore, to the differences in the position, tensions, and behaviours of fathers (Gorell Barnes et al., 1998). In the 1990s, more serious attention was given to families going through separation and divorce (Dowling & Gorell Barnes, 1999). More attention was now given to "two family systems" that, through conflicts of interest and the earlier dissolution of couple ties, would necessarily have to incorporate new learning and develop significant differences with the family system as formerly defined. More recently, I have continued conversations with fathers about their own changes throughout their life transitions. Do they see themselves as being intrinsically the same? What have they learnt along the way? Is fatherhood always work in progress as the transitions of life continue?

In the chapters that follow, some of these questions will be addressed by fathers, mothers, and children themselves in a variety of different contexts.

# CHAPTER TWO

# Attachment theory, child development research, and mothers' and fathers' connections with children in everyday life

*Linking to the past in the service of the future:
individual meaning and wider family processes*

A ttachment theory initially developed in the UK in the post-war context described in Chapter One. Bowlby (1951, 1953) offered a way of linking what goes on inside people's minds to their emotional responses in their everyday relationships, thus making links between past experience and present-day responses. Bowlby proposed that childhood emotional experience is mediated over time by "inner working models" which later organise adult emotional responses. Attachment behaviour is, itself, biologically based, initially described and defined in relation to infants seeking closeness to a figure of safety in the face of what they perceive as a threat in their immediate environment, as any young dependent animal does. The instinctive expectation of the seeker is that the protective response of the attachment figure will remove the stress created by fear, soothing their alarm responses, so that their minds can settle and continue to process experience. At that time, due to post-war social expectations, as discussed in Chapter One, the central attachment figure for a child was likely to be his mother. While attachment ideas were later expanded in child development research into a framework in which it was slowly recognised that soothing in response to a child's fears could encompass other family members—fathers, older brothers and sisters, grandmothers, and others in addition to mothers—the pre-eminence of the mother–child bond remained a central tenet of attachment research itself, which developed its own trajectory, independent of the various models of infant upbringing currently co-developing in a changing society. Clinicians working with children and families, who recognise that people living in close proximity set up patterns of interaction which mutually influence one another, agree that these include a wide variety of ways of "bringing up baby". Relatively stable sequences of emotionally infused speech and behaviour surround the newest member of any family, become processed by her internally, and she, in turn, interacts with, and influences, others as they grow. Attachment researchers did not extend their framework to include the family as a whole for several decades. Their focus remained on understanding the many variations of processing emotion and understanding through the unit of mother and child, and the effects of these variations on subsequent development of a child's mind, often to the exclusion of all other intimate interpersonal influences.

For those who live in families, the interactive patterns of their own behaviour with others, their attachments to one another in sibling relationships, as well as to their parents and grandparents, the mental processes that go with these attachments as they are repeated during development, create a useful meaning context through which problems can be viewed. Family patterns act as both cause and effect, generating feedback loops that create a fit between context and the problems that arise within it—"circular patterns of interaction". The relations between parents also carry reflections of relationships from earlier generations modelled within them. Their own behaviours, thoughts, and feelings are, in turn, constitutive of (contextualising the development of) patterns that will contribute to the inner working relationship models of the next generation. Recent ongoing research into how these patterns of safety, attachment, and discipline become coded within each family and how they are recognised, translated, or misunderstood by individual members of different generations in everyday family life, has been categorised within a framework of "domains" of family living (Hill et al., 2003, 2014).

### Cultural variations in attachment theorising: different positions for fathers or no positions at all

Using attachment ideas can help us to understand emotional patterning in families as well as throw light on idiosyncratic difficulties for some individuals in becoming and being a parent. As long as the significant model of family predominantly favoured by early researchers in the field—the mother–child unit—is not viewed as the universal model for how children should be raised, attachment models can offer a valuable clinical lens through which to view both good and bad aspects of parenting. There are many ways that attachment theory, and the study of infant security and the developing mind, developed as a body of work which privileged mothers so strongly over fathers that it denied both the potential value of fathers as a human resource and many fathers' own particular experiences of caring for their children. Fathers disappeared from research vision altogether for a decade or two and grannies, aunts, elder siblings, and other caring kin whom we know to be bringing up children have only recently entered the frame of attachment research in the context of a wider epidemiological focus exploring resilience in communities (Patterson & Vakili, 2013).

An attachment frame for family work always needs further unpacking through a range of cultural lenses. Many years ago, Krause, from an anthropological perspective, enlarged attachment ideas within the systemic field, to include cultural practices:

> socially and culturally constructed themes of thought, emotion and action are anchored in the ontology of human beings caring for and being attached to one another . . . the content and details of these interactions are shaped by and embedded in culturally patterned practices. (1998, p. 79)

This book focuses on a small but changing cultural world, the UK, in the context of one female lifetime, and none of the things I discuss should be taken as an attempt to "totalise" the experience of any group, but merely as one (white, Anglo-Greek) woman's partial lens. Women of the same generation of all ethnicities within the UK are likely to have certain common social experiences as mothers, independent of family culture, as well as highly idiosyncratic ones: becoming a certain kind of mother in relation to a particular father and particular child. The plurality of intersections of ethnicity, class, and cultural heritage mutating through different generations, and mutually constructing one another, mean we should never subsume any descriptions of the practices of child rearing under a single, culturally assigned "heading". Larger dominant discourses about men/fathers and women/mothers, always need to be unpacked within each new family or child rearing collective of parent figures in order to understand who is doing what for whom within the necessary matrix for a baby and developing infant. Attitudes towards fathers between different female collectives also influence one another. Further particularities have developed within gay and lesbian family lives, which have, in turn, offered new lenses for reflecting on families, attachment patterns, and the positioning of fathers.

In spite of widespread professional recognition of social and cultural diversity in child rearing, the preferred presumption of attachment theory as it evolved throughout my working life was that infants and mothers had the primary bond through which security of emotion, intelligence, and mind are constructed in the early months. This conflicted with many cultural models of early child rearing based on larger group and kinship care. Fathers were positioned as secondary across the spectrum of family life, or, in many cases, ignored as irrelevant to the child's wellbeing As well as marginalising the roles that fathers were actually playing in many households, this idea of the singularity of motherhood is at odds with much of the reality of most women's daily experience, once pregnancy and paid maternity leave is ended. The challenge for translating attachment ideas into clinical work with families is, therefore, important. Rather than a previous emphasis on child deprivation being primarily related to the absence of mother, the theory needs to be recast in terms of systems of reliable relationships that are available to an infant and the damage to development which occurs when these break down. Breaking down would signify that a child is either no longer being reared within a protective collective (as, for example, with unaccompanied child refugees) or no longer held in the minds of parents or caring elders (which might not be the case for refugee children, but might be for others who had been ignored or abused within their families from a very early age and had later been removed from them).

There are many variations on attachment breakdown. Dunn, in the Bristol and Avon study of family lives in the 1990s, studied breakdown in relation to family separation and reconstitution, and examined the question from children's point of view: when a child might themselves feel "forgotten", or no longer attached, in the light of post-divorce family reconstruction and/or step-family living. She found that while older children can embrace a wide range of relationship constellations and retain a sense of where they belong and who they are becoming, there is also always a strong wish for connection with biological parents, or those to whom they were originally connected as infants (Dunn, 2002; Dunn et al., 2004). The actual experience of being forgotten, or not held in mind by anyone in particular, is common among children who are later looked after by the state, and is sometimes described by fathers who are attempting to parent but have not had positive family experience themselves.

## Thinking about fathers in multiple family contexts

With an awareness of multiple differences in cultural family practices, the following questions can be asked: first, how many people might constitute the "internal working model" of family for a child ? Second, is there a limit in numbers for that same child to still develop safely? What are the positions of fathers in these different contexts? How will these positions be differently regarded in a family structure based on a matrilineal model of child rearing, or in households that are women-led for a variety of ideological or personal reasons? How, within any child-rearing group, will there be distinctions based on economics, education, partner choice, and other idiosyncratic variations? In my own family, for example (following a good principle of female sociology to work from the bottom up), my upbringing network consisted of a mother working full-time, a working father whose work life I often shared, a live-in Irish nanny/companion, a Greek grandmother and aunt whom I visited more than once a week, and an English granny with whom I spent much of my pre-teen school holidays. In spite of multiple kin care, I have no doubt that my mother "held me in mind", but each of them also held aspects of my mind in their minds. My father held me in mind, but his thinking was usually disqualified within the female collective. From my professional perspective, the wider knowledge held by relatives and reflected back into the developing identity of the child is not sufficiently taken into account, either in psychoanalytic thinking, in attachment theorising, or, indeed, in many aspects of the systemic approach to working with families.

## Fathers and social psychology research: the 1960s onwards

Although social psychology research acknowledged fathers' presence in families from the 1960s onwards, fathers did not influence the main thrust of attachment research itself, and they were marginalised within it. Researchers who did pay attention to fathers challenged the notion that children do not form strong attachments to them as early as the first year of life. Pedersen and colleagues also reported on mothers' views that infants responded positively and enthusiastically to their fathers' return from work, with boys showing particular intensity (Pedersen et al., 1980). In nearly one third of the families studied by these researchers, the primary attachment was to the father, the breadth of attachments largely being determined by the social setting. Lamb determinedly undertook further investigation of attachment hypotheses in relation to fathers in the 1970s and made lengthy in-home observations, concluding that, as early as seven months old, infants showed no preference for either parent over the other on attachment behaviour measures, although all showed preference for parents over strangers (Lamb, 2013). He speculated that playfulness was the key to father–infant attachments and that, in the absence of playful cues, infants develop clear-cut preferences for their primary carers (usually their mothers).

### Co-constructing parenting and role

Further studies in Europe and America confirmed the—perhaps obvious—notion that increased paternal involvement does strengthen infant–father attachment, but only when the care offered to children by fathers is supportive of mothers and also responsive to the child's cues. The presence of father in itself is not enough. It is the increased responsiveness within mutually shared frameworks, a shared ideology about parenting and role co-constructed by mother and father, that counts towards a child's wellbeing. Father's presence in contexts that are not endorsed positively by mothers can have a nil or negative effect on a child's measured wellbeing. This is of particular importance in the context of fathers seeking contact after any kind of parental separation where neither children nor mother find that this presence contributes to harmonious family life.

## A father's special role?

In the absence of mother, a number of familiar others can stand in as "stress relievers" (fathers, elder siblings, grandparents, nannies, and key nursery workers). However, for certain periods of the child's development, a few key figures are likely to be essential to the child's sense of security. If a father wishes to retain a primary parental status, he needs to take part in his infant's life on a regular basis from the beginning. If he is not there for extended periods, the special relationship given to primary carers by an infant and then held on to within her mind can suffer by his absence. This is central to many dilemmas faced by a father who does not take this need for proximity and regularity into account. The regulatory rhythms and strength of the relational bond is likely to be vital to the ongoing construction of "parent" in the father's mind, as well as to the child herself: "that elusive sense for patterns which we humans inherit from our genes involving all the mechanisms of representations of knowledge" (Hofstadter, 1979, p. 694). In the absence of these instinctive, joint regulatory rhythms and the subtle knowledge and recognition held of the other person that develops within these, much subsequent fathering has to be worked out in the head, rather than being held in the body on a day-to-day basis.

## Dwayne and his grandfather

Dwayne, a young father of Caribbean origin, described his own large extended family as comprising four families, with his great-grandmother as the common matriarch. The household he lived in consisted of his grandmother, his grandfather, four aunts, one uncle, and twelve or thirteen other children kinship cousins. His grandfather did "an amazing job" and was a role model for him. However, in his own opinion, this extended system let him down in relation to his own fathering of children as, although he had admired his grandfather, he had not been able to work out which of his qualities had allowed him to commit to his children on a daily basis. Dwayne felt that he had let his own daughter down by not staying in touch with her, though they had met up in her teenage years after a gap and were now good friends.

## Proximity and special carers: theory and daily life

The debate about how much the central and exclusive relationship with mother is necessary for infants to become secure and develop "evenly" has been regularly challenged by researchers from other disciplines, such as anthropology and sociology, as well as by daily life. Hrdy argues that multiple caring ("alloparenting") is a crucial step in the evolution of modern humans' capacity for thought, language, mentalization, and conscience, asserting that infants with several attachment figures grow up better able to integrate multiple mental perspectives (Hrdy, 2009).

The realities of the need for two household incomes, the available child day care structures, and the real life experience of women and families provide the alternative realities within which children grow, and which offer them multiple mental perspectives. Day care patterns when women return to work are various and range from kin care to paid child minder to nursery. In those lives, children develop relationships with a range of figures, not all of whom are regular and ongoing, and mothers and fathers ideally remain constant alongside them. Infants monitor the proximity of their preferred carer and, within the second year of their lives, are able to hold on to the idea that a special person who is not there may come back (play peek-a-boo: hiding face, taking hands away but knowing that the other person, even though hidden, will still be there . . . the pretend mode of disappearing). A fourteen-month-old who is preverbal can, none the less, "know" someone is going; for example, take their shoes to the door, wave "bye-bye", and shout "hiya" when they come back. These are the foundations of implicit memory, which develop as a consequence of everyday repetitive experience. The idea that even though someone is not there at any one moment does not mean she will not be available at another moment links to a child's developing idea of continuous relationship. It also links to the idea that the person whom he holds in his mind can, in turn, be able to hold him in her mind. In many families discussed in this book, a loved and wished for father— good or bad—does not come back at a critical developmental time. In addition, following many such disappearances, the psychic reality of his presence is not maintained for the child in a positive way in the mind of his mother. This is very different from how fathers were held positively in a mother's minds during, for example, the war years or, in a contemporary setting, a father who works away from home on an oil-rig or travels in the context of his work. A source of early disappointment, such as the loss of a father, might contribute adversely to later expectations and to consequent behaviour within intimate relationship patterns. This early loss could enhance a wish or longing for something that did not, in fact, exist in an earlier relationship.

## Negative interactions between fathers and young children

Main and colleagues took forward the concept of "internal working models", expanding thinking about these to include emotional experience over time, and speculating how the mechanisms for these experiences were carried forward (Main et al., 1985). A young child's relationships will be formed out of a long and cumulative experience of his interaction with a parent, and of his parents' interactions with other people. The mind builds up pictures, or schema, or stories of interactions and responses, which include, over time, the feelings that go with these, as well as the sense of control or helplessness that the reciprocal sequences of interaction have generated (Stern, 1977). While everyday interactions between a child and his parents can be benign and learning orientated (shutting and opening doors, taking people their shoes to put on before going out, turning taps on and off), in dysfunctional family or child care contexts they can also become imbued with emotion and fear (the doors are slammed, a finger might be trapped, shoes can be thrown across the room). Infants' experience with neglectful or cruel parents or carers can mean that simple acts become imbued with negative emotional experience and dread.

## Principles of intimate relationships and "mentalization"

The work of Fonagy and his colleagues over the past twenty years has illuminated many ways in which distorted attachments in parents' own childhoods affect how, as adults, they think about each other, as well as their children. The capacity for intimacy is linked to the term "mentalization" and to the concept of "intersubjective mind" (a mind developed and shared within a mutually influencing system of relationship (Fonagy et al., 2004; Gorell Barnes, 1995; Trevarthen, 1979). The framework of mentalization has been conceptualised in terms of the connections between secure attachment, the capacity to think and reflect about subjective experience, and clinical processes that facilitate family members in thinking about the minds of other human beings close to them (Keaveny et al., 2012). Fonagy has linked the well-developed capacity for mentalization firmly to security of attachment and concomitant regulation of the brain system: emotional regulation in the self over time is, in his opinion, a core outcome of a well-regulated infant–parent relationship. This, in turn, relates to faster development of cognitive capacities, to a sense of confidence that distress will be met by comforting, and to a clearer sense of knowing oneself (which connects to being able to understand others). We can enlarge the concept of "attachment system" away from a two-person system to consider the principles of which the system is made up: loving care, positive regard, attentiveness, and attunement and responsiveness carried out within a regular group of different people throughout the child's pre-school life in addition to a mother. These are key aspects of the parental care necessary to maintain relationships with young children. If a father and his child have had significant breaks in daily or regular contact, it will be important to reinstate and maintain these aspects.

## Attachment theory and post-war yearning

Attachment theorists' often poetic formulations of "the infant's mind" bears little congruence with the experience of many children who have multiple carers. It might be possible, if irreverent, to consider how adherence to the model of attachment to a "good" mother was itself a strongly wished for model of relationship for all humankind, an earlier "earth mother" wish. At the time of the early development of attachment theory, a large proportion of children in Europe had been evacuated from home without their parents during the bombing of civilian populations; fathers were away from home fighting, often for many years, as well as many suffering in prisoner of war camps;

the Holocaust and the extermination of six million people was beginning to be absorbed into the public psyche, and a huge longing for secure "family life" was centred around the person of mother and home (Bowlby, 1969, 1973, 1981). Similar human need for love and security might have been differently constructed in societies that, through ongoing awareness of environmental risk and danger, had long decided that the survival of children lay in safety in numbers of caring kin and elders. It is, therefore, always important in our thinking to translate the core principle of "secure attachments" for children to the cultural models preferred by any family we are working with and to make flexible assessments of how the necessary developmental requirements for the child are being observed and carried out.

## A focus on fathers: daily affect regulation for infants and for fathers' own selves

The gradual acquisition of emotional regulation capacities begins early in the first year of life. What are the detailed interactional processes between children and their fathers that can amplify or diminish the successful development of emotional regulation and synchrony (Feldman, 2007)? Systems theory and neurobiology can intersect usefully when considering transactions between a baby or small child and the daily interactions in his life that structure early experience. These lay down the earliest mental representation systems on which the working models of later years are formed. During the early intimate exchanges of everyday life, strategies for affect-regulation, and, subsequently, self-regulation, are co-created with others. This process involves recognition and naming of emotion in the infant's self but also in the parents' selves. Fathers on site can be active in this way in developing strategies to control levels of arousal in the infant. During these processes, some discover the self-regulating properties for their own affect arousal and for better management of these by mediating infants behaviour with their mothers, or others, and, in turn, being mediated by them: "Let's take you for a little walk, while mummy has a break", or "I'll change that nappy to make you more comfortable while mum has a shower." Pride and joy also play a part in a preverbal infants naming of good and bad actions and understanding of a father's part in them. Teaching fathers positive reinforcement and reflecting on the outcomes—"good boy" accompanied with a big grin, or "well done", "thank you", or "aren't you a clever boy then"—are all small common everyday exchanges that regulate both father and child. Work that has focused on early parent–infant interaction provides vivid experimental confirmation of the ways that infants learn interactive and communicative patterns from the earliest months of life. Ramchandani and colleagues (2013), from their recent research in the UK, suggest that boys might be more susceptible to the influence of their fathers from an early age. By eighteen months, it is generally agreed that each child in an ongoing family system will have a pattern of expectation and reciprocity in place within a small number of familiar environments.

Affect regulation—the management of emotions so that they do not peak out of individual control and do not harm others—is probably the most difficult feature of parenthood, occupying much professional attention in most social care and therapeutic settings. A father's experience of his own parents' capacity to look after him as a child, with or without tenderness or awareness of his mental states and wishes, will, in turn, influence his mental state as a father, triggered by the needs and wishes of his own child(ren) at different ages and stages. A father's capacity to mentalize—to imagine what the child is communicating—is particularly critical in the earliest months and years, since non-verbal behavioural cues are the child's primary means for communicating his or her own mental states. The child's wellbeing will largely depend on his parents willingness and readiness to understand these cues and respond to them appropriately. Sensitive carers, whether parents, elders, siblings, or nursery staff, respond to infants "cues" or distress with vocal and physical gestures that enable babies to develop a "language" around their own feeling states. For many children, such understanding is limited or lacking due to a parent's own limited emotional availability. Bifulco and Thomas (2013) have also drawn attention to the role of antipathy as a parental attribute and the effects of antipathy on children's insecurity. Antipathy is a factor remembered by many fathers as an acutely painful aspect of their own childhood experience, and is further considered in the chapters on violence and mental illness later in this book. Depending on the degree of misfit between what is sought by a child and what is given by a parent (contingent and non-contingent interactions), a child will be more or less able to organise himself in congruent ways and to control impulses, and have a more or less clear sense of himself in relation to others.

### Fathers and affect regulation as adults: early traumatic relational experience

If, in early interactions, responses that a child wishes for are not forthcoming, or result in hostile or abusive exchanges from parents or carers, a child is likely to become anxious and his capacity to mentalize becomes compromised. Attunement is replaced by hyper-vigilance. Kraemer has highlighted the vulnerability of boys, stating that infant boys display more distress and demands for contact than girls, that boys are also more sensitive to maternal depression than are girls, less easily soothed, and find it more difficult to tolerate stress, as well as being more reactive than girls (Kraemer, 2000). Unkind aspects of adult to child interaction range from repetitive unresponsive behaviour to more distorted responses. Some of these earlier unmet or distorted experiences are often still held within the minds of fathers who come for therapeutic work. Current negative behaviour with a partner or with children might be relocated in an earlier context. Main, in a later development of her work on the roots of attachment disorganisation, formulated a theoretical model. She demonstrated that an infant or child becomes disorganised when experiencing the carer simultaneously as "the source of alarm and its only solution". The child who seeks comfort from the parent finds instead that the parent is frightened by him (Main & Hesse, 1990). A "frightened" response from the parent to the child creates further threat for the child, who then experiences emotional unavailability in the "frightened and frightening" parent. The researchers argued that such contradictory experience induced "approach withdrawal" conflict in the child (subsequently leading to "disorganised behaviour" in the specific context of seeking proximity). A large body of research has subsequently explored and confirmed aspects of these disorganised interactional experiences, resurfacing in a variety of contexts that include aspects of what children with parents suffering from major mental illness can also experience (see Chapter Twelve). This knowledge can usefully inform our thinking when working with violent and disorganised relationships between adults in intimate relationships, as well as in acrimonious Court procedures relating to children (Chapters Nine to Eleven). Disorganised attachment appears to be the most powerful and long-lasting subcategory of insecure attachment and the associations appear to diminish very little across age (Fearon et al., 2014a,b).

Fathers who, as children, have had deeply insecure attachment patterns might have trouble regulating adult emotional states on their own. As a result, they can place inappropriate expectations on others with the implicit, but often unconscious, wish that others will regulate them. They could experience excessive anxiety and a longing to be taken care of, which their children cannot meet. Some fathers presenting with anxious, jealous, and over-possessive behaviours have narrated childhood memories of emotional dislocation and ill treatment: for example, being locked in the "coalhole", having their heads "put under the cold tap", "being locked in the outside lavatory", beaten regularly for many years "for my own good", made to eat out of the dog's bowl on the floor. Other fathers have been recounted by their wives as "howling" and "curling up" in their children's presence as they get back in touch in a physical sense with their own earlier deprivation or mistreatment through an upset developed with their own child (a traumatic experience "relived in the mode of psychic equivalence" (Fonagy et al., 2004). Schore proposes that cumulative relational trauma deriving from early poorly regulated attachment experience is imprinted in the right brain, and connected to children's use of dissociation (Schore, 2001). This later relates in adulthood to an impaired ability to regulate intensity of affect. Lack of opportunity to develop language about early experience, which characterises boys' upbringing more than girls', connects with a subsequent inability to recognise, label, and articulate feelings that have lain dormant. Experience of similar painful emotion in adulthood might lead to a reliving of the earlier experience in the mode of "psychic equivalence". Psychic equivalence means that the retelling of an earlier tale of terror might not lead to any relief because there is an absence of any developed reflective pathways between childhood emotional experience and later strong emotions that might be re-experienced in life as a parent. Whereas many childhood fears can be mediated through games, films, stories, or shared experience with friends, sometimes internal trauma retains its power and is context specific within the intensity of family life. The mental representations of the past, re-emerging in current interactional reality in family life, can bring a parent for therapeutic help to disentangle the pain he or she is feeling and the damage he or she might be doing.

### Disorderly love and therapeutic conversations

Within clinical work, we know there are a great range of insecurely attached relationships, which range from "avoidant" to "highly disorganised" (Zeanah et al., 2011). Most of these should not, in my opinion, be equated with a failure to love, but can lead to loving in ways that are inappropriate for children at different stages of their development (further explored in Chapters Nine to Eleven). Within this range of "disorderly love" lie a large number of the problems and problem behaviours many fathers seeking help might bring. These include unmodulated aggression and poor impulse control as well as unrecognised impaired emotional development that can lead to only partial understanding of the needs of wives, partners, and small children. There might be controlling behaviour as an unwelcome way of dealing with their own anxiety. There is likely to be poor self-image, a sense of not being wanted or loved. There could be violence to try to enforce love and control or as a way of dealing with a sense of helplessness. There is likely to be depression as a result of sensitisation of the neurobiological systems due to long-term stress adaptation. Prolonged experience of verbal abuse, ridicule, humiliation, and disdain from the elders in their own lives, which is regularly reported by fathers with depression and other mental health difficulties, can also contribute to abnormality of brain function. It has been found that harsh childhood corporal punishment was associated with reduced grey matter volume in the two brain regions that are central to higher cognitive processing, such as working memory and to aspects of social cognition (McCrory et al., 2011).

### Internal working models can translate the past into schema organising the present: talking with distressed fathers

Discussing both stress and resilience pathways with fathers, taking some of these researched factors into account, can be meaningful to them in reflecting on their own lives. This is particularly so when this thinking can be applied to current and future relationships with their children. Research supports the idea that preverbal experiences remain encoded in the brain and can, in cases of ongoing trauma, affect functioning through life. To know that strong attachment relationships in infancy contribute to providing fundamental mechanisms and strengths for the social regulation of stress can give a distressed father a new sense of purpose in maintaining regular connection with his child. The knowledge that our own early fears are still within us and can be reactivated when we are exposed to new traumatic stress (even though we often have no memory of how the fear was acquired) is a more useful formulation for a father than believing he is going "mad". The notion that, in subsequent family life lived as a parent, the context in which the original fear was constructed can be retriggered through interactions with partners or children that are similar in pattern and intensity of affect is also helpful. Such current experiences, when they occur, can be compared and contrasted with a father's knowledge about his own earlier experiences and separated out for focused thinking. I might access such experiences by asking "When was the last time you can remember it [his own unregulated emotional storm] happening?" and, having located a recent memory, continue with "And what do you remember about it happening before?", thus backtracking from the present. Loneliness, fear, powerlessness, injustice, confusion (a list produced "off the top of my head" by two fathers, both sent away from home, one to boarding school and one to a children's home) can resurface as emotions in contemporary family contexts where there seems little rationale for their appearance. Memories are on a spectrum from parental lack of interest, including antipathy and withholding of love, to material and physical neglect. This can lead to discussion of more distressing experiences such as physical abuse or violence, psychological abuse in the form of disorganised behaviour, or persistent negative critical commentary, and, more rarely, sexual abuse. Here, disorganised attachment has become connected to secrecy and to satisfaction of a repetitive physical experience which is analogous to an addiction.

*Fathers and negative behaviour towards children and mothers: discussing back stories and future change for children*

An attachment orientated model sustains the idea that both father and child are involved in co-creating regularities of interaction and pattern, and that both can suffer from lapses or breaches of the rhythms they have formerly developed. Fathers' selves have been constructed in mutual interaction with others in their childhoods and many might have developed defensive strategies to deal with tough experiences, strategies which are later in conflict with the requirement of "being a good dad". The conflict this induces is worth unpacking and separating out. The knowledge that early stress primes a child's brain to be more responsive to subsequent stress throughout life can also be used to encourage fathers to diminish the stress they currently create around their children, while simultaneously allowing a framework for their own vulnerability to be considered respectfully (Shonkoff & Garner, 2012). For a father, the idea that his child's brain is influenced by the environment into which he is growing, including those negative relationship patterns of which he, father, is a part, is particularly useful in engaging him more directly in situations where he and his child/ren are estranged. It gives him tools to think about himself as having responsibility towards his children in relation to his own behaviours around his child, rather than creating dramatic scenarios around "rights" which are being "denied him". Ideas about adversity, children's development, and resilience can be explored in ways that are both culturally specific and culture-free, and have, therefore, been found acceptable in contexts where "Western jargon" has been rejected by a father.

I have been influenced in the direction of open talking on the basis of science by witnessing the success of formulating mental illness in comprehensible ways to children and parents, with the aim of children being able to perceive their parents' behaviour as "external" and not automatically connected to the child (Cooklin, 2006; Streeting, 2013). This has further underpinned my belief in the value of ongoing therapeutic conversations where knowledge and experience are shared, which has always been a part of my clinical approach. The structure, function, and development of the nervous system and brain, and how these biological components affect behaviour, emotion, and cognition are, in an everyday human sense, everybody's "right" to be informed about as tools towards understanding the human condition. While we still know very little, some of what research has discovered is valuable in understanding ourselves better. I use neuroscientific ideas in rudimentary ways with some fathers who struggle with emotional dysregulation, explaining the limitations of my own understanding, and working out with them how they see past and present life stresses affecting their emotions and cognition. Normal aspects of emotional dysregulation can include anxiety, fear, forgetting what has just been said, having an "over-crowded" mind, "fuzzy" thinking, not feeling able to control "rising feelings" when stressed or overwhelmed, going "off on one", or "losing it".

### Social deprivation and developing organisms: socially adaptive organisation and attachment disorganisation

Developmental psychopathology has now brought together some of the developments from neuroscience, the internal organisation of the body and mind, with what then happens to the infant in the outside world. The relationships between specific genetic traits in infants and the sensitivity of the early parenting that children receive is of particular interest to all mental health professionals, indicating, as it does, the powerful effects of social deprivation on developing organisms— small vulnerable beings in the making. The metaphor of "cascades" (Luijk et al., 2011) has been adopted by a body of researchers in developmental psychology who think about the individual as an active and purposeful part of a larger, integrated, biodynamic (person–environment) system, within which the parts mutually influence and trigger one another. Interfering in the development of negative cascades can be included (Lenzenweger, 2010) as a purposeful activity by any of us as part of our work with parent–child interactions in any context. Where these are regular and repeated, they give rise to increased synchrony (harmonious interaction and expectations of interaction by a small child which are, in turn, increasingly corresponded to by larger aspects of their social environment). Neural development and social interaction are inextricably entwined, and aspects of brain development are relationally constructed within systems of responses to the infant's expressions of need. A recent body of research has focused on how genetic and environmental influences further shape the development of self-regulative capacities in young children (Cox et al., 2010; Propper & Moore, 2006).

Whereas the secure attachment pathway is only one of a number of self-regulation pathways, it remains an ideal and idealised beacon in the multiple complex routes for child rearing that come to the attention of family workers of all kinds. Longitudinal studies involving parents and children (Zeanah et al., 2011) rarely include the multiple developmental hazards that the idiosyncrasies of daily family life present. Rutter, who has long maintained a vigilant critique of attachment theory, has recently pointed out confusions in the way debates which use attachment principles are put together (Rutter, 2015). Different life experiences will always be able to mediate earlier attachment experience and difficulties in intimate experience in adult life should not be attributed only to insecure attachments and poor early experience. This punctuation is important in reminding ourselves of the human capacity for resilience and being able to pick up positive threads to sustain resilience along the way in our work. However, acts of remembering, and the quality of negative and distorted memory, seem to be particularly powerful where negative childhood experience continues to influence an adult's own parenting behaviour. The way childhood negative experience continues to be held within the body as well as the mind has now been shown to be one of the most powerful influences on adult intimate behaviour, and it might be in the zone of disorganised attachment as a child that the power of trapped emotions has the most powerful consequences for parenting as a father. Disorganised attachment appears to be the most powerful and long-lasting subtype of insecure attachment, and the associations appear to diminish very little across age. This is further explored in Chapters Eight to Ten, on violence, and Chapter Eleven on fathers being mentally ill.

# Becoming a father in non-live-in fatherhoods

For many men, beginning life as a father does not go hand in hand with living in the same home as the child's mother. Some of the larger social and family hazards facing young couples who do not live together during the period in which a father might be trying to construct a relationship with his newborn child contribute to fragile attachments. About four in ten babies are now born outside marriage in the UK, and non-live-in, non-wed fathers are more likely to lose touch if they separate from partners than those fathers who married before they co-habited and had babies (Kiernan & Smith, 2003). In the two chapters that follow, I discuss some of the challenges and difficulties faced by fathers who wanted to become connected, stay connected, or reconnect to their children when they have never been married to the children's mother. Some might have co-habited for only a short period. They have usually moved out of the mother's life, but often kept up an intermittent contact with their child, the relationship being kept hidden or unclear for the child. The majority of the fathers I have seen in these circumstances have been referred through legal aid by solicitors, and subsequent work has depended on the goodwill of both mother and father to try to reach some positive arrangements for their child. This goodwill is often absent, and the complexities that might set in are further discussed in Chapter Four.

Over the past twenty-five years, a loose public and political consensus has emerged more clearly in the UK around the importance of fathers in children's lives. Research itself has offered confusing and often discouraging messages to fathers about their own value to children. At the end of the twentieth century, Lamb summarised research on parenting as showing that warmth, nurturance, and closeness were associated with positive child outcomes, regardless of whether the parent involved is a mother or a father. The finding that it might be the qualities of a second person (but not necessarily a father) that is important to a child and his or her social and emotional development was additionally confirmed by Golombok and colleagues, whose ongoing work records the lives of children in lesbian partnerships (Golombok & Tasker, 2015).

Fathers seeking to maintain relationships with children were acknowledged by social researchers to have a potentially important role in children's socialisation and wellbeing, providing there was no harm to the child involved in a continued relationship. The idea of "harm to the child" was backed by research considering the impact of parental quarrelling and aggression and the negative effects on children, and conflicted with the notion that fathers were valuable in their own right. The development of the "best interests of the child" ethos gradually expanded in the 1990s to include a more liberal position developing in the family court on how a father could continue to carry out some responsibilities to children even when a mother might be uninterested in his participation (Collier & Sheldon, 2008).

## Elaborating the range of fatherhoods we hold in our minds

Dunn and colleagues (2000) categorised the range of fathers in their large-scale study of family living in the west of England in the following ways.

1. Father: the birth father of the child who may be living in the household or a non-resident father if he is living in a different household from the child.
2. Stepfather: if he is not the birth parent of the child and the mother has children from a previous partnership. In addition, he might also father children in the current partnership at which point a

father will be acting as both biological and stepfather simultaneously (stepfather is used interchangeably with social father in much research).

3.  Complex step-families: both mother and father have brought children from previous relationships so both are acting as biological and stepparents within the same household. Additionally, there might be further children from the current partnership at which point a father will be acting concurrently as both biological and stepfather.

4.  Father-led households: single-parent households of which a percentage (around 11–15%) are father led.

From the fatherhoods considered in this book, I would add those listed below.

1.  Fatherhoods conducted primarily from outside the child's home as a result of "freely given/no ties" sperm donated initially without any projected claim on fatherhood but subsequently reconsidered and followed through (sometimes internationally by means of social media).

2.  Dual fatherhoods in which a man has children in one or more households, one of which might be legitimised by marriage or regarded as the "public" family while the other is hidden (to be distinguished from families where a man has children in more than one family as part of a "cultural" pattern, notionally legitimised within its own social history, as has been the former structure of many British Caribbean families).

3.  Serial fatherhoods with progressively younger women, where a father's latest partner could be as young as his older children from an earlier relationship.

4.  A range of gay and lesbian–gay family households with further fluidity around gendered parenting, some of which is called "fathering" and some households which reject gender-specific naming.

## A father's thoughts about himself: nuances past and present

Within these multiple contexts of fathering constructed through varied relationship transitions, how do fathers think about themselves and the commitments of love, responsibility, and hands-on practical care they can offer (Walters, 2016)? Individual constructions of their potential roles as fathers will be influenced by the way their close social networks think and talk about their own positions as fathers, in turn influenced at multiple nuanced levels by culture, diversity, and intersectionality. Geography, urban or rural living, and social media can all play a part. Whereas in some Inner London boroughs female-headed families (with or without visiting fathers) form over fifty per cent of the family population (and female couples are socially accepted), in one north of England family I worked with, the child in question was the only child in his class to have a "second" mummy and found his visiting father's position hard to explain to his school classmates. Some fathers engaged in a serious quest for an appropriate role in their children's lives have also talked about their own growing up without a father, and their difficulty in developing ideas about their current potential role: 'I've never seen a dad in action, only my mate's dad, like, so it's hard."

Many fathers consulted to did not see how a dad who is unemployed, or who does not live with his baby, can still contribute to his child's life in important ways. Peer exchange is not necessarily supportive. It can include doubts about staying connected to children with whom you do not live: "It does you good to go down the pub and have a moan with your mates . . . easier than catching the train to see them sometimes." The separation of conception from fatherhood through sperm donation, and the multiple constructions of how family life can now be done, has further challenged any "taken for granted" arrangements for the father of the twentieth century discussed earlier. It places a new and different requirement on fathers to engage one by one in thinking about the importance of their part in children's lives and what being a dad will mean.

### How does a father "know" what to do? Messages and meta-messages on thinking

There are many myths and traditions in relation to "being a dad" that are largely unspecified and held loosely in a general social narrative about what good dads are for. These can be invoked by children and by mothers to promote action from men. Some of these come from basic human wishes for reassurance and security: "A dad is someone you should be able to snuggle up to and he will say 'it's OK; everything is going to be all right'." Others are culturally essentialist messages about fathers as providers and "heads of the family". Other sets of messages about "becoming a man" are organised around standing up for yourself and showing courage and bravery. These messages often need translation from the context of combat, whether in the playground, street, or warzone, to the intimacy of family life The notion of courageousness or bravery in building the skills for becoming a dad is a useful one for fathers who are able to compare and contrast between different settings when they have had to find courage in their lives (Barnes et al., 2005)

Gender and fatherhood, as part of the fabric of family and childhood life, are woven into a boy's idiosyncratic view of himself in relation to future fatherhood, and usually become updated in subsequent contexts in relevant ways. However, these contexts might not themselves include the translation of older cultural ideas underpinning manhood into what it takes to develop successfully as a parent. Family cultures are also organised by myths, legends, and traditions, and children take these in both consciously and less consciously through the rituals of family life over time. A child's perception of the relationships between all the gendered family positions—power over others, entitlements and rights, duties and responsibilities over more than one generation and the way the family handles these—as well as the many conversations in which gender is directly or indirectly discussed or alluded to, will offer either rigid or more fluid ideas on "knowing" how to become a man and father.

Bateson pointed out ambiguities in the word "know", addressing the many levels of "knowledge through which thinking needs to shift": learning and knowing through the senses as well as recognising, perceiving, and naming. Knowing about fathering is no less difficult than any other form of knowing. Too often the idea of fatherhood, or the principles by which a father believes he should be relating to his child, are cut off from knowing through the senses for many reasons.

> Our life is such that its unconscious components are continually present in all their multiple forms . . . in our relationships we continuously exchange messages about these unconscious materials, and it becomes important also to exchange meta-messages by which we tell

each other what order and species of unconsciousness (or consciousness) attaches to our messages. (Bateson, 1973b, p. 114)

Meta-messages often get lost or misunderstood when fathers are
disconnected from their children and no longer have such rich layers
of multi-level exchange available, either with the mothers of their children or with the children themselves. Communications in these
circumstances can become reduced to fragments, "tokens", which are
frequently misinterpreted and misunderstood by those for whom they
are intended.

Research evidence has indicated that, in western cultures, even as
recently as thirty years ago (influencing men who are the fathers of
today), the socialisation of emotion had marked gender differences
from infancy onwards. Parents responded differently to anger in boys
and girls, showing more tolerance and even encouragement to boys as
part of the development of "toughness". Such behaviours, first
encouraged within the home, then became reinforced at school,
further shaping ongoing gender differences. Boys were more likely to
fight it out, whereas girls attempted to come to consensus through
discussion. Boys were more likely to blame others, while girls were
more likely to blame themselves. The autonomic nervous system for
boys is known to be more sensitive to arousal (Hetherington, 1989,
Kraemer, 2000), but boys' upbringings, which emphasise damping
down of emotions, are less likely to provide mediating outlets for
emotions to be translated into words and thoughts about self in relation to others. These distinctions between boys' and girls' upbringings
are still a key difference for professionals to be aware of, since it still
has implications for work they undertake with parents aged over
thirty, although probably less so for parents in their twenties where
gendered ideas are likely to be more fluid. Discussions with boys in
sixth form college now also demonstrate the wide range of sexualities
that young people are thinking about and discussing, so that these
intersections will bring their own variations to who does what in
family life and how fatherhoods are named in relation to parenting in
the future.

When drawing on any theory that makes gendered distinctions
about emotionality, it is important to remember that many adults we
are now invited to work with are likely to have complex models of
intimacy and managing stress that often do not fit Western European

gendered norms. They might have been without kindness in family life, or might have been dispossessed of family and, increasingly often, of country. In addition, the stresses of managing traumatised existence in countries ravaged by totalitarian regimes or by war have constructed new parameters for men and for women in relation to their visions and perceptions of the role of father.

### Fathers and newborn babies: some research findings on what creates close connections

The orthodoxies of fatherhood in which any individual man might be trapped are now likely to be continuously challenged by the expectations of women, as well as the snowball effect of positive new experience generated by babies. Public ideas about the ability of fathers to enjoy tiny babies have changed totally in the past forty years. In the 1970s, when fathers first entered hospital birth rooms in the UK, fathers' importance to young babies began to surface as a subject for research, as Raphael-Leff observed (2008). Until then, sixty per cent of live births were conducted at home, which meant that men's feelings about their newborn babies, such as tenderness, protectiveness, and overwhelming love, remained private and did not contribute to reshaping public beliefs about fathers' emotionality and capabilities. Once the powerful effects of exposure to birth and fathers' connectedness to the baby, previously believed to be the domain of mothers, became available to researchers to study, they provided new information in the field of ideas about fatherhood. A meta-conversation about fathering as an intimate activity had nuanced research available to back it (Greenberg & Morris, 1974).

Studies showed that around the time of the delivery of their children, levels of testosterone in fathers decreased, while levels of prolactin (the hormone producing milk in mothers) increased (Storey et al., 2000). Men could be seen to be "wired" to engage in intimate hands-on parenting given the opportunity to be present (Grossman et al., 2002). The encouragement of skin-to-skin contact with fathers as well as mothers in hospital delivery rooms facilitated this. In many studies with infants and children, no difference has been observed in levels of maternal and paternal sensitivity. Research into the emotional reactions of expectant fathers also drew attention to the ways that a father's own presuppositions about fatherhood, foetuses, infants and their needs, and his fantasies and beliefs about these in relation to how he himself was looked after, are all important indicators as to how well he will engage with his infant (Raphael-Leff, 2008). Studies of families in which the father is primary carer indicate that differences between maternal and paternal handling are negligible when intimate familiarity with the baby is taken into account (Doucet, 2006; Pruett, 1993). Fathers are often aware of the needs of their babies and their partners but require encouragement and help in attunement. Hands-on involvement is enhanced by preparation and greater responsibility, which increase competence.

## Mutual influence in families where fathers live elsewhere: the study of positive partner relations and mutual influence in child development research

The systemic influences at work within unmarried families, and the pull between families of origin (usually on the mother's side) and fledgling beginner families of procreation, were rarely studied until the past decade. Now, social research projects from America have enlarged the scope of study of family and father to include the effects of the social environment on family life in African-American families and the involvement of fathers in non-married couples (McHale et al., 2012). A mother's positive regard for a father and the ways in which this can influence his participation with his children is significant, and a number of studies also emphasise the ways in which good fathering correlates with positive partner relationships (Matta & Knudson-Martin, 2006; Ngu & Florsheim, 2011, Perry & Langley, 2013).

## Developing a new identity as father: living separately but parenting together in the context of wider family tensions

When a father is neither married nor co-habiting, and he or his partner, or both of them, still live with their own parents, there can be complex issues around how to develop a common identity called "family". From the start, family life has to be shared with the grandparent generation. A father's own model of what fatherhood can entail will have been shaped by his own gendered family development. His family of origin, however, might not have equipped him to manage the expectations and requirements of another family system, that of his partner, with its own ideas about gender and role. Differences can blow up between a father and the family of his child's mother. A father then has the difficult job of developing his own practices of connecting to his baby within an extended family that is holding on to its own traditions and standards.

### Rituals and practices for an "out of house" father that fit with a mother and her family of origin

What rituals and practices can help a father construct a sense of connectedness, "ownership", and being a dad with his baby? Do the resources he provides, economic and emotional, entitle him to bonds with the baby in a mother's and grandmother's eyes? Fathers of all ages, but particularly young, uncertain fathers, in part define their role through the giving of gifts, clothing, equipment, and toys, as well as hands-on care, and can establish an "out-of-house" role in the baby's life. Discussions about equipment for the baby, arranging space for the baby to sleep in, discussing what kind of buggy to buy, are all important ways of anchoring a father to the coming life. They keep him connected to the mother, establishing a conversational and emotional domain that is shared. An alternative, less welcome pattern is one where marginalisation begins by mother holding discussions only with her "live-in family" and her women friends.

A father might also want to do things with his baby that are considered unsuitable by the mother's family, such as taking his baby for a beer with his mates, or to the pub in the pram to watch the football. His baby might be born in a context where there are many pairs of watchful and potentially disapproving eyes on him, limiting his freedom. Many court cases, driven by the desire for active fatherhood, have had their origin in these watchful and oppositional family contexts.

*Example.* Adie told me, with sadness, that his own father had moved out when he was a child and that he knew what it was like not to live with a father. He had seen his father "about once a month" from an early age. The idea of a fatherless child was a strong theme in his story about himself. It lay behind the inappropriate ways he had been trying to enforce a contact now prohibited by his son's mother and grandparents. "I had such a strong relationship with him, and they (Bex's mother Kaylee and her parents) have killed it. Bex doesn't want to know me now. Kaylee wants me to walk away, but I'm not going to . . . whether it takes two years or twenty years . . . kids need to know their father." Towards this end of "not walking away", Adie stood accused of a range of threatening incidents, stalking, threatening to walk off with the baby in his pram, and "poor parenting" (evidenced by a neighbour who had seen him "slap his son on the leg"). There were a number of rumours circulating against him on the estate, including that he was concurrently raising a baby with another woman.

In the face of his total denial of the poor fathering behaviours attributed to him, and his clear wish to be a presence in his children's lives, I talked with him about using his courage and determination in a different way. How could he turn his commitment to more positive tactics that would win Kaylee over to recognising his good intentions? I suggested that he might try and work on clearing his name if he wanted once more to be included in the family home of Kaylee, her parents, and Bex "so that Bex could be told a different story when he was older". I suggested that if he tried, he could put the record straight. Adie proposed to find out about Bex's likes and dislikes, write him letters, and maybe do a video diary. I attempted to help him think about the difficulties he had to face in developing a relationship with a two-year-old: as long as he had these stories being told against him by Bex's family it would be unlikely that Bex would feel he could make a relationship with him in the future and he would need to address Kaylee's concerns. Adie had the idea that if he could find a picture of himself doing something nice with Bex, then Bex would feel more like seeing him. He did not seem to take in the strength of the many narratives of his own "bad" behaviour that were being told about him on a daily basis by the family to whom Bex was closest.

Having a strong desire to be a father is not, on its own, enough. By demonstrating poor parenting (smacking, neglect, or inappropriate behaviour such as drinking or smoking dope while looking after his child), a father has to face up to its effects and take responsibility for change. A mother's tolerance depends largely on how a father behaves towards his children and his level of competence when with them.

The way he actually carries intentions through into positive actions is the significant indicator to a mother and her family of his capacity to become and to remain a father.

### Employment as a factor in a father's sense of self-worth that may influence his commitment to his child

The scaling down of permanent employment and the growth of zero-hours contracts, currently on the increase in the UK, could also contribute to a father's sense of not being able to plan for a separate future for his new family. It is likely to lead to mothers in uncertain economic and housing circumstances to depend equally or more on their own family of origin (if they are present in the country) than on the father of the baby. A young father might hunger for work as part of his own identity, but find he is deprived of it. "Earning money is still a crucial part of my role as a dad: it's come down the generations . . . but sometimes I sit and just look at my mobile all day waiting for a call to come through to tell me where to go today. And sometimes the fares are more than I can earn in the time I am given" (young father, Spring 2015). "In my family it's been usual for the man to earn more, but now just can't get work . . . and what do they [the men] have to offer the kids . . . yes they can look after the kids but still that's something they're just not as good at as the mum. It's better if you're both working, fairer, more even that way" (father in a family where his partner can earn more than he can, Summer 2014).

In families that have made the transition to systems of shared work and childcare, a different ethic can develop, with fathers sharing responsibility with their partners not only for emotional and financial support of the family, but also for direct and more equal involvement in the care of their children. This quality of sharing is one that many young fathers yearn for. They feel, and are at risk of becoming, estranged from children whom they love or would like to learn to love, but they feel anxious and disadvantaged. They might become caught in a paradox where the behaviour they need to show the mother of their child to gain her trust can best be learnt in the context of the developing child from whom they are estranged, as recent research from the Fragile Families Research Project in the US shows (Perry & Langley, 2013).

## Non-resident fathers: the benefits
## of involvement for children

Flouri's study of adolescents showed that boys benefited from father involvement, as evidenced by lower social difficulties. A father staying involved to age seven predicts lower likelihood of involvement with the police in teenage years as well as improving teenagers' academic motivation and general feelings of happiness. When assessing the interactive influences on fathers' continuing involvement, she cited contextual factors: the father–mother relationship and the child himself, emphasising that no universal claims can be made about the impact of father involvement on outcomes for children. Rather, studies show that certain aspects of father involvement in certain groups of fathers are associated with certain groups of outcomes for certain groups of children (Flouri, 2005; Flouri & Buchanan, 2002).

## Fathers who do not make it: does it
## matter to the children?

Evidence from the Fragile Fathers Study (Carlson et al., 2008), in addition to other studies cited above, indicate once again that it is not the frequency of contact with non-resident fathers that makes a long-term difference to children's wellbeing, but the nature of the non-resident fathers relationship with the children's mother and their ability to co-operate around the children. Greater frequency of father–child contact, engagement in father–child activities, and shared parental responsibility apparently lead to no essential measurable differences in children's wellbeing. Whereas live-in father involvement is positively associated with pro-social behaviour in children, where fathers live separately this is not the case and children's social behaviour might be more related to the relationship between them and their social fathers. Resident social fathers can often be involved as heavily as biological resident fathers with the children of their partners, and, in such cases, their involvement is equally beneficial for the children's development and behaviour. The role of other male relatives and their regular participation in the lives of children, could also be more beneficial than intermittent relationships with unco-operative, non-residential fathers.

*When there has been no family life—promoting connected fathering in the first two years of life: discontinuous change and new epistemologies*

It is obviously important, therefore, to promote genuinely co-operative parenting when parents live apart. When couples separate before any rhythms of living with their child have been established, working with them on the basis that both will continue to be involved in their child's life helps establish a joint epistemology or approach to the raising of their child across the different domains of development, even though they are living apart. The knowledge they both require includes developing some understanding of the internal logic of each other's emotional processes, which the children can later access and comprehend themselves. While this can be hard work even in families who have lived together for a long time, it is even harder work when a couple do not live together and never have done so. Most of the learning described in the changes in couple interaction of Rob and Jan (below) involved new learning: "learning about the context and acting according to a (shared) understanding of the rules and premises of the context in which learning takes place". Bateson argued that learning acquired in early life is likely to persist throughout life because of the self-validating nature of the behaviour that ensues. This assumption is based on stability in the system itself. If fathers are to gain or regain a relationship with their child following dissolution of a partner relationship, they have to become capable of new learning. This includes the rules and premises of the evolving context that they wish to become part of, as well as managing future discontinuous change in the evolving family context. Mothers rarely remain static in their own assumptions and behaviours around living with their children, and fathers' often desperate attempts to keep things "fixed" can become a burden, which contributes to more negative co-parenting.

*Rob and Jan: regulating complex conflicts of interest and constructing a framework for co-parenting*

Poverty, lack of housing, insecure employment, social adversity, and social exclusion, which weigh heavily upon families in the UK today, are ongoing stressors not yet fully accounted for in physical, mental, and emotional health. For young fathers who have been exposed to chronic stress in their childhoods, the concept that experiencing adversity and mishandling as children could still impact on their stress responses now can be useful to them in reducing reactive and hostile responses to their own children. The adverse impacts in their own lives can be referred to, thought about with courage, and worked with in ways directed towards responsible parenting. Hyper alertness and vigilance, products of early hostile environments, which might have been adaptive for "father as child", protecting him in a particular family or enabling him to be "street wise", do not assist in adaptation to the pace and rhythm required for looking after a baby.

Adverse early experience and the adaptation from hyper-vigilance and reactivity to connected fathering were among personal changes Rob had to contend with in deciding to become a father. Following a relationship of very short duration with his girlfriend, Jan, she became pregnant, and they were planning to move in together. This ended when Jan found out that Rob had been double-dating her best friend, Lal, while Jan was in the third month of pregnancy. Her rage was complicated by his assertion that he still wanted to be a fifty per cent father to the child, an idea she could not tolerate initially. She decided to continue with the pregnancy, although her "friends" were telling her that he was a "frightening manipulative bastard" and his "friends" were telling him that she "had stitched him up" by retaining the baby.

Over the last three months of her pregnancy, she came to recognise that, although unfaithful sexually, he was showing commitment to her as a pregnant woman. He demonstrated courage in standing up to his laddish friends and it seemed that the idea of coming fatherhood was generating an independence of thought and a new trajectory for his own behaviour. Rob brought some of the same flair he had previously developed in his own business start up to the idea of becoming a dad. Referred through his solicitor, the two of them came to ask for help in negotiating a contract for parenting their child "separately but together". I saw them individually, as well as jointly, to work with their ideas about how they would bring up their child, keep the level of acrimony down, and establish rhythms that would fit with a real baby and the real world.

We developed agreed goals around establishing a "good enough", orderly, secure attachment to both parents, rather than the disorderly, emotionally dysregulated attachment that Rob had experienced in his own childhood, where he had grown up in an impoverished and violent household. They both wanted to move from hyper reactivity to tolerating each other "well enough", so we drew up measures of polite behaviour that would not be upsetting to Pip (their child) on future visits and contact handovers. Rob welcomed the idea of learning about how to construct a secure attachment framework, taking up the idea that insecure attachments are more likely to create a greater inability to regulate stress and contribute to seeking multiple, often inappropriate, relationships later in life (as he had done himself). The concept of attunement—co-ordinating his child's expectations with his own responses—and taking into account the movement between two families meant that he would also have to take into account differences between Jan's way of doing things and his own, and the effect of these differences on Pip's nervous system. He took on board the nuances of promoting the regulation of his and Jan's stress systems, the way they managed these during visits, and the fact that this would relate to Pip's ability to regulate himself both in the present and in the future. He made lists and kept notes. He spoke of his own abusive childhood briefly—a combination of neglect, emotional extremities, and extremely violent discipline. He did not want to relive the emotional experience. In describing but setting aside his childhood, he asserted that he was determined to give his own child a better experience than he had himself.

## Establishing predictable patterns

We settled on the model of frequent and predictable visits by Rob to Jan's home (twice a week for the first six months). Early attachment work in the context of post-divorce visiting with children under three (Solomon & George, 1999) highlighted that a particular risk for this group of parents is whether a mother, herself distressed by the visit of a father for whom she might still have strong ambivalent feelings, is able to lessen any distress a baby might show at handover. Therefore, we worked on civility between the couple as well as normalisation of information-sharing around Pip. Over two years, we all learnt a lot as we went along: establishing safety structures for Pip's twice-weekly transitions from his mother's household to Rob's; securing equipment (safe car seats, highchairs, stairgates, etc.) and establishing feeding routines that met Jan's standards. Rob wanted to know about Pip's health each week in detail and a shared diary was established. Jan wanted formalised rules about communication, the leaving of phone messages, and the maintenance of pleasantries, asking Rob, for example, "Shall I ring you every couple of days and talk about Pip . . . would you like that?", and he answered "Yes, absolutely, but try not to be confrontational and sarcastic because it will shatter both of us." We focused on the behaviours that could lead to negative emotional escalation. These included clear financial agreements and record keeping on both sides. Rob wanted gratitude for the provision he had made (to be called careful, not "mean"), and Jan wanted him to realise that she was spending the money he gave her on Pip: "He doesn't have any proper understanding of the cost of this baby." They each had to learn to accept that the other would never see them the way they wanted to be seen. Jan knew she would always see Rob as a liar and, a year on, could not accept that her son Pip spent his weekends with "another mummy, Lal", but agreed not to "go on about it".

In maintaining the relationship while Pip developed, I spent time moving them from narratives of grievance and complaint about one anther towards narratives of pleasure in Pip and his development. For Rob, "Crawling around, gurgling bath-times, stroking the dog together, seeing the progress with physical activity . . . I keep a diary so I can record the progress." Jan said, grudgingly, "I can see that Pip really 'does' dad, it is odd the way boys 'do' men." The grievance–happiness balance changed as Pip reached his third year, by which time Lal had a baby with Rob. This was hard for Jan to cope with, and she fell back into a despising narrative of Rob as a man which was hard to shift, "A sad bugger who wasn't smart enough to see that we could have had a lovely family life who surrounds himself with younger people who probably think he's a sad old tosser . . ." Of contact, she said, "I'm prepared to recognise the role he has to fulfil in the future, playing ball with Pip and all that stuff, but I would worry if he becomes like him, rude, arrogant, and weird." As with many other mothers, it was very hard for her to witness the place she had hoped to occupy as his wife being filled by another woman with her own baby. Rob kept up his commitment to Pip, and a chance encounter in the street eight years later confirmed that father and son had maintained a strong relationship.

## What did Rob, as a first-time dad, take from his relationship as a father?

Rob's family had no money when he was a child, and he had gone out to make money in his teens and done well. What took him by surprise in relation to Jan's pregnancy was the strength of the feelings he developed towards his coming child, and the degree to which he wanted to prioritise him in his life. The security he gained from learning to "be a good father" helped him repair the damaging and depriving experiences of his own childhood. In prioritising fatherhood in the context of couple breakdown, he was able to pick up and go with the emotional growth potential in his own life, interrupting the negative trajectory of his former abusive emotional experience and ceasing to look for multiple attachments, as well as creating a secure future relationship with Pip. However, support for Jan was essential until the relationship was firmly established, Jan could see no harm coming to Pip, and, furthermore, that Pip positively loved his dad.

## Ann and Rick: assisted fertilisation and fatherhood "disposability"

The transformation of possible motherhoods through the growth of assisted fertilisation has led to changes in law in which the requirement for a *father* in a family has been replaced by the recommended *"value of a second parent"*. Simultaneously, choice of "designer" fatherhood through sperm donor sites has led to a specialisation of choice of "ideal" father by mothers not seeking live-in relationships with men, some of whom do not wish to live with women, either (Sheldon, 2005).

In the biological drive to have a child, there are many ways for a woman not to recognise a partner as an equal parent in the processes of conception, pregnancy, and birth, as Rick's experience showed. Ann was increasingly aware of the ticking of her own biological clock. She had worshipped her own father and, following his death, she decided her own child should have the image of a "good father in her or his mind". She recruited Rick, an old friend from her college days, who agreed to conceive with her on the condition that he would become a responsible father to the child, not be kept invisible. He believed that

Ann would come to love him enough to make this possible, although she did not wish to get married. They moved in together. Ann insisted on artificial insemination rather than intercourse, but expected Rick to assist in giving her regular hormone injections as part of the "joint project". When the pregnancy was well advanced, he sought consultation because he was afraid of the hostility Ann was showing towards him: "She is obsessed with her bump, and there is no room for me . . . I feel like the spare man in the system, the technician, very distant from the process."

In a joint interview, Ann told him that she could not find "space in her mind" for him at the moment, but she hoped this feeling would change once her baby [girl] was born. However, when Em arrived, Ann actively discouraged Rick from getting close to her. He persisted, with my encouragement, and they did set up rhythms around bath-time and bedtime, which meant he developed a relationship with Em. "Em sleeps with Ann, so Ann is exhausted and Em will only nap during the day if Ann is with her. It is very hard for Ann and I to have any time on our own together, and Ann has decided it's probably easier if she just gives in and keeps it like it is. We can never leave Em with anyone to get some time to ourselves . . . if Ann and I do separate, then Em won't be able to stay with me." He found, to his distress, that Ann had been telling her friends that she got his sperm from a donor website. When challenged by Rick, she denied this. She subsequently went on holiday with her mother and Em without Rick, though continuing to live with him (sleeping separately) in their flat. When I invited the two of them to consider what stories they would tell Em in the future about her early days in the world, Rick said, "I would tell her we loved each other very much and decided to have a baby together", and Ann said, "We wanted you but it didn't work out between us."

Rick continued to yearn for Ann's approval in the face of evidence that it would not be forthcoming. Ann said that she was not sure that she wanted the "burden of life with a man", and in the following year Rick moved back to his old flat. "My relationship with Em suffers . . . when I lived with her I would come back from work and be greeted with a beaming smile. Now she is more likely to turn to Ann. I only get to spend two evenings a week with her." Unfortunately, Rick's narrative of self-pity militated against him either getting closer to Ann or having more time with Em. He construed Anne's lack of affection to him on his visits as evidence that he would not be of importance in Em's life: "Why do I bother . . . she is not bonded to me and it all seems a bit pointless and just easier to walk away . . . it feels as though all the joys of parenthood will be denied me . . . a live-in father gets more time in a weekend than I get in a month . . ."

The questions raised by Rick and his experience are more widely relevant for fathers. There is no requirement for a "father" for assisted reproduction to be legally authorised, and a co-parent or other significant adult can be found instead. How the relationship with a "significant other" is presented to the baby in a mother's mind will vary, and in her fantasy might include a former loved person (such as Ann's father). This denies recognition of the feelings of a real father, which develop alongside the life of his growing child. A legal recognition of paternal responsibility might have to replace a "natural" recognition if the father wishes to continue in his relationship with his child.

### Parental mental illness and early fathering for live-out fathers: creating secure attachment pathways in difficult contexts

In this section, the hazards posed to a father by managing a mental illness in his partner alongside staying connected to his newborn child are discussed. Never-married fathers, temporarily acting as primary carers in the context of a mother's mental illness, have to pay particular sensitive attention to regulating her distress, especially where there is no wider family to support her. Many parents (now grandparents) do not live in the same country as their children, as with the two couples described below. A father can form a very close attachment to his child when a mother becomes disturbed following the child's birth, and can "step in" to protect both mother and baby from major distress by providing some stability in relation to the interactions around the new baby. For some mothers who already function with high emotional intensity prior to becoming pregnant, recovery can be very long and, in some instances, their rhythms do not rebalance following the birth of a child (Joyce, 2014; Ramchandani et al., 2009). An emotional equilibrium, which was adequate when only one person (the self) had to be managed, is tripped into disequilibrium by the presence of a dependent and demanding being—a child. A father can step in and act as a protection here while the mother heals, and a mother–baby relationship is formed more slowly, as Quentin was able to do below. However, in other couples (see Aisha and Bashir, who follow), the illness that develops is too great for the holding capacity of the couple, and the child (and the emotional relationship with the father) remains at risk.

## Emotional distress or mental illness

How mental illness is to be conceptualised has been a controversial consideration in much clinical work, used in ill-assorted ways in both private and public discourses. In private contexts, partners are frequently noted to define each other's behaviours as irrational. This definition usually has at least two components: a failure to recognise the mind-set of one partner by the other, as well as a tendency to define the degree of intensity or extremity of emotional responses of the other as beyond normal thresholds—"out of it". Once the concept of the "irrational" has become ongoing currency within a relationship, it can move on to considering the other as suffering a disturbed mental state (even if unlabelled). It might then be a further short jump to labelling this as mental illness. The definition of mental states of great intensity as linked to categories of mental illness remains controversial.

Quentin and Guilia described a complex state of disequilibrium when they came for a consultation on how they could hold their parental relationship together. Guilia had a difficult pregnancy and a caesarean, which she found "of mind-blowing proportions". Quentin took two weeks off and sat with her in hospital. He worked from their shared home for the following two weeks: "The only time she was really happy was when she was totally looked after . . . the outside world didn't exist. No one else saw Sam [the baby] for two weeks because I literally did everything around her. Her mum came over for the next three weeks, but as soon as I went back to work it started unravelling." A year on, he reflected, "I have never met anyone else with such anger . . . two years of relentless anger punctuated by brief bursts of happiness. She threw me out a dozen times, attacked me frequently, tore the buttons off my shirt, bit me . . . I decided eventually it would be better for Sam if all that anger wasn't constantly aroused." He moved out when Sam was one: "It was the hardest decision I have ever made. To start with I continued to visit daily."

Guilia confused him with alternating invitations to come closer, wishes to start again, followed by derogatory attacks and "abrasive revilement". Most visits started with goodwill, then dissatisfaction set in "an attitude of aggrieved hostility". Guilia said of herself and Quentin during a second meeting, "I couldn't bear the conflicting emotions, on the one hand wanting him to be there, on the other wanting him out of my sight." In spite of declaring that she wanted to work in couple therapy with Quentin, she subsequently decided she could not face it. She showed an increasing "active malevolence" towards the relationship between Sam and his father. She refused to let Quentin put him to bed or to take him from Quentin (she made Quentin put him down on the floor before she would pick him up herself) and if Sam was clinging to his trouser legs, she would say "This is your life now Sam . . . look how your life is, Sam."

### Interrupting negative cascades

Quentin decided to focus on maintaining strength and stability for Sam in the face of this escalating disturbance, because he believed only he could make a difference to the instability in Sam's experience. He assured Guilia that he would stay connected to Sam, in whatever changing context. Two years and many journeys later, he reported that Guilia's pattern of love and hate towards him continued but that, through the efforts of lawyers, mediators, and therapists in three countries, he had kept the relationship going. This included changing his work life to accompany Guilia to her home country for a year. "My relationship with Sam is blossoming. We have a brilliant relationship. He enjoys his time with me and often asks if he can stay longer, but equally I know he loves his mum and finds the process difficult. I would love to see him more but at least I see him every week now and we have an intimate and trusting relationship . . . it's my relationship with him that has made the struggle worthwhile in the long view."

### Bashir and Aisha: father's love for his son bypasses respect for mother in her mind

Quentin was able to take Guilia into account in his determination to live alongside Sam. In his mind, he could "keep her safe", containing some of her more ferocious and damaging moods. In other circumstances, in taking the mother into account as the "gatekeeper to the child", a father can risk the mother's enmity and, in periods of greater mental fragility, extreme reactions: "You do not know how to harness the goodness in me", Aisha yelled at Bashir. She chided him with his inability to understand the paramount importance of her position as mother, "You're not at the same emotional level with him as me." As he described it in our joint couple meetings: "The very lovely Aisha with whom I have been in love for many years and still love, can turn into a black hole . . . all evil things rush in and she treats me with total contempt." For many months, they struggled in therapy together to achieve some emotional co-regulation of their tempestuous relationship, and the emotional violence they drove each other into. "It's wired into our brain"; "We just can't change however much we want to"; "We can't always be friends and that's why we don't live together . . . we get on better if we are not together, but then we have to come together again . . . we exchange terrible insults . . . including those of madness."

Aisha showed greatest hatred for Bashir not allowing her pre-eminence in the struggle for parental ascendancy: ". . . who is the most important parent? Don't forget I am." Her own mother had always called her father "useless", and she herself had been encouraged by her mother to abuse her father. Her instinct to abuse Bashir was very strong. Bashir said, "I do not want to become a 'doormat' for her." They had quarrels over the upbringing of Rafi: "If he says I am too strict I put my hand over his mouth and say 'if you ever say anything bad about me I will stop you coming to see him'." These exchanges could escalate to pushing and reciprocal shoving and hitting. She said of him, "You do not think of me, of what I need . . . there is a way you love our child which discounts me entirely . . . you go straight to the love for him and bypass me . . . think before you do anything . . . you are the only one who will miss out."

The respect a father is able to maintain, and show to the mother of his child, remains key to making co-parenting work for the children even in these difficult conditions. Coming together for couple work held Bashir and Aisha together in a containing way over eighteen months, but without significantly changing the pattern between them, as it seemed they could not bear either to get closer or further apart. They decided to have another baby to see if that would improve their relationship. Five years later, I learnt that they continued in much the same way, each of them having different intermittent partners, but unable to let one another go.

### Reflections on how managing the "illness or dysregulated component" in the two relationships was managed differently by the couples, as well as by me

What was the connection Quentin needed to make in relation to the "disorganised/distorted aspect" of Guilia's attachment (the space in her mind in which there was no room for a relationship with him and a complex one of alternate closeness and rejection of Sam). Quentin was able to retain respect for Sam's love for Guilia throughout the four years I was intermittently in touch with him (by email and by phone when he was not in London). He came to recognise the limits of Guilia's capacity for closeness, to him as well as to Sam, which made him work hard on retaining neutrality rather than displaying criticism or emotional involvement in her presence. This, in turn, led her to feel recognised by him as Sam's mother and allowed a parallel, though unstable, respect from her towards the relationship between Quentin as a father and Sam.

What was similar and what was different in the relationship between Bashir and Aisha? Bashir was too often provoked into retaliatory and critical exchanges with Aisha for her to feel there was any respect on his part for her own relationship with Rafi. She would also constantly try, by any means possible, to extract recognition from Bashir for her as a *woman*. This would lead to her becoming close and seductive for a period, thus confusing his attempts to maintain a more neutral fathering relationship with Rafi and transforming it into a relationship based on desire for Aisha. In turn, this would subsequently make a separation on both sides essential, as the critical, over-involved, and hostile, but yearning, relationship was too much for both of them and led to destructive interactions in front of Rafi.

With each of these couples, I felt warmth and respect for their painful and volatile struggles and held on to a strong hope that they would negotiate these on behalf of their children. However, in both cases, I had to learn the limits of what I could achieve in any moderation of the powerful emotional effects of their relationships with each other. My natural inclination, which is to engage emotionally with a couple's dilemmas, had to be tempered to a more dispassionate stance in the face of emotional woman abuse to male partners, a resonance from my own childhood. Both couples were able to experience my belief in their developing capacity as parents and gave me feedback on this following the end of our work together. "You were able to show us you could hold on to the possibility of us remaining good parents even though we often wanted to hurt each other."

These fathers had built recognition of unpredictability into their own work patterns as well as their romantic and parental lives. In the instance of Quentin, and of three other determined fathers partnering women with mental illness or extreme forms of unregulated emotional behaviour with whom I worked over several years, the capacity to work from home or to take their work across the globe made a significant difference to their continued fathering.

# CHAPTER FOUR

# Getting connected after a long absence—fathers re-entering their children's lives: conflicts of interest, belief, and attachment

G reater attention is now paid to ways of protecting and encouraging non-married fathers' links to their children following any form of parental separation. This has come about through the more assertive claims of fathers themselves, network support groups (Fatherhood Institute, 2012), a heightened awareness of children's rights to an ongoing relationship with both their parents, as well as to a human rights ethic within family law on the right to family life (Collier & Sheldon, 2008). Legal links between unmarried fathers and their children have been strengthened by the inclusion of fathers' names on a child's birth certificate, and legal responsibilities that go alongside this have been enacted. In the social domain, promoting fathers' involvement to address youth crime and boys' educational underachievement has tended to rely on mobilising ideas of masculinity, authority, and power quite different to those ideas informing policy agendas aimed at engaging fathers in a relationship with young children. These are based on intimacy, nurture, and connectedness. Lewis et al. (2002) noted this ongoing dichotomy of fatherhood; fathers as strong but uncaring, necessary for their contribution to order and discipline *vs.* eager and caring, but rejected by hostile mothers. In daily family experience where fathers and children are connected, emotional co-regulation can develop within a framework in which exploration and attachment lead on to the development of age appropriate discipline, so that both nurture and authority are incorporated and these aspects of fathering become joined up (Hill et al., 2014).

## Mothers want fathers to change and fathers do not keep up

Lewis and co-authors (2002), in the small-scale but detailed study of fathering following cohabitation breakdown, enquired specifically how fathers had carried out care and responsibility towards their children while living together with their mothers and further explored how, on break-up, residence, child care, and contact arrangements had been decided. The study found that, in spite of couples having set up as non-married families with a bias towards being unconventional, the absence of many conventionally expected skills in the fathers of their children subsequently contributed to women leaving them. The growth in earning power for many women has also led to a readiness in some mothers to "let a father go" if he does not meet her expectations. These decisions are separate from decisions taken within a context of domestic violence or partnership aggression. They are just a feeling that "he isn't worth the hassle". Where a mother subsequently objects to a father wishing to make contact by legal means, using the umbrella of parental "rights to contact", often following a long absence, the family situation might be felt by the courts to require assessment. In this context, I came to work with fathers seeking further contact and mothers who were ambivalent or doubtful about any value that a father could bring to their children's lives.

## Biological fatherhood relationship breakdown and social fatherhoods that follow

Whereas biological paternity can now easily be proved, the ideas of a young child having active, face-to-face exposure to their biological father of whom they had no earlier direct daily experience could remain problematic for a mother, especially when she has re-partnered and the child has a "committed" social father. Preference in law has usually been given to the best interests of the child and his or her psychological and emotional capacity to benefit from the relationship, rather than to the father seeking connection and his own wellbeing. A clear definition of what is "best" is usually a summation of many complex variables. A father's own life circumstances might have changed since he conceived his child, leading him now to acknowledge his wish for active paternity and the determined quest to establish such a possibility. Social and financial circumstances might have improved, equipping him to feel more empowered to seek out his child again and take on some economic and emotional commitment. The wish for a relationship with his child might have grown in significance over the years, and a longing to be recognised by his child and be known to him or her has set in. The structures available to fathers through law have meant that if his recognition by a mother who primarily sees him as an irresponsible parent is to succeed, any emotional distress on his part can often only be packaged as "father's rights". The paradox of a rights-based approach is that as a dominant discourse, it can construct negative images of "dispossessed fathers" as angry, and sometimes even foolish, people in the minds of the public and can further prevent a father being seen as a desirable parent by a mother.

### Life's wear and tear: stress and the concept of allostatic load

Life damage, wear and tear to a father's body and mind, has to be taken into account in assessing some fathers' capacity to take future responsibility for a child. The cognitive skills and affective functioning of a dispossessed father, his state of mental health, and the emotional or social resources he possesses to manage a reintroduction into the life of a child who is already happily settled in a family context without his presence will all need to be sympathetically considered (Howell & Sanchez, 2011).

In working with many of the highly stressed fathers I have seen over the past twenty years, the concept of allostatic load has been useful in thinking about a diminished capacity in some fathers to form emotional relationships and, in particular, to support future emotional relationships that are appropriate for children in realistic ways in their own minds (Cicchetti, 2011; Ganzel & Morris, 2011). The term allostasis was coined to describe the body's response to shifts in biological systems and refers to the wear and tear undergone by physiological systems to maintain stability in contexts of extreme protracted stress. Allostasis is distinct from homeostasis. Whereas homeostatic processes promote stability by working within the established ranges of physiological systems, allostatic processes modify these ranges (Beauchaine et al., 2011). The concept was originally developed in relation to immune system responses and has since been expanded to include adaptations within other biological systems, as well as changes in psychological functioning in response to a range of environmental challenges. Fathers who have been in states of acute anxiety could become significantly depleted, and the psychological adaptations they have made over time, their allostatic load, can be likened to the wear and tear on the body of repeated adaptation over time. Such wear and tear can shape future responses to stress and might well result in responses that become maladaptive. While the literature is too enormous to reference with respect, key papers on motivation, mood regulation, and social affiliation are of relevance to some of the relational work we do with fathers and families in prolonged stressful circumstances (Beauchaine et al., 2011; Patterson & Vakili, 2014).

Many women do not wish for continuing paternal involvement, particularly if they fear it will upset a life they have developed following the earlier separation. The revival of a father's interest can be for many different reasons. Sometimes, such a quest is a logical extension of what is felt by a father to be a "natural right" to develop a biological relatedness with a child into a social relationship, a trigger jolted by recognition that to be connected to one's own child and his or her development is one of life's joys. Other reasons might be more malevolent, like the wish to spoil a family life of which the biological father is not a part, or revenge on a woman whom he cannot get out of his system.

## Sally, Rowan, Aileen, and Tom

In the Family Law Reform Act of 1987, the Law Commission considered abolishing distinctions between married and unmarried fatherhood, but subsequently recognised that granting full parental rights to all unmarried fathers might undermine a mother and her children, and any family unit she might subsequently form with a new partner. In daily life, defining "father" might be unclear. This applied to Sally's family. As Aileen said about the "awkward" situation between herself, Rowan (her child Sally's biological father), and Tom (her husband and Sally's social father), "When you're not married he doesn't have any rights to the child, his name is not on the birth certificate . . . yes, she's our child, but Tom has had the bringing up of her."

Rowan's approach to Sally, his daughter, demonstrated both a wish for his daughter and a wish for her mother. Following an overseas term of duty in the army, where he had received a bad head injury, Rowan decided to make Sally part of his life in spite of the fact that Sally already thought of a friend of his as her dad. Aileen, Sally's mother, had subsequently partnered with Tom, who became Sally's social father from birth. Rowan, however, believed Sally "knew" *him* as her dad, reporting that she had looked him in the eye and said, "I want you to look after me, but you don't want to", during a teatime visit to his own mother when she was three. He had pursued Aileen intermittently, sending her sexual invitations confused with threats, and behaving as though Tom had no place in Aileen's life. Aileen had approached the courts both for a protection order to prevent Rowan from harassing her, and to establish a procedure for assessing whether Sally had any feeling for Rowan as her dad.

### Fragile stories of a connection that was wished for but not carried out

The occasions on which Rowan based his own story of Sally's attachment to him were fragile and unevidenced. They relied on intermittent professions of love on his part and belief in Sally's returned love, rather than offering evidence of time spent together during which any solid bonding might have taken place. Rowan's ideas of what he would contribute to Sally's life were clear, even if his language was confused. "I have got that love that I want to offer her . . . and I think she might have that for me. I would like to take her swimming, and kick a ball around, and maybe help with her education."

Aileen feared Rowan's intrusion into her now stable family life. "It is more for his own good than for Sally's." She also worried that Rowan wanted to get closer to *her* rather than believing his stated intention that he wanted to be a father. Sally's social father, Tom, declared, "While I don't bear him any grudge, I have been there for Sally since she first poked her head out into the world . . . I was there and I have looked after her ever since." He thought the way Rowan had built an imaginary relationship with Aileen was very strange, "like a man pining for his wife of long standing".

### Assessing Sally's responses in relation to Rowan as father

Sally and I met under the banner of sharing her current school project on "different sorts of families". Her mother did not want to say anything about the truth of the situation to her but had prepared photographs and drawings of different families which we built on in our meeting together. Whereas Sally guessed all the photograph relationships correctly, she said of one in which she appeared with Rowan, ". . . I don't remember who he is", although she recognised the kitchen dresser behind his head and said, "That might be Betsy's" (correctly naming Rowan's mother). She showed no awareness that Rowan might be in any relation to her other than as a "friend of my mum's".

Aileen had come to recognise that she would have to bring Rowan into the family at some point, but thought that when Sally was eight it would be better, as she remembered her elder daughter becoming more "sensible" about this time, and "you could have a good discussion with her". Rowan became upset and angry at the idea of a wait, and said that Aileen was still trying maliciously to impede his contact with his daughter. "I look at her picture every day and cry . . . I would just like to be her father . . . she'll be able to talk to me and I'll be able to talk to her, and she will understand me better now than when she was little." I helped him refine this into something he could share with Sally when they met. "You were a happy surprise and looking back I would say you are the best thing I have to look to." He went on to add, "I would say mum and Tom have done the best they possibly could do in the circumstances to bring you up . . . I don't want to take that away from them, I just want to be part of your life."

### Keeping me away from my daughter and "telling lies"

However, one of the difficulties of sustaining a story with a positive intent on Rowan's part was that he would swerve in his mind from his good intentions towards Sally to bad thoughts about why Aileen did not recognise his potential as a sexual partner. Details of the many frightening incidents in which he had accosted, confronted, or assailed her with letters, phone calls, etc., were set aside by him for an alternative rhetoric of his rights as a father. I used a developmental approach, which, as a "third thing" in a conversation about a child, can be useful in interrupting other distorted trains of thought about a former or current partner. I invited him to think about tempering his own impatience as a grown man against the needs of a little girl who has to grow up a bit herself before she can make sense of it all. Rowan responded positively to this, reflecting on how recovering from his injuries had made him more patient, as had learning new skills. Although despondent at the wait, he agreed to it in the knowledge that he would know his daughter more fully in the future.

### Reflections on my involvement

What was happening in Rowan's mind? His inability to take into account the mind of Sally's mother, Aileen, as a mother initially prevented him from understanding the probable future effects on Sally of his appearance as a father if he insisted on being made known to Sally now. Rowan had unfinished business with Aileen, which he seemed unable to take responsibility for and agree to manage, and this strong sexual yearning often interfered with the stated primary goal of wanting to become a responsible parent. Sex, rather than parenting, would become the higher order principle of engagement. His sexual yearning for her remained a presence threatening the goodwill she might develop towards him as Sally's father. The recognition that Aileen found his pursuit frightening, and that this militated against his success as a potential father to Sally, required some vigorous debate as well as sympathetic acknowledgement of his longings for love.

### Does the child having a social father affect a biological father's chances of making a successful connection with his child?

If a father is not present in the child's early construction of intimacy, the idea of a relationship with father as of a higher importance than other relationships in a child's life is likely to suffer. If a social father is present during this time and has formed a strong attachment to the child, a father's "comeback" will need to relate both to the child and to the generosity of spirit of a social or stepfather (as with Rowan and Tom, above). It is also important to note that securely attached children can make a great many relationships with other adults without their primary bonds with the father who was there for them from the start being threatened. So, the answer becomes "it depends".[2] When absent fathers are not present (in the mother's mind or in the narratives of others, such as grandparents, uncles, and aunts), a child is likely to be uncertain what to make of such a person if he subsequently appears. In the absence of a surge of attachment feeling in a younger child or an ongoing curiosity in an older child, guidance from known parents is likely to be the primary influence. Much of the success of a father's approach for ongoing connection will, therefore, depend on his acceptance by a mother, and by any other relationships central to the child's life, including a social father. A father who has become disconnected from his own children could discover himself as a bit player within a powerful context of wider family relationships that his child now belongs to, the strength and security of which he has not anticipated.

Working with children who do not know their fathers, but whose fathers want to enter their lives, allows unusual conversations with younger children about what a child expects of a father. "What is a daddy for?" is a conversation with different parameters at ages four, six, nine, twelve, and in the teenage years. Exploring with fathers what they believe they can bring to a child's life is also a delicate and often fragile process. For fathers who have had an early period of "hands-on" caring for their child in the first year or two of their lives, the positive qualities in the backstory of their early attachment to their child, and any detailed knowledge they might have of their infant's earlier development, can increase the probability of a subsequent relationship. The child might also have a shadowy awareness of them. However, again, if a long period of absence has followed a parental separation, following which a mother has re-partnered, the earlier parental attachment might be in conflict with the subsequent attachments a young child has developed, and these, if they are ongoing, might now be preferred by the child. A child's readiness for a father is a powerful aspect of reconnecting, to be understood in each attempted relationship, and is discussed further in the different responses of Chloe and Shane that follow.

*Wished-for relationships with children.*

When assessing the family and the two current separate worlds of a mother and a father, and considering the changes that would occur for the child if a father were to become more present, making use of an attachment-related model in a schematic way is useful in considering the future. The importance of a specific dynamic model within a father (his representation of child and family in his inner model of family life) are part of a framework for considering the reality of his intentions and wishes in relation to a potential real relationship with his children. The strength of his wishes (usually for a particular quality of intimacy and "specialness" in the child's life and mind) and the reality of what is possible might be far from one another where a gap has been sustained over some years.

*Fathers and mothers differing accounts of why life together did not work out*

In post co-habitation breakup, lack of clarity about the reasons for the original breakup has been marked. The nature of the father's own real-life attachment to the child and the amount of hands-on care he was able to give before the separation is important to clarify in detail to assess whether a father–child bond has some reality to work with. Even one year of a committed relationship with an infant can make a significant difference to how a father and child subsequently reconnect, and where there has been no such period, a relationship and how it will be constructed takes on more of a new supportive exercise (as with Rob and Jan in Chapter Three) than a reconstruction.

## Is it ever too late to come into a child's life?

Fathers who have taken up a relationship with their child following the early years, in some cases not previously knowing the child existed, challenge the notion that it is not possible to make an intimate relationship later in the child's development. The success of this attempt is likely to depend largely on the commitment a father makes once the mother has signified acceptance of his presence in her child's life. Walt, for example, found that a former girlfriend, Johanna, in Australia, had a child who, from the images he had seen of him, looked remarkably like himself. When he questioned Johanna about this, she denied that the little boy was his child. As Johanna was by then co-habiting, he accepted her statement, although as far as he knew no other father for Ollie had made his presence known. Two years later, he saw a further image of Ollie (on social media) and could no longer deceive himself; a key moment in his narrative. He decided to fly over and meet him. Johanna had now ended her relationship, and felt more prepared to receive Walt and allow him into Ollie's life. In spite of there being no prior "attachment relationship", there was an instantaneous recognition between them. Ollie was wary that Walt would disappear again. However, the quality of the relationship rapidly changed as he realised that his father's commitment was to becoming a permanent presence in his life. "I think what actually happened, if I'm honest, is that all the things that I've been brought up to believe, this actually said to me, 'OK, what way are you gonna jump?' You've got to sort those contradictions out now. You have to. Now it's your turn to actually, in terms of this little life, to actually prove to yourself, as much as anything else whether you actually do believe the things you say you believe, about being a reasonable human being" (Walt, 2014, personal communication).

## Negotiating distance and closeness

As a child gets older, the degree of closeness or distance he is willing to accept from a newly appearing father will vary. I have known fathers who have moved back into live-in relationships, sharing households, but not beds, with partners from whom they had earlier separated. They have found that children who were very small when they left required time and commitment before the child would trust them in the role of "daddy". While the attribution of "mother as gatekeeper" is widely used, there is often little accompanying discussion of what is encompassed in the term. It is likely to include a mother's wish to protect her child from the disappointment and pain of further relationship breakdown, and a natural tendency to tread warily on behalf of herself and her own relational world, as well as the social world that she has put together for her child. Children who have missed a father's presence are likely to share her wariness or to have their own.

### *What have fathers seeking a role in their child's lives through the court said they would like to do with their children and contribute to them?*

What are the things fathers say they want to do with, and on behalf of, their children? The fathers I have met who had not lived with their children at all, or who had left before they were two years old, did not have clear ideas about a future role, but among their goals were elements of the things that, as research demonstrates, generate wellbeing for both children and fathers. These include play, responsibility, and "watching over" the next generation: "Read a story at bedtime, go to the park, help with homework, kick a ball around; give them a bath, teach him/her to ride a bike, go shopping, have a meal together, help with computer, watch him/her do sports, go to school events". Snarey (1993), in a four-decade study of working-class American men initiated in the 1940s, found that a father's greater involvement with his children fostered children's educational development and later career competence in the lives of both sons and daughters. Fathers' own wellbeing related to satisfaction with their paternal roles and to a sense of "watching over" the next generation. The desire to be connected to the future through being part of the development of their own children has, in my own experience, been a strong part of fathers' drives in seeking out a relationship with them. Equally strong to the success of this venture has been children's sense of their own control over the terms and conditions of taking a father into their lives.

### *Suspending any formal ideas about what a father should be*

In the examples given in this chapter, we can see different contexts for constructing fatherhoods.

1. Fathering a child born as a result of uncommitted sexual liaison, which the father then decides several years later to turn into a living relationship, in one instance failing to pay attention to the child's mother having re-partnered.

2.   A deliberate decision by a mother to create a baby with a man who was not committed to co-residence and "an open mind" approach to his relationship with his child.

3.   An initially mutual commitment between a couple, which broke down within the third year of the child's life for disputed reasons. Inevitably, ideas about being a father within these different contexts are diverse.

Working with would-be fathers, who are uncertain about what they want to offer to the children they fathered at a different period of their lives, requires a suspension of any formal idea of what a father should be in favour of promoting as good a relationship as is possible between the father that is present now and his child. Children have different responses to the approaches of a person called "father" and different curiosities, both about the man himself and about what they, as children, might become in relation to a man they do not yet know. The process becomes a co-evolvement of relationship, with evolving parameters, mediated between child, father, and mother, and any current partners, and wider relational systems.

### *Living alongside unpredictability—Adela, Chloe, and Harold: intermittent sightings and uncertain phone calls*

Harold had three children in different parts of the world, two daughters and a son, maintaining an emotional but erratic relationship with each of them in which there were no rhythms or reliabilities that each child could take for granted. At the time I first met Chloe, his younger daughter, when she was six years old, he was living in Canada. Chloe was aware that he was called her "father", and had seen him once or twice a year for two or three days at a time. Until she reached the stage of school when everyone aged seven was required to do their family history, and found that most of the girls in her class had daddies who came home at the weekends (if not every evening), she had not voiced any particular expectations of him (according to her mother). However, she obviously had wishes, fears, and imagination, which she demonstrated in modelling and doll play when we met. In most of her three-dimensional constructions a tame animal, or princess, was surrounded by a castle, and wild animals were guarding her from the outside world. Following the class project, she became both more curious about what a daddy was, and more exacting in her expectations of him. My consulting room offered a place where her uncertainties could be thought about and discussed, at first very obliquely, but becoming more straightforward as she engaged in the idea that she had a voice in the process herself.

Her mother, Adela, retained an open-hearted affection for Harold, but demanded a discipline from him in relation to Chloe which she had been willing to forgo for herself. She described him as "Very odd, bright . . . not quite right . . . his feelings are always right in your face and there is a hidden side. . . . Ninety-five per cent of what he says may not be true, and when I press him his story crumbles . . . it doesn't make sense and that is what Chloe picks up now . . . I was terrified of having a baby with someone so weird, but I went ahead out of deep warmth for him . . . he was perfect for me at the time." Adela was the main earner. She talked about the "raw nerve of lone mothering", which had been tapped by the family map exercise at school, and had made up her mind that she should maintain the thread of the relationship between father and daughter, however ragged.

An important feature of making Harold's visits work over the following two years involved Chloe in setting up some of her own rules for managing his unpredictability, and subsequently coaching her father in how to keep to the rules: "Bring your own food for lunch, only take pictures of me with your phone if I want you to . . . go when you're not wanted . . . do not lie to me, 'cos I know when you're doing it." Initially, she asked me to pass these messages on between meetings. On Harold's request, I set up a "talk" system with him by phone. We discussed what made Chloe uneasy, and what she wished for in coming visits: "Give her all your attention when you are with her; please remember that, although very grown up in some ways, she is only seven years and one month old; she wants you to stop teasing her." Talking on demand with a neutral third party (me) who was child focused, being recognised as a daddy with a serious intent, as well as talking developmentally about Chloe, encouraged Harold to persist in the relationship and take Chloe's child-size wishes into account.

Questions of expectation and entitlement arising from Chloe's curiosity were an ongoing discussion point. What might Chloe be entitled to expect from a person called "daddy"; what knowledge did he have about what other girls in her class have in the way of time with their daddies, and how did this compare to her, Chloe's, experience? How do daddies get on with other people in the family, such as grannies? "So you see, Harold, a lot of it is compare and reflect." In subsequent conversations with Chloe and Adela on his visits to London over two years, which included the three of them coming together "as a family", Harold stated openly that he had no understanding of developmental difference; that Chloe at seven could think differently from Chloe at three had been new to him. However, as long as ideas could be made active and concrete—"specific examples, please"—he would do his best. Chloe, in turn, began to sculpt their times together and invite him to do specific things that other daddies did, with her "stay for bedtime and read me a story."

In my early meetings with Chloe she was nearly seven, and was puzzled. She knew she had a half sister and brother because her father would tell her about them, but she felt threatened by these unknown blood ties and what she was supposed to feel about them, "I don't know a single real thing about Havana and Zak . . . Havana has a mummy who my daddy married and then he divorced her very soon . . . he flew over to see me when I was a baby and now I am eight he wants me to go to see him in Canada." By eight, she could say, "I wish he could come and see me a bit more", and "When he comes to London he should stay near us . . . a normal daddy would say 'oh I'm coming to London, shall I come and see you', and then stay near me."

### A family interview: Chloe takes charge

An extract from one family interview when Chloe was eight shows Harold's thinking being developed by his daughter. Chloe had decided to challenge him about his infrequent visits. Harold declared that the limitations on his visits were based on an (unevidenced) conversation with a judge, a friend of his, his inner gold standard of a good father's behaviour . . . "two hours a month, that was the recommendation, which adds up to two days a year", to which Chloe replied, "Daddy, if you don't come more often I will feel more and more shy of you." Harold said, "Two hours a month was the recommendation", and Chloe said, "That was then; six years ago . . . things have changed." Of his assumption that she would be like Havana, his elder daughter, she said, "I am a child not a teenager, I would like you to know. I am different from Havana, and my mummy is different from Havana's mummy . . . every child is different from each other." Harold said he would feel more comfortable, and come more often, if he could see her on her own, not supervised by granny, and she said firmly, "I don't feel safe with you, you turn your phone off so I couldn't call if I was scared, and I don't think you're safe crossing roads yourself let alone looking out for me. I only feel safe with you in the house." Harold complained that he felt bossed about, and Chloe said, "'I order you around because I don't trust you", and she added, "I don't feel you like me very much, I don't feel like you are my dad."

Adela and Chloe continued to "educate" Harold in how he could remain "himself" (one of his preoccupations) but become a father with whom Chloe could have a stronger relationship. He admitted his own lasting inability to predict how the mind of a nine-year-old was working, "I gauge the meetings according to how I am feeling, *I cannot take her mind into account, but I am trying.*" This intermittent, collaborative family work continued into Chloe's teens. Adela had decided with Chloe that although her dad "could drive me mad, I want you to know him enough to make up your own mind about him." Harold observed of Chloe, "She has been delighted to see us, her mother and father together and think she has a father . . . it seems good for her to see us together and getting on." Over two years, Chloe became further connected to her father's wider family, his sister, and her own half sister and brother.

## *Reflections on my involvement*

What were the missing links the third person—myself—as outsider to this recalibrating system could provide? Each person in the family found it hard to consider the ongoing situation from the other people's point of view. Intersubjective sympathy, as an ingredient of managing the strangeness of the arrangement successfully, was missing from the parents' relationship with one another. As Harold also said about himself, he had no understanding of development and the resulting change in a child's capacity to think and, while always delighted to see Chloe, had previously had no ideas of her as a thinking being. I was able to help him develop his ideas piece by piece, in a non-threatening way, using Chloe's own lead. Adela used me and my telephone conversations with Harold to maintain a resilient approach to Harold herself, without "losing it" at what she saw as his chaos. Chloe took up the organisation of her relationship with Harold, on behalf of her own wish for a proper daddy, because, in my view, she recognised his goodwill, which meshed with a longing in herself for a person she could call daddy. This also included an exasperated acceptance of what he could not understand, which she seemed willing to try to "shape up" for him. It did seem that Chloe was able to get on to her father's wavelength and recognise his idiosyncrasies without feeling threatened by them.

## What is in the child's best interests?

If we take as the highest principle the best interests of a child, in family situations where a "hidden" father wants to change the definition of his relationship into becoming an "acknowledged" father, there will be highly conflicting views about what best interests will be. A father seeking establishment of relationship and meeting resistance from other adult parties responsible for the child is likely to see himself as a victim of circumstances beyond his control, or, when feeling more hostile, as within the control of the mother, who can become defined as acting against him. In some cases, mothers have new partners, by whom they might also have children, as in Sally's case. There will be conflicts of interest involved that have to be acknowledged from the beginning. This sudden "threat" of new relationships which might rearrange all the meanings on which a child and family have built their lives can be greatly feared by a mother who might also feel guilt about the "long-term lie" she has been living in relation to a child's "real" paternity. Most fathers seeking contact have a core belief that their relationship with a child will act in their child's best interests. Their stated intention is likely to be that they want to change their lives to "be there" to protect and nurture their children. That their intentions do not convince the mothers of their children can then become one of the greatest sorrows a father could experience.

Intermittent sightings of a biological father occur in many families where a father has not been officially declared as father, and are often contrived. He might have been placed within the child's social orbit, unnamed, sometimes known as "Uncle", or "mum's friend". A mother might feel she wants the child to know her father, but also wants to prevent this other relationship from becoming open or having any power in her child's life. The question of whether there is space for such a relationship in the child's mind will vary also, depending on who else is taking on a role of parent. In some instances, a father is half experienced by the child, who brings this unconscious knowledge to any assessment process that might happen later along the line. If knowledge is withheld, the way in which the idea of relationship with a father develops in the inner life of the child might become be distorted and confused in his or her mind. This was the case with Shane, who follows.

### Dad viewed across the playground: are "mum and grandpa" good enough?

Shane, aged eight, resolutely maintained that he did not want a father in his life. He pointed out to me that many families consist of a mother, a child, friends, as well as a grandparent. "I've already got a granddad, and he looks after me a lot." He said he thought his life was "pretty perfect", and that if he had a dad he would probably have to play fewer computer games and do more homework, like his friend's dad made his friend do. He protested on the one hand that any man in his life at home would make him uncomfortable, but affirmed on the other that he liked his mum's current boyfriend because he was good at computer games and he made his mum happy. He asked directly why, if his dad, Dave, wanted to see him so much, he had waited until he was eight, when he could have called him any time. He also asked why he did not pay the maintenance he was entitled to. (Whereas his first question can be seen as legitimate from a boy of eight, the second one is more likely to have been influenced by his mother's questions about his father and conversations stirred up between them by the approach from Dave,)

A complicated story of relationship break-up marked the telling of the story from both parents, Dave and Dana, with recrimination about sexual infidelities and money demanded and money owing. Dave told me that he gave up attempting to maintain contact with Shane when he heard that his son had formed an attachment to Dana's new boyfriend, Keith, but when that relationship was seen to break up

three years later, he resumed his attempts to see his son. The degree
to which Dana had formerly pushed him away was unclear, but Dave
showed me a letter in which she asserted that Keith was "ten times the
father you could be to him". Dave said he had been told that Dana was
not now influencing Shane against him, but he did not really believe
this. However, he also admitted his own failure to come forward in a
positive way for his son over the years. He used to see Shane in the
school playground, as his new partner's children went to the same
school. "I could have strolled over to him and had a chat and made
things go a different way. I didn't want to upset him; I've regretted it
and been cross with myself ever since."

Like other fathers seeking a future attachment, Dave was very preoccupied with the reasons why his son did not want to see him now.
He did not seem to accept responsibility for his own past failures to
connect with his son to Shane's present "lack of interest" in him. "It's
causing a lot of turmoil and upset. Even if I never get to have regular
contact, I want peace of mind about it all." In an interview between
Shane and Dave which subsequently took place, Dave sought for
Shane's understanding: "Basically, the only way I could see you was if
I came to mum's flat where Keith was living and she wanted you to
think of him as dad and call him dad, and I thought you would be
confused." He said tearfully to Shane, "Not a day goes by that I haven't
thought about you. I have the love for you that I have for my two
girls. I used to drive by the playground just to look at you." Shane said
that he also used to go out and look for his dad. They both laughed
ruefully at the fact that they had each been so hesitant, and had a
brief moment of shared painful emotion in which, however, Dave
failed to take responsibility as father for the troubled times of the past.

## Progressing future contact

Meeting later with Dana, Dave, and Shane, I asked Dave to find the
right words to explain to Shane why he would like to have him back
in his life. Dave said to Shane, "I always feel there is something missing in my life," and repeated that "there hasn't been a day gone by
when I don't think about you and wonder what you are doing," Shane
was fidgeting during this exchange between his mum, his dad, and
himself, a novelty in his life. Dana talked to Shane about Dave's
computer skills, skills that she told Shane he had inherited from his

dad, suggesting Dave might come over to their home and play some games with Shane. Shane initially agreed to this, but subsequently decided he did not want his father on his "own turf". Rather than wishing to learn anything from Dave, he became very competitive, declaring he would definitely beat his father at most games.

Shane agreed to undertake a trip to Legoland with Dave, planned between Dave and Dana. A month later, I met further with Shane and Dana to assess how things were going between Shane and his father. Shane had taken up a new clear position against Dave, asserting that he had been "horrible to my mum". In elaborating this idea, he thought this was "about four years ago" and said he still had memories of rows about money between his mum and his dad during a period when his mother had no employment, and they were dependent on Granddad for a weekly shop.[3] His mother reassured him in the meeting: "We were both horrid to each other . . . it was a horrid time." Shane then said he was frightened of being kidnapped by his father. His mother said, "Don't be silly, it's obvious he's not a kidnapper . . . getting to know your dad isn't taking anything away from you, its making your world a little bit larger. There are so many aspects of him in you . . . you are the child of both of us." Shane replied that he did not want his world to be larger. "I don't care what the law says about having a dad as well as a mum." I asked Dana to tell Shane in what ways she saw aspects of Dave in him. She said that Shane was headstrong and did not give up easily, and that this determination had helped her, his mother, develop her own negotiating skills: "You are a good talker and that comes from him, not me."

Shane surprised Dana at this point by asking her, "How come I can't remember him from when I was a baby?" We talked about how, as the brain develops, new memories and associations often come to overlay early memories, and commented how confusing it must be for him, being asked to get to know a dad of whom he had no good memories. To show what he thought of the new relationship, Shane said, "I could make a time machine on my computer, and this would kill him off; and then I wouldn't have him in the future."

### Who's the king of the castle?

In reflecting on how resistant Shane was to the idea of meeting further with his father, we (Shane, Dana, and I) thought together about the way in which the whole system on which he had built his life was in disequilibrium. Shane was used to being the "king of the castle" at home (Dana's words). He had a strong relationship with his mother, and his developing verbal skills were increasingly leading him to be in charge of situations at home, as he could now defeat her in arguments. If "being in charge" was the most important thing to him (the highest context marker for security from his perspective), then a relationship with his father might lead to the balance of power within his world being upset. Although he had already had two other men in his life whom he had been asked to call "dad" by the age of eight, neither of them was still living in the home, and he was the "man" who remained mother's continuous companion and also her friend. The introduction of a person, Dave, who had previously been narrated only as unreliable in his household, both by granddad to his mother in his hearing, as well as to him directly, and the recruiting of this person into "relationship rights" over him, did not seem to him to have any advantages. Dana was determined to persist with Dave in their life at this point, but the omens looked unpromising. My own involvement within the court process was over.

Shane and his father met for three further outings together, but Shane remained doubtful about the purpose of continuing with the relationship. In his own words, "I don't see why I need a father in my life. Lots of kids only have a mother and her family. I have got what I want and need, and I have got a good grandpa and he looks after me a lot. What is the purpose of a dad that I haven't already got?"

## Reflections on my involvement

In this family, the narratives of both Dana and Shane shifted backwards and forwards during the time I knew them. While Dana became more positive towards the idea of the two of them developing a relationship, Shane's tentative curiosity about his father subsequently reversed. The first factor was his anger that his father had not made a move to come back into his life sooner, and, by doing so now, upset the current equilibrium of his life. This, in turn, related to his reluctance to have his own position as "king of the castle" threatened. The actual experience of being with his father on a day out did not kindle his own enthusiasm.

The second factor was his mixed memories of a father as a "bad" rather than as a "good" man. Jenkins, whose work over the past twenty years has analysed in detail the effects of parents' angry behaviour on children, has shown that it is not just the direct experience of anger and violence that has negative effects on the child's mind, but also the witnessing of angry behaviours between others on whom they depend (Jenkins, 2003; Jenkins et al., 2005). The memory of quarrelling voices can be retained by a very young child, although the subject of the quarrel might not have been known or has been forgotten. The witnessed behaviour of his father towards his mother, both before separation and on any subsequent visits, is key to a child's own interpretations of his father as a "good man".

The third factor was his assertion that his grandfather had been solid in his life. Questions raised by Shane's preference for his connected grandfather over his disconnected father point to the importance of including grandparents in some family assessments. Equally, it could be that his grandfather's dislike of his father in the past influenced Shane (who was still close to his grandfather) in the present. How does a grandfather "stand in" as father in ways that make up for the absence of a father in many families? What difference will it make to Shane's development and potential omnipotence as a man not to allow his father to challenge him? Will his very able mother offer a different, but satisfactory, model of socialisation (like 2,000,000 lone parent, female-headed families in the UK at the present time). What different outcomes may there be for Shane when he, in turn, becomes a father?

# CHAPTER FIVE

# Fathers, children, and conflicts in family arrangements following divorce

In answering the basic but complex question, "What is contact for", I look again here at how a father's earlier relationship with a child continues to affect how he and his child maintain attachments following both separation and divorce. A major difference for separated fathers who have been *married* to the mothers of their children, compared with those who have not, is their own more defined legal responsibility for their children's welfare, growth, and development. However, this legal responsibility is not necessarily followed through in many families where professionals become involved. In answering the question: "What is good for them about coming to see me?" children's views include: "staying in touch"; "it's part of how I know who I am", and fathers say, "I am one of the building blocks"; "I am part of her growing up". If we look at the joint framework of love and intimacy within which a child gains knowledge of relationships in the world, we need to add, "What is good for the child is also good for the father."

> What's good for them about coming to see me? . . . when they do they experience love, and I think that's good for everybody . . . when they come and see me I experience love and you know that's . . . it's as simple as that really. If you love them and they love you, the usual

arrangement, father and children relationship, and that, that love is good. It is good for people to feel relationships. (Simon, quoted in Gorell Barnes & Bratley, 2000, unpublished manuscript)

It is estimated that almost one in three children will experience a parental divorce before the age of sixteen. Parenting plans (CAP, 2014) spell out sensible and reasonable ways for parents to proceed with making care plans for children. They do not, as yet, cater for parents who have either mental illness or acute problems of high emotional irregularity that complicate divorce processes further. Fathers who determine from the start that they will maintain regular frequent childcare after a divorce, and discuss and settle these arrangements with their former wives (the ongoing co-parent for life) are, unsurprisingly, less likely to have difficulties than those who do not think the post-separation arrangements through. Many adjustments have to be made in any life, as new family epistemologies evolve, and some fathers find such flexibility very hard to accommodate.

Many factors play a part in men maintaining strong parenting in their children's lives. A new partner or spouse to either parent who is positive towards maintaining family connections makes an important difference to ongoing engagement of a father who lives away from the household. Conversely, rivalry between a biological dad and a social dad can wreak havoc in a child's weekly experience, and witnessing distress to a child can influence a father away from maintaining contact. In thinking about the changes in a father's role following divorce, it is useful to have a systemic understanding of the emotional context in which his identity as father was shaped within the partnership. What were the cultural and individual expectations that went into the development of his role as father, and what will the interpersonal processes that transform these into successful or unsuccessful post-divorce fathering be? What are the conflicts of belief between the system of care now surrounding his children after separation and his own inner image or identity as "boss" or head of the family, a role which many men take years to give up in their minds? How realistically has he made plans in his mind for offering love and fathering for his children on a changed basis that takes other influences into account?

Working with families where the parents have been separated early in a child's life, before a child has a good working memory of his or her own, allows the witnessing of ongoing subtle distancing man-oeuvres within the conversations of a mother who does not want the ongoing involvement of a former partner and her immediate family. These might become part of the child's everyday experience (see Chapter Six). Family conversations might develop dominant patterns, which often exclude positive possibilities of a future relationship with the father. Such outer dialogues can become inner monologues, voices in the family becoming conversations in the child's mind ("he's a bad dad because he made my mother cry"). As described by children, such inner monologues can be powerful and confusing and restrict any desire for a relationship with a father. They often reflect the active ambivalence a mother herself is experiencing at the idea of an ongoing relationship with the man from whom she would prefer to be separated: "What's a dad for, a dad can't do anything a mother can't do, I don't want one."

The pathway towards an estranged father's own future fathering is rarely straightforward. There are two differing hypotheses discussed in the literature about where father's skills in parenting develop. The first is that a father might become highly involved with his children as a result of his imitation of available and supportive fathering in his own childhood. The second hypothesis is that having unavailable and unsupportive fathering themselves leads fathers to wish to do better with their own children, without having a sense of the steps necessary to do so. In post-divorce fathering, both hypotheses might be secondary to what a father has already learnt in the marriage, as well as being able to incorporate the understanding of specific behaviours expressly wished for by his children. Learning what being a hands-on dad involves from various contemporary sources includes the children's mothers themselves, grandmothers, and intimate relatives and adult friends of both genders in conversations that keep them focused on the child as an active participant in the process of shaping their future relationship.

### Transitional systems and a father's continued attachment

The Avon Longitudinal Study of Pregnancy and Childbirth (ALSPAC) (Dunn, 2002; Dunn et al., 2004) highlighted variables affecting children's development within different family groupings, and showing that post-divorce living has many variations (Fabricius et al., 2010).

These included the number of relationship transitions a father makes and the importance for children of him maintaining strong relationships with them in spite of multiple re-partnering himself. Children under eight who placed their fathers as "not close" on a simple family map indicated implicit dangers of distance from their own fathers, and were assessed as being three times more likely to show behaviour difficulties than children who placed their fathers in the central circle (Dunn & Deater Deckard, 2001).

## Bad attitudes and irresponsible behaviour: multi-levelled processes

Significant changes have been achieved relating to the gender and power struggles in the lives of women in the 1950s and 1960s, but the devaluation of women in everyday life, the sexual objectification and wider abusive communications about women have not gone away. Men seeking fatherhood following an acrimonious separation often do not wish to moderate their own rage at former partners, still concurrent parents. Their anger about women can still be seen to interfere with their more hopeful and loving feelings towards children. While many men have made social changes, more primitive aspects of male beliefs about women continue unchanged in aspects of fantasy about how women should be and behave, heard when men get together and drink, expressed widely on social media, and sometimes shockingly acted out in rapes and attacks on women's bodies in the street. Negative beliefs about women inevitably permeate work with men who believe they have been "wronged" by women and have to be tackled without amplifying the ongoing latent anger. Each professional will develop their own repertoire depending on their age, gender, and confidence. My own stance as an older woman includes incredulity at how such attitudes can still be held (expressed directly) combined with distilling a father's outrage to focus on specific incidents on which it is based. I then try and find ways of us examining together the inconsistencies between the father's quest for relationship with his child and his anger with the child's mother, and practise reflecting strongly with him on how anger might interfere with the wished-for goal of coming back into the child's life. In return, I have experienced outrage at my failure to be "on his side" but also attempts, however limited and painful, to face up to the contradictions and do some work on them.

Some of the different ways a father can create difficulties with his children even when a good contact relationship has been under way are shown in the extracts from family work that follow. Lack of responsibility and lack of awareness of children's needs can be demonstrated in diverse ways: through sexual relationships and sexually inappropriate behaviour in front of the children; through bad behaviour (such as drinking too much in the children's presence); through not showing enough consideration for mothers who are continuing to do the larger part of raising the children, including financial withholding. There might also be bad-tempered or disrespectful behaviour to their child's maternal grandparents, who now play a large part in caring for the children. One piece of bad behaviour that has not earned a place in research, and that stretches across cultures and diminishes a father in the eyes of his children, is the badmouthing of a mother's mother, a common occurrence when an irate father believes his children are being kept from him with a grandmother's backing (see Mike and Amba, below).

## Conflicts and irrational behaviours

There are many forms of conflict contained within post-divorce wrangling between couples. Some have a long history of marital or partnership difficulties, often involving extended families prior to the divorce (as in the third example below). Others become bogged down, and dependent on court processes, as a way of one or both of them maintaining identity when former roles are threatened. Either group can remain in disputes for years (Blow & Daniel, 2002; Gorell Barnes, 2005). Staying in conflict and the recurrent use of the court over years can be a way of remaining connected to former family and role when all other methods have broken down. In these situations, it is important to assess the value that the court is offering parents as an emotional regulator, and to balance this against the effects of continual emotional arousal on children and on fathers. Court processes may in themselves contribute further to the dislike or "alienation" of a father who is persisting in his efforts to achieve recognition of his "rightful" position, both in the minds of the children and that of his former partner. Some couples have few or no models for peace-making, and men who have lower autonomic nervous system arousal in situations where they are threatened with loss respond reactively so that anger is likely to overcome any stated good intention (Hetherington, 1989).

## Attachment, loss, and anger

As with other family relationships discussed in this book, the capacity for high emotional exchange, independent of any categorisation as "mental illness", can be a marked feature of post-divorce processes. Divorce challenges both intimate patterns of attachment and the secure bonds with children on which many fathers rely for aspects of their own mental health. Anger at potential loss of the most loved others, the children, is brought to centre stage (Byrne et al., 2005) Over the past two decades, since the Child Support Act of 1991, many fathers correctly saw law and legal processes as embodying a presumption of children's primary residence being with their mother. There was a lack of political commitment to dealing with the specific difficulties of separated fathers at a legal level. Very high levels of conflict have been estimated in about ten per cent of all divorce cases (Bream & Buchanan, 2003), with three per cent of parents who use the courts repeating the use of court as a form of mediating strong, and often chaotic, emotions between former partners (Trinder et al., 2008). Working within the family court process, fathers' rage at exclusion from children's lives often presented as impaired mental health. We do not have mental health services within the current structures of National Health provision that extend to the particular needs generated by loss of children and anger at loss—attachment anxieties and often highly irrational angers and disorganised behaviours occurring in the context of the disruption of attachment bonds on which many fathers rely to keep them feeling sane and secure in the world.

In assessing conflict behaviour and violent acts in the post-divorce period, it is important to note all instances of dangerous behaviour, how often these have taken place, and whether things are getting better or worse. Bumping the car of the child's mother, stalking the mother at work and the child at school, phone harassment and harassment through the use of friends, including threats of maiming, and other demonstrations of jealousy and disorganised attachment, are common (Davis & Andra, 2000). Some partners, when confronted with the implications of their behaviour for the future of their children, are prepared to commit to safe methods of managing flashpoints and make agreements around the safety of children. However, for such changes to be maintained, a father needs to take genuine responsibility for his actions and give a commitment to work towards change (Cooklin & Hyde, 2014).

## The Children Act 1989 and the Child Support Act 1991: implications for fathers' "natural" relationship with their children.

The fact that the Children Act of 1989 made no presumption of *shared* parental responsibility became a sore point in fathers' fight for equality in post-divorce parenting. The Child Support Act of 1991 could, at the time, be seen as a coming together of concerns about family values as discussed in Chapter Three: absent fathers, a rising "social under-class", and crime and moral breakdown being widely aired concerns (Collier & Sheldon, 2008, p. 151). When this became law, there was agreement across political divisions that fathers should formally pay mothers for the upkeep of their children. However, the workings of the Act subsequently became the object of considerable anger from fathers, repositioning them as "victims" among those who chose to use it as leverage for "fathers' rights". Anger focused around the specific discourse of payment not equalling right to contact. The emphasis in legislation was on responsibility, not rights, but for many fathers this emphasis was opposed because they saw it as unfair. While the Act recognised that once a parent always a parent, it did not include any notion of entitlement for fathers to continue their relationships with their children as a natural part of their ongoing life process. That such a division in the assumptions about men and women in relation to children and their upbringing had developed as a social norm reflected a lack of recognition within the longer-term politics of gender about the importance of keeping men and children connected. Fathers who had wished to establish and maintain meaningful relationships with their children after separation had to struggle for this in the face of mothers' ability to resist any contact if they believed this not to be in "their child's best interests" (Collier & Sheldon, 2008, p. 163). The failure of law to accord fathers equal time with their children was portrayed by many men as a psychological injury to their sense of their own worth, not only as fathers, but also as men.

The system of separation from family that the upbringing of boys had long maintained in the upper and some of the middle classes of the UK was an essential feature of the institutionalised masculinity common in the late nineteenth and the twentieth centuries (discussed earlier in Chapter One, and later in Chapter Nine) and shaped many men's thinking about fatherhood. We can reflect on the relationship between the absence of thought about positive fatherhoods in law making and among the judiciary as a possible further extension of this. The beliefs and social values about gender that developed alongside the positioning of the male role as defender of nation, women, and children prioritised these roles over fathering and intimacy, as well as affording them greater social and political power. The legislation of 1991 could be said to have shown a time delay in relation to contemporary fathers' potential as parents, fathers who wished to be intimately connected to their children, a lag which the past twenty years has, to some degree, made up as gender positions have become more fluid and the relationship between men, women, and work continues to change.

### Post-divorce living—struggling to develop new ways of doing dad: conflicting epistemologies

In post-divorce parenting, fathers and mothers can often move rapidly away from one another towards practices of fatherhood, motherhood, and family life that might have acute differences from one another—new epistemologies, as noted in Chapters One and Three. The systemic interdependence of the married state, what each one relies on the other to be, do, and represent, can, after divorce, be overthrown by one parent, hankered after by the other, and missed in its totality by the children. A father's fierce recognition of impending loss and his sense of disequilibrium could also lead to new performances of "being a devoted dad" that a child might not have previously experienced while the parents were together. Such a turnaround happens particularly when children are very small, five or younger at time of separation, and a father becomes suddenly aware that he might lose their trust unless he now puts in regular and more extensive time with

them. Such shifts in hands-on commitment, and an intensified performance of fathering practices, can lead to complex paradoxes in childcare arrangements at a time when a mother wants to consolidate her
own new rhythms of living. Expanding her new stories of self will be
complicated by the regular presence of a father who is no longer part
of the live-in household but wants to be there for intimate time with
the children (supper, bath, story, and bed). Where fathers have had
less hands-on experience of parenting during the marriage, such
fights for more intimate contact following a separation might not
succeed. A father might find that he has not "earned it", either in the
eyes of his former partner or in the eyes of their children. The ideal of
co-parenting can serve to fuel conflicts between separating parents in
cases where fathers' continued presence is seen by mothers and children as a product not of co-operation, but of legal coercion through
court accorded contact time.

### Father's presence and children's wellbeing: denigrating family and social discourses

In working with fathers seeking a relationship with their children, I
have come to focus with as much precision as possible, within the
time allowed, on the details of how fathers attempts to become part of
their children's lives have been accepted or rebuffed by the wider
family. The ways in which stories are told about how an absent parent
"conducted himself" when living with his family, as well as how
stories about a father's functioning and intentions as a parent are
recounted, not only by the child's mother, but also by other relatives,
might develop a litany and rhetoric of their own. This is discussed
further in Chapter Six, in relation to processes of alienation, and also
applies to emotional work with families where there have been con-
flict-laden separations with arguments about money and housing, as
well as parenting. The same phrases and rhythms in family discussion, as well as descriptions of former events, might be heard, often
word for word, when told to an outsider (such as myself) on different
visits. A father might become positioned by these negative narratives,
often of single instances of bad behaviour, in ways that overlay other
potential stories of nurture, love, and responsibility. Where a family
has closed against a father, the narrative of his "badness" is likely to

have become an essential component of self-protection or self-justification within the closed system.

There is also a range of wider social discourses about men and about fathers, as discussed in earlier chapters, in which men are portrayed as of less significance to children than mothers, and sometimes discounted as having no relevance at all. While this can contextualise collective distress for women in comforting ways, "dick-led dad, that's what I call him, dead loss as a father" (Anna, 2016, personal communication), it can also amplify a larger, overarching denigrating social discourse about men as fathers which is unhelpful to the potential development of a nurturing and responsible role on an instance by instance basis. The blame for this negative outlook belongs to neither gender alone, but is a product of the discourses of each about the other, over time, in multiple cumulative contexts.

The current popular vote, as well as evidence from research, as noted in Chapter Four, has come down on the side of fathers having an important role in the socialisation and wellbeing of children, providing they are working alongside mothers. Responsibility rather than rights has prevailed as an idea legitimising fatherhood, and has a central and distinctive higher order legal role in encouraging good behaviour in parents. Fathers-4-Justice has long argued that the best way to meet children's needs in family life after divorce is by sharing out both care and residence equally. However, research in the last two decades has not supported this belief. Research has shown, overall, that the presence of a father in a child's life is not, in itself, enough to distinguish a family *with* a father as having greater probabilities of positive outcomes for children than for children in a family without a father's presence at all. The key message, therefore, is not whether men or women make better second parents, but that fathers only make life better for their children when they attend to the necessary features of their involvement in their family lives. Once again, the quality of paternal involvement and his awareness of his children's needs, rather than the frequency of visits, has been found to be the significant indicator for children's long-term wellbeing, with active involved co-parenting found to be the best co-parenting. However, children's longing for their fathers also has to be given emotional weight, though largely absent from research on children based on performance outcomes. Children who are now mothers themselves have spoken of this longing to stay in touch with their fathers: "I can't make the longing go away: I'd love to but I can't . . . I have spent much of my life recognising and talking to that longing" (Rosie, May 2015, personal communication). Fathers' longing for their children and the longer-term effects on their mental health of the loss of their own relational development through responsibility and nurture also requires additional research weight.

## Conflict and children: how does children's meaning-making affect a father's chances of re-entry into their lives?

Conflict experienced during the period of separation alone has less overall effect for children than ongoing adversarial exchanges between parents (Cummings & Davies, 2002; Jenkins et al., 2005). It is now widely accepted that former experiences of parental conflict, as well as stories about these conflicts and who was 'to blame', are likely to affect how children of any age subsequently appraise and respond to disagreements. The effects of conflict are cumulative, so that any new conflict is amplified by a child's former exposure to acrimonious episodes. What grannies and grandpas say about what is going on can elaborate understanding or increase negative perspectives of fathers. Children's capacity for meaning making with their siblings also begins at very young ages, so that the opinions of older siblings about their mother's and father's behaviour, can affect a younger child's own thinking and expressed views (Dunn et al., 1991).

## Fathers and vulnerability following divorce: contextual variables

Is fathering more vulnerable to loss than mothering following conflict and divorce? As with other research questions regarding fathers following separation, much of what happens to a father depends on his former position in the intact family system. A fathering vulnerability hypothesis has been advanced to describe some of the negative effects of marital conflict on fathers by Cummings and colleagues (2010), who found that father–child relations following separation were more vulnerable to the negative effects of marital discord than were mother–child relations. However, fathers who have strong

attachments to their children prior to separation and are able to maintain a contact based on direct connection to their children are less likely
to be vulnerable than those who have to rush to create a new strength
of attachment in the context of panic about losing their children.

Within a post-separation restructuring of time and energy, some
women become impatient with the details fathers can attempt to elicit
in micro-managing family arrangements for fear of being left out, or
in order to maintain the illusion that the family can still be run in the
same way. For fathers, the emotional dimensions of managing part-
time parenting, the stress of coming together with children and then
having to say goodbye, the absence of ongoing involvement with the
minutiae of children's daily lives, which they formerly took for granted, are often more powerful than some can manage rationally. Former
insecure or disorganised attachment experiences can well up with
redoubled force. This is particularly so where the children's mother
has a new partner and a father fears that the children will come to love
the new partner more than they love him.

Research has suggested that because mothers generally have a
more clearly defined role with their children than do fathers, they are
able to compartmentalise stress in their roles as "mothers *vs.* spouses"
more readily than fathers following separation. At a clinical level, we
can observe that this is not necessarily the case when it is a *mother* who
leaves home and the children stay with their father, or when children
believe their father to have been unfairly treated by their mother and
are determined to have residence with both their parents. Another
suggestion from research is that men use social withdrawal as a more
common response to stress than do women. Men are more prone to
becoming emotionally overwhelmed when experiencing distress, and
social withdrawal might be an effort to alleviate this. Once again, a
clinical perspective indicates that where fathers have had strong and
active relationships with their children within the marriage, they are
less likely to withdraw following a separation.

## Role re-assignment in the family following a divorce: helping fathers acquire necessary skills

In my work with parents over the past twenty-five years, I have, in principle, taken the position that there is no necessary fixed relationship

between a parent's gender and what they are able to do or not to do on behalf of their children. However, it has also been necessary to recognise how ill equipped many men are to take care of the minutiae of domestic and caring lives. Following separation, parental tasks that have to be managed include the stabilisation of two households in which children can develop and flourish. This could mean that tasks formerly allocated to one parent might also have to be learnt and practised by the other. While some mothers will encourage their former partner to learn new skills such as cooking and washing clothes so that their children can reliably stay overnight, others will not do this, especially where they blame the father for the separation. If a father has his own mother or sister, she might be willing to be recruited for such teaching or early days' supervision, but, at times, it is only the kindness of others, which might include girlfriends, men friends, neighbours, or professionals currently working alongside the family, who do this. I have stepped into the remit on several occasions where a father had been accused of child neglect, sometimes supervising childcare at home where neglect was a contested issue, teaching a father how to keep children safe while cooking their tea, or making sure they were able to give a child a wash-down safely without being accused of inappropriate touching, in addition to thinking about wider safety issues in the home or the street. Direct assessment of whether a father does indeed have the necessary capacity to look after a young child is, of course, an important practical part of any work where the safety and wellbeing of children is paramount.

### Different stories where a father is held to be at fault: kincare, conflicts of belief, and emotional family processes

In the remainder of this chapter, the focus in the examples is on emotional family processes and conflicts between the two parents, as well as the larger family acting as guardians and gatekeepers. Examples have been chosen in relation to the different developmental ages of the children both to contribute to wider thinking about what a child can understand and to show ways in which families reorganise to protect children. The capacities of children to make their own judgements about parental processes in the early years (under five), middle childhood, and teenage years are included. In fathers' own rhetoric, much emphasis has been given to the negative effects of mothers on fathers' contact with the children, but below I extend thinking about the issue of "gatekeeping" to include the wider context of all the relevant family relationships that reconstitute themselves around a mother and children following a separation where the father is seen to be at fault (Schoppe-Sullivan, et al., 2008).

## Some principles of working with estranged fathers

In exploring some of the painful relationship conflicts around parental care, the issues that I work on with fathers include the following.

1.  Their own capacity to work on the likely effects of former or current violence, emotional abuse, and financial irregularities that have disadvantaged the family: (a) the effects on the child, (b) the effects on the mother's concerns about future contact between father and child.
2.  Their ability to work towards at least a minimal position of understanding the other parent's position, in the service of promoting the child's best interests in becoming able to develop a good enough relationship with each parent in the future.
3.  Their understanding of children as unique beings, who carry their own repertoires of making sense of the world around them.
4.  The child's wish to reconnect and what might be impeding this.

A systemic approach, in which the mutual influence of all family members involved is openly looked at and explicitly stated, usually makes sense to a separated parent thinking about the children, as, indeed, it does to children themselves. Sometimes, however, a father simply wants what he sees as his, his child, and refuses to recognise the point of view of others involved. Anger is usually the first emotion that has to be recognised and addressed. So, I begin with recognition of this, followed by attempting to increase a father's understanding of his child's position, and then, through his understanding of the child, I move to thinking about the mother. In working with a mother, I move carefully through the web of alternative caring that is set up, always using respect, but maintaining a right to question arrangements (a right accorded by the authority of the court).

## Working with a family to re-establish a positive relationship with a father: allowing a father back into a child's mind

*Dirk and Daisy (in their forties), Mike aged five, Sue aged twenty-eight, May and Bob (in their sixties)*

It is hard for very young children to retain their own positive memories of their father when they are removed from one of their parents in negative circumstances, and before they have acquired speech and can ask questions. Where family members in their new daily environment continue to emphasise negative aspects of a father's behaviour or intentions to the child, consciously or unconsciously, on a regular basis, the child will need to have a legacy of good memories or a source of stories about the good aspects of a father to construct an alternative narrative that will take them through the anxieties attendant on court proceedings. Children might have positive experiences embedded from former living alongside their fathers, but such experiences might not be talked about later, or thought about within the domain of the child's post-separation home. In a therapeutic conversation in the context of assessment, the complexity for a child of different levels of feeling and knowing about a father can be discussed in a more neutral way.

### A story of pitfalls in troubled post-separation arrangements

Mike had been separated from his father before he was two years old and moved several thousand miles away from him to live with his mother's family of origin in England. His mother, Sue, had married Dirk, as she later said, "out of a sense of adventure", coming, as she had done, from a "gentle and protective" home, and marrying young to see "more of the world". Sue and Dirk settled in Canada on Dirk's family farm. Following a violent incident between Dirk and a farmworker, which upset Sue, she had removed Mike and flown home to live once more with her parents. Within her family, it was asserted that Dirk suffered from "personality disorder", and Mike's grandfather had taken out a prohibited steps order through the court. This naturally aroused strong feelings in Dirk. Sue would not allow unsupervised visits, despite the court finding that he was not suffering from psychiatric or personality disorder. However, she agreed to Mike going away with his father for supervised holidays. Sue's own parents, Bob and May, had told her that Mike would not miss his father, that he would become attached to them, and that Sue could remarry and replace a male figure in his life that way. A pattern of infrequent but regular visits twice a year continued over two years, with Mike and Dirk staying with family friends. When Mike was four, Dirk took a girlfriend as his holiday companion, ostensibly to cover the order for supervision. Mike returned disturbed and began to show signs of sexualised behaviour. This was interpreted, by mother and several health professionals whom she consulted, as possible sexual abuse. All further contact was then refused; neither would Sue allow Mike to talk to his father on his weekly phone call. A "siege" with phone calls on a daily basis began, with rudeness and hostility on both sides. After many further months of checks, assessments, and reports, the accusation of abuse was set aside by the court. The professional consensus was that Mike had been upset by witnessing father and his girlfriend engaging in intercourse. Sue became willing to consider some mediating family work with Dirk, and this was the point at which I entered the saga. Sue conceded openly that Dirk had never hit or shown physical aggression to either her or Mike. Later, I learnt that a history of abuse in May, Sue's mother's family, made that family particularly sensitive to sexual abuse as a possible interpretation of upsetting events for a child.

### Wider family system work: what was needed before Mike could think openly about his father?

The grandparents, Bob and May, needed to believe (1) that Mike would be safe in his father's company, and (2) that they would themselves be freed from the earlier forcefulness of Dirk's telephone behaviour, and from accusations that they were deliberately withholding Mike. Sue herself required some sustained help in separating her hidden, more positive, parental relationship with Dirk from the views of her parents (on whom she was also partly financially dependent).

### The sub-system of Sue and Mike

Sue needed to take back authority from her parents for Mike as her child and spend serious time thinking about whether she could believe contact with his father was of benefit to her son, and Mike himself (now five years old) needed a space to get back in touch with his dad in his mind, as thoughts about dad had been prohibited for a while, and to think about whether he wanted to see his dad again.

## The sub-system of Dirk and Daisy (his second wife)

Dirk believed the whole accusation of abuse was a manipulative plot to prevent him from having contact with his son, created and maintained by mother's parents. He had not previously made a connection between the behaviours of shouting, and "sex to make up", which Mike had witnessed, and the behaviour that Mike had subsequently shown, which in detail closely mirrored the patterns of adult behaviour. Dirk's position towards the family in which his son had been living for nearly four years was that it was a hostile environment in which the grandfather Bob was more like a "rival father figure" to Mike, as he had always wanted a son of his own. Dirk had been very upset to be told by Mike on the phone that he now had a "new daddy". Dirk claimed that Bob and May had always sought to prevent him from having a closer co-parental relationship with Sue, which he had attempted throughout (and which she later concurred she had secretly collaborated in maintaining). He referred to his new marriage to Daisy, and asserted that residence should now be transferred to him. In an emotional manner, he deplored his loss of the early years of his son's life which could "never come again".

## Disentangling the voices

All the family work took place in Sue's family home until she felt secure enough to meet Dirk in the local CAFCASS office. Within the house, I used different rooms to work with different individuals and subsystems, including talking with Mike in his small tent on the back lawn. Bob, the grandfather, took me aside (on a landing on the stairs) to whisper that he had never uttered any words or behaved in any manner that would lead Mike to feel his grandparents did not like his father. I took this as a statement of future intent rather than a truth about the past. May, the grandmother, asked me to consider (in the kitchen) that even though the accusation of abuse had been set aside, Dirk was not and never had been a gentleman ... "he might be triggered into violent behaviour by Mike himself at any time." Both grandparents, concerned and protective but acting without any evidence that Dirk was a threat to Mike, thus had subtle but powerful voices that militated against the possibility of good co-parenting with Mike's father in the future. (They were also making clear their intentions not to stand in the way of what the court had now ordered: that Dirk be able to find a way back to his son.)

### Sue finds her own voice

In working with Sue and her parents together (in the sitting room), it was noticeable how, when her mother was present, it was difficult for her to speak (literally) with her own voice. The conversation between her and her mother became intertwined and often they would finish one another's sentences. Eventually, with my continued encouragement that she finish her own thoughts and sentences, Sue said boldly, in front of her parents, that she had always wanted to promote Mike's relationship with his father, that she had secretly continued to send him monthly bulletins of progress (from her computer at work), and that she wanted to do what she could to make things work between them. She said further that the meeting in which she had actually been face to face with Dirk in court had brought to her mind some of her original attraction and love for him as well as reminding her that he had always been a good father (sentiments she had always found it hard to express in front of her parents). She told me that she had told Mike that the court had decided daddy had done nothing wrong; that now he would meet Daddy and Daisy and Daisy's own little girl, and that a lady (me) was going to help them all talk about it so that Mike would be able to go on holiday with them. In reply to my question, "What preparation do you think Mike would need before he met his father", she thought he would need some strategies to deal with his own feelings of anger and sadness because he thought that he had not been seeing Daddy because Daddy was angry with him. Now she had told him that he would see Daddy again, the taboo on speaking about Daddy was lifted and he had already begun to say, "There is some good in Daddy and I would like to see Daddy again."

### Attachment issues and contact: a focus on Mike's confusing experience

Mike had experienced several week-long periods away from his mother while with his father during contact visits as a young child (under four), and on his return from these had displayed many of the usual behaviours of children who have no internal explanation of why they have been removed from their mothers. On return to her, he had been cross with her, alternately clung to her and ignored her. This had, in the grandparental mind, been interpreted as evidence that he had been "disturbed" while he was away, as at those times he was not the "sweet, easy boy" he normally showed himself to be. He was, as he said to me later, "only a little boy", but all the adults around him expected a lot from his understanding.

## Mike's understanding

Mike had a number of fixed points that he clung to and repeated many times in relation to what happened in the holiday. He did not understand how grown-ups behave when they are angry (no one in his mother's family household ever performed anger, so it would have been new to him). Sex was also new to him. He confused intercourse with a deliberate attempt by father to hurt his girlfriend, and this had frightened him.

Most of my interview with him alone took place in his small tent into which he had invited me, obviously feeling it was his personal space. I introduced the story of his father, that his father really wanted to see him again, and that he had sent a video of himself and his second family in Canada. Mike said, "Mum wouldn't want me to go all the way to Canada", and I said, "Well, she doesn't mind now she has decided you can be safe there and if you won't be frightened." He showed me a puppet he had made with strong legs for walking "a long way". I said he had a lot to deal with in his young life and had needed his strong legs, and I congratulated him on all he had done and been through. He said, "Sometimes I am like a young man and sometimes I like to be a baby as well", and I said I had guessed that from reading some of the many reports. "Come on now", he said, "let's go and look at the video . . ."

## Watching the video and making the phone call: a biochemical cascade

Sue and I had previously agreed that we would watch this video without her parents, as the film related to her married life away from them. It seemed to me very important that Mike should reawaken any memories he might have of a place where there had been a shared life between mother and father, even if this was in the first eighteen months of his life, as he currently had no recollection of there being any good relationship between them. The video of the early days of family life on the farm was a great success, with Mike recognising some images of the house itself as well as the farmyard atmosphere, especially the farm dog with its long wagging tail, which he lit up with excitement about, ". . . yes, oh yes". After a few minutes, Mike and Sue began to join together in the idea of him visiting and playing with the dog in spite of her former anxieties. He said, "I'd like to see Daddy, I'd like to talk to Daddy", and, seizing the moment, I said to Sue, "Shall we ring him now?" We managed to get through straightaway on my mobile, to Dirk's enormous pleasure, and the two of them began a conversation about what Mike had seen on the video, which swiftly moved to future visits.

While there is a range of ways that an uncertain father's relationship with his child can be sustained, successful indirect contact through phone, Facetime, Skype, or social media depend on a young child's capacity to visualise and feel safe with the parent with whom the engagement is being attempted. I had thought it important to make this call with Sue present, so that the conversation with daddy was sanctioned and approved by mummy. Rose (2003) has proposed that learning evokes a "biochemical cascade" that permanently alters the brain when a memory is activated. In my experience in family work where a divisive structure has been maintained in order to justify a particular family arrangement, the wider constraints of system change have to precede and accompany such an individual possibility, but, once the taboo on thinking is lifted, changes can take place very fast.

### What did I learn with this family: reflecting on the work

The family can optimistically be viewed as a learning forum which enables the child's mind to open in the context of the family's own changing attitudes. Some patterns, fixed against the idea of father's presence, started to shift rapidly. Mike was then able to make a new relationship with his father with a free mind. He subsequently met his father's second family in the presence of his mother, and went to spend a month with him later in the year. A strong early relationship was available to be rekindled.

Throughout this rapid piece of work, it was notable that Dirk showed no recognition of his own impact on any aspect of the process that had taken place, or to the force of his own personality and its potential effect on the rather shy and nervous young woman, Sue, who had moved from the world of her family to the far away world of her husband and then, rather quickly, within three years, moved back again. Dirk was impatient, demanding, and intolerant of views other than his own. I had to be clear about my own direction and pace and not be bullied by him. I constantly felt under pressure to carry out his "orders". I was able to understand the grandparent's experience, but I was also able to see how their evasiveness and deceptive strategies had driven Dirk, a man who wanted the shortest way through to his own end point, into a state of often uncontrolled anger. Dirk was also very quick to learn. Directing his thoughts towards the wellbeing of his child and demonstrating my thinking to him on a point-by-point basis helped him to contain his impatience in the more hopeful context of seeing that the pattern of relationships that had been closed against him was changing. In this process, he was supported by Daisy, who brought greater patience and calm to our meetings and encouraged Dirk in his expression of love and thought for Mike, rather than anger towards his grandparents.

## The development of moral judgement in children

### Gary, Halima, and Jalil (aged seven)

Fathers who leave a marriage secretly because they have been sustaining a dual relationship with another woman, or who have a gay lover and then decide to "come out", have not allowed the child's mind and emotions to engage with the changes taking place, so that the children suffer on two counts: loss of a parent and the absence of any explanation. The emotional experience of a young child when a father leaves might remain raw and unmitigated, at a time when he is also witnessing the distress of his mother. A father seeking a relationship has to be helped to face up to finding words. He also needs to give attention to a framework of relationship with his child that is acceptable both to his former wife and his child, rather than falling into the rhetoric of "father's role" and "father's rights" that he has, in effect, forfeited in their eyes by leaving.

Jalil, whose father, Gary, had left his mother, Halima, the previous year in order to live with his girlfriend, Stacey, believed he had left because it "was something I had done". Gary was uncertain about whether Halima had stuck to the agreed telling of the story of separation or not—"Is she influencing him against me?" Anyone who has worked in these situations in detail will know that the question of influence is extremely delicate and difficult to discuss productively: "Jalil can see in my face what I think of Gary but I can't get rid of that."

*Individual meetings*

In thinking about how to proceed in a situation with multiple misunderstandings, I always see each family member on their own before bringing them together to look at points of factual difference and conflicts of belief about the "facts" and the behaviour of the other. An individual meeting with a father might include questions such as: "How do you think your son is thinking about his mother's life at home now you have gone?" as well as exploring his own awareness of his child's understanding about the preceding events. Future orientated questions around "What do you think you could say or do that would make things better for your child[ren] now/by next year?", etc. help to move thinking forward.

*A couple meeting to define future parenting arrangements*

Gary and Halima had agreed to a formal meeting as a couple. Each came with a prepared agenda that they had formerly discussed with me. They agreed on a wording for Jalil: that Gary did not love Mummy that way any more but that he wanted to be her friend, that it was nothing to do with Jalil. Gary added, "I would seriously like to be on speaking terms with you in a positive way" and Halima replied honestly, "I have been civil to you, you have dragged me through court processes, and you still want me to like you. I will say hello and goodbye but I can't be nice to you . . . the way you left was trashy, you weren't friends at the time." However, in her eyes a father was important: "You will have to teach him again that you are his dad, he doesn't call you Daddy any more." Gary said he would take all the responsibility for the telling and for his future relationship with Jalil.

### Looking for an explanation that frees a child from self-blame and acknowledges his upset

While the explanations Gary gave Jalil helped him formulate a sense of the misunderstanding between his parents, from Jalil's point of view, it did little to alleviate his deep sorrow for his own loss of his father. "The bad thing is that he left . . . he can't have left because of Mummy because she's a very nice mummy, and I'm cross that he left such a nice mummy so it must have been because of me, something I've done. And then he stopped coming to see me every day and he never said why." They had enjoyed weekly contact in the park together for six months, but then dad spoilt that by saying he wanted him to go overnight, "and I didn't want to leave mum . . . I don't really think she'd got a reason why dad left either. She might have been lonely. When he wanted me to stay with him I wasn't going . . . I think he's a bad person and I don't like him and I'm never seeing or going with him." None the less, when his upset had been expressed it subsided, and he agreed to meet his father again.

### A family meeting: the family together

The incident of "staying the night at dad's flat" was reframed by Gary as, "All it meant was that I wanted to spend more time with you." This provoked the earlier unspoken grief in Jalil, ". . . if you wanted to spend more time with me you shouldn't have left." At this point, he was crying bitterly, and Gary made a prepared speech about it not being his fault in any way. Eventually, Jalil allowed Gary to cuddle him with Halima's encouragement.

### Further contact

The court proceedings were dropped and contact continued on a weekly basis for the next six months. On follow-up, Halima reported that, in many ways, Jalil had moved away from his father towards her own family of origin and her brother in particular, "He's decided that this man, his dad, walked away and now *he* is walking away." She did not think that Gary had sufficient understanding of the impact of what had happened on his son, and was happy leading a "bachelor life" with his new girlfriend: ". . . there's not a lot upstairs and there's a big mouth. He's a good man, but he couldn't resist flattery from another woman . . . it may not even work out for him, he didn't have to lose his family . . . I even feel sorry for him at times. We have moved on now and are able to talk to each other without flaring up, but he still wants a little bit of emotional attachment from me which I'm not up for."

### *Reflections on the limitations of what could be attempted in this process*

In many ways, this was a straightforward post-divorce case of a father seeking a contact where a mother was angry with him for leaving her. What made it unusual was the clear participation of the child as a strong voice. Working with Jalil, between the ages of seven and nine years, it was apparent that a continuous process of moral reasoning was taking place in his mind which, while necessarily concurrent with his observations of his mother, and, therefore, never independent of anything his mother or her wider family said, could be seen to be the workings of his own mind. Gary found it hard to take account of any criticism Jalil might voice and was enjoying his new freedoms. Gary's inability to talk about the contradictions in his own relationships and the effect of these on his son's life, once I was no longer part of the process, meant that he continuously failed to discuss questions in Jalil's mind.

### *Children: their moral position in a context of family feuding and shifting parental positions*

To access the goodwill of his child, a father will necessarily need to take account of the child's understanding of his intentions towards the child's mother (depending on his age and understanding). In the Peterson family, the "moral" reasoning of the boys, Alastair, thirteen, and Mark, eleven, was highly developed and placed forcibly in front of their father, Ron, in a continuous attempt to get him to change his intermittently unsympathetic behaviour to their mother over the previous years. Meribel suffered from a debilitating long-term autoimmune codition, which sometimes rendered her unable to move, and the children had cared for her, with the help of their grandmother, since their father had left. Mark said, with conviction, "If dad could find it in his heart to change . . . has he got a heart? . . . then he's got to show he is nice to mum in two ways: he wouldn't drink beer and he should phone mum up and say 'Honestly and truly, Meribel, I am sorry, can you make it up to me if I can make it up to you?'" Alastair added, "If we could see him apologising to mum through the door, or hear him on the phone saying 'I am sorry for all the silly stuff I did' . . . if we could actually see it and hear it, we could forgive him." When they were asked, "If you are to give dad a second chance, what would he have to change?", Mark answered with a clear list: "(1) learn to listen, (2) learn to take us seriously, (3) treat me like a son . . . he treats me like a competitor and if he's 'got me' he's winning a competition over mum."

The children's grandmother, Pam, had her own grievance and wanted to emphasise how, when they were married, Ron had kept her and Meribel, her daughter, apart. Pam also reported that Ron's parents were overindulgent towards him, especially when he was "under the influence of alcohol". Pam declared that she was "man enough to take action" if Ron was in any way to threaten her daughter and she was willing to go to prison on behalf of protecting her daughter and her grandchildren. Meribel herself was not so vociferous against Ron and wanted to engage in reminding the children that she and their father had enjoyed their lives together. She said warmly, "He was a lovely man, and I fell in love with him." The two families had lived alongside one another and the two parents had been to school together. Their parents had been, and remained, the major influence in their lives with each other. Meribel said she "adored" Ron's parents, but thought they overindulged him and did not make him face up to the effects of his drinking or to his responsibilities to them as a family. Ron's repeated position was, "I want time with my children on a regular basis . . . Pam's to blame."

## Changing the frame

I was unable to make any difference in the negativity of the narratives on either side of the two household extended family, though both parents seemed to be offering some wish to have a continued relationship. I decided to change the frame of "fight" for the children, and offered Ron and Meribel a couple interview on their own in CAFCASS offices away from their home town. The precondition was that neither was to tell their mother or their children beforehand. Ron and Meribel agreed eagerly to participate in such a meeting (to my own surprise). In an alcohol-free environment, with none of the grandparents present, they were able to relate warmly and emotionally around their own separation issues and their attachment to the children. Ron said, "We've both been hurt in our relationship, some things I am truly disappointed about and I am sure you are the same." Both of them said they did not trust their own mothers to behave, and became serious around discussing the things they thought affected the children, growing physically closer to each other through their shared experience. They requested some time alone together, and I left them cuddling on the sofa.

Following this meeting, Ron withdrew from court proceedings and the couple decided to manage the ongoing contact dilemmas on their own. Ron was reinvited into mother's home to build up trust with the children and enable them to see that their mother and father were as one around their belief that it was in their best interests to see him. Contact went forward on a more secure footing for the following year, in spite of Ron's continued drinking. Meribel wrote to me a year later to let me know of the boys' successful academic achievements, of which both parents were very proud.

*Reflections on this piece of family work*

When a grandparent has been recruited as a carer, it is obviously important to engage with the grandparent in the process of re-establishing a connection between the children and their father. However, that same grandparent might be looking for a different outcome to the mother herself. Pam had a strong investment in keeping her daughter and Ron apart, but Meribel still yearned for Ron romantically. The recognition of this romantic tie, and giving permission for it to be spoken about together (and later with the children in the absence of their grandmother), allowed a new trajectory to be developed between Ron and Meribel.

*Taking a moral position: the competing influence of grandparents and peers on a young person's willingness to see her father*

In the Singh family, Rasheeda, mother's mother, had been invited over by Ishtal, the children's father, shortly after he left home, because of his concern about the children's wellbeing in the context of their mother Rosanna's extreme depression. Over the year of Rasheeda's presence in the family, however, Ishtal had lost his temper at her outspoken remarks about his own infidelity, and, in losing it, had said "unforgivable things" which the children had heard and repeated. In a family interview to discuss contact, Rosanna explained to the children why she still thought their father was a good person for them, that he wanted to see them, and she wanted them to see him. "He is a nice man, he has a good sense of humour . . . I still trust him, he is your dad and he loves you . . . I think you will have fewer problems as you grow up if you see your dad . . . ideally a child needs both parents together, but in the long run, two happy homes rather than one unhappy one might be a better thing." Her daughter, Amba, who was thirteen, chose to take a different position, and argued her own case about conditions for future connection with her father with her mother. "I would like you and dad to be friends, mum . . . most parents are divorced in my class but their parents are still good friends. This would make it much easier. You must change too, whatever granny Rasheeda says." By the end of the interview, we clarified (with Amba firmly guiding the negotiations) that the three younger boys would see their father but that Amba would not. Amba told me that her peer group of friends at school were a powerful influence in encouraging her to take a strong position on behalf of the women in her family. "They say, 'don't let your dad push your mum around'."

*Intercultural conflict: the foolish female messenger*

In discussing the children's views with Ishtal, I identified how his daughter had voiced a position about his behaviour in leaving the family; "She did not say she does not love you but she does not like the way that you live with another woman and badmouth their granny." Ishtal was very angry with my failure to "win over" his daughter, and shouted that he thought someone with my training and experience would be able to see through all the lies and cant, and that it would be obvious to anyone that his children were maintained in a regime of fear by their grandmother. He yelled that Rasheeda was doing black magic on the children, "blowing dust and bitter liquid ... goes into the kitchen and puts things in the food." He went on to say that his daughter had been "taught to lie from an early age and was simply the next in a long series of generations of lying women ... I am giving her up. Rosanna can take our daughter back. Each child is a shackle, I will have only my sons, but [cooling down a little] we need to have it so that the relatives do not interfere. They must shut their mouth."

*Reflections on the work*

As part of my own professional development in post-divorce dispute work, this heated intergenerational and intercultural exchange between father and daughter, with Amba taking the part of a modern young British girl and myself behaving as a naïve older female messenger, strengthened my belief that much of what we can usefully do with fathers requires a practical stance. An educative conversation debating with an angry father the rights of his children to different points of views as legitimate can be possible and is often necessary. In this instance, disadvantaged by his anger as I was, I focused with Ishtal on his own thinking and choices, placing his daughter in a London school that had educated her into a different culture, with different ways of thinking about gender and role. I pointed out that he himself had placed her in this context for developing her mind and risked suggesting that he might himself have to "catch up" with her changes, rather than continuing to insist on traditions of respect and obedience to him in the person of "father". The paradox of his position, simultaneously presenting his daughter with an image of a father who was breaking the family morality by choosing to live with a woman other than her mother, was apparent to him. All Amba was asking for in these difficult circumstances was that her parents behave as friends, and that he stop badmouthing her granny. This reasoning turned out to be a useful approach, and led to a better outcome in connecting him back to Rosanna through his young sons. Amba, however, hung out for the changes she had overtly asked for, friendship between parents, and an apology to granny and, within my time, she had not acceded to his request for contact.

# CHAPTER SIX

# Processes that alienate one part of the family from another

*Patterns, habits, and the loss of reflecting minds*

T he previous three chapters have considered difficulties, social, emotional, and familial, which can get in the way of a father's good intentions towards being a dad. This chapter considers interpersonal processes that might deliberately influence a child away from a father. If the family is viewed as a potential open learning system, which can allow the child's ways of construing relationships and his relational world to change in the context of wider family changes, the converse can also happen. Bateson long ago described habits in thinking as "the sinking of knowledge down to less conscious levels", and posited "the unconscious contains not only the painful matters which consciousness prefers not to inspect but also many matters which become so familiar that we do not need to inspect them" (1973b, p. 114). Much of what we do as therapists is to restore the capacity to think and reflect in contexts where these important human capacities have been subordinated to habit. We inspect habit and wonder how such habits developed, and what is concealed by their maintenance. What is gained and lost for whom? We look for habits in patterns of behaviour and speech, and the ways family members behave, which are not necessarily responses only to the current situation, but have become laid down over time. We then try to decode the meanings that seem to be at odds with current scenarios. In alienating processes, these disjunctions between the person seeking contact, their apparent "good" intentions and the usually inappropriate response, create interactional misunderstandings that amplify. Each person is moving towards the other with different intentions, without checking if there is any common ground. For example, Mimi, a four-year-old girl, greets her apparently amiable father's attempt to give her a present in the following way: "I can see you're giving me another rip-off present . . . I mean a rubbish present . . . a packet of pens . . . I mean what kind of present is that . . . a packet of pens . . . pens aren't very exciting!" Later in the meeting, in which she has constantly tried to engage him by drawing pictures of wild animals that she then throws at him, she says randomly, "You didn't give us the money that you should have." Thus, her view of a "rubbish present" is also coloured by the financial irregularities which have played a large part in family stories that she has overheard. Later, she adds an opinion: "When I get married I'm going to have a husband that's way better than you . . . a saddo like you", and later still offers him threats. Handing him a drawing of a tiny boat and a large shark, she says, "I want to put you in a boat to China and it would sink down to the bottom very, very deep and you'd be eaten by a shark" (Gorell Barnes, 2015).

### Tactics of control in conflicted discourses: sanity, identity, and court processes

Analysis of family discourse from related fields (Ochs & Taylor, 1992) orientated me twenty-five years ago to tactics of power and control in routine daily family conversations. Then later, during court work, I observed mothers, grandmothers, grandfathers, and children talking in family situations where fathers were collectively held in a negative light, which illuminated the subtle ways that children's thought can be turned away from any value given to their fathers' visits. When observing alienating processes in the room, a professional also has to hypothesise in her mind about possible conversations that are not currently being had, but may be taking place elsewhere. The extreme states of mind that many parents, mothers as well as fathers, fall into when threatened by distance from their children can be compounded by a belief that their former partner will have more influence in shaping their children's minds than they do, and the fear that a child might then turn against them. These extreme states of mind can be framed as "illness" in a variety of ways, which then further complicate potential connections and attachments between fathers and children.

### Why does Cherry (aged ten) say, "Tell the judge I am never going to see my daddy again, never"?

On occasions, I have been asked to attempt a "therapeutic mediation interview" by a judge or solicitor desperate to achieve a resolution of a case that has returned to court many times over many years. In the interview below, Cherry's parents, Rose and Aaron, have agreed to meet to try to agree a more realistic format for contact between Cherry and her father in the context of court disputes during the past five years—half her current lifetime. Cherry has now also refused to see her father's family, her granny and grandpa and his sister and her family, "I won't go and see them, I won't."

Cherry's mother, Rose, started with the best of intentions but became progressively more random in her assertions about Aaron's "controlling" behaviour and the way that he "upsets" her. I asked her to describe what Cherry might see that showed that she, Rose, was upset by Aaron, when this happens. Rose said, "She sees my moods." I asked her, "What does Cherry actually see?", and she replied, "She sees that I'm drained and exhausted." I asked, "How does this show on your face, in your behaviour?" She replied, "I become tired and snappy." I asked, "What does Cherry do when you're tired and snappy?" Rose replied, "She walks off in a huff . . . she might also see it too if somebody phoned, and I was having a conversation with them about my upset." I queried, "How do you think seeing you upset might affect Cherry's own thoughts about seeing her dad?" Rose insisted (contradicting her earlier statement) that she never had a conversation in the same room as her daughter, so Cherry would not be affected by her upset. She claimed that she always "walked off" and had the conversation in another room. However, she agreed that Cherry's older half brother and half sister, stepchildren to Aaron, would often talk about their dislike of their stepfather at family meals, which is likely to have had an impact on Cherry's perceptions. Rose asserted that the children had never got on with their stepfather. Aaron said, "Yet again, Rose's recollection of events is imperfect. I would never move in with a divorcée without having a good relationship with her children." Rose yelled, "That's right, Aaron's always right and Rose is always wrong. I'd like you to step back and stop being so disparaging." Aaron asserted, "We had a good relationship until it started to deteriorate. I used to take Lulu to school every day." Rose yelled, "What you mean is you drove out of the gate before she'd even got into the car and shut the door." Aaron was silenced and sat back.

Three minutes later, Aaron asked Rose whether she "did not always have a very bad memory for detail". She answered sarcastically, "Yes, unbelievably bad." She said, "The way I used to deal with things was to say 'if that's what they [i.e., Aaron and his mother and father] believe, let's just go with it'. I know the truth, I know what I know, and I'm going to stick with it. He's trying to label me mentally ill again. I haven't got mental illness, and I haven't got parental alienation syndrome." Aaron said, "You see and hear one thing, and I recollect another. I went to the GP for help to try and keep us together." Rose snorted and said that it was the GP who had told Aaron that she was mentally ill. Suddenly changing position, Rose asserted to me, "I will never undermine Cherry's relationship with her father. For me it is important that she has a mother and a father in her life. Cherry is her own person."

I commented on the anguish they both seemed to experience in trying to talk to each other, saying that an intimate relationship that had gone wrong had become a battleground for the truth. Rose replied, "I was actually looking forward to coming here and working together on a positive future for Cherry, but there is no give and take. As with many times, I've been beaten, there is no reciprocation . . . [to Aaron] "it's because you disparage people, I'm quite devastated . . . [to me] I want Cherry to have a good relationship with him but if he can speak in such a disgusting manner as he has today, then Cherry won't want anything to do with him." Rose added that if Aaron could treat her with respect, there might be some hope.

Reflecting on the progress of this interview, I could feel from my own experience of being in it how this couple had the capacity to drive each other into a state from which they could see no return to a middle, collaborative position. This predicament, in my experience, is very common, when alienating processes become a core component of the patterning of family life. I commented on my experience, and on the confusing effect of the conversation on my own mind. I suggested that Cherry's refusal to participate further in family life with her father might reflect the effects of the conflict between the two of them, not only as they played it out as we had just seen, but also in an ongoing way, in her mind. Whereas both presented as reasonable and well intentioned people individually, when Rose and Aaron were together in the same room the capacity for rationality was replaced by constant sequences which led to one being driven into a highly irrational position by the other. In Rose's case, her emotionality became so high that she would lose the main thread of the narrative of the interview. The end product could, and often was, then framed by her ex-husband as her inability to control her emotions, with the implicit or explicit implication from Aaron that this was part of a mental illness (see the discussion of this in Chapters One and Twelve). However, as I saw it, the key frailty was less a product of mental illness than part of the context of Rose's long struggle with her ex-husband for the definition of her mental reality. The constant attempts by each of them to claim the "real" definition of the relationship with Cherry, as well as with each other, had become of a higher order of importance in this long struggle than the wellbeing of their child.

I was invited late into these proceedings and my experience in the six interviews that I had was that the strength of the battle between them was likely to be greater than the strength of any single intervener. Alienation can become ferocious, as unconscious processes that can also confuse an incomer to it can show. Cherry had already taken up her position and my belief was that she was unlikely to change it until she became much older and stronger, could feel she had some real choice in the matter, and could be less stressed herself.

Little is yet known about the long-term effects of specific stress in childhood on adult life, in spite of an enormous literature, including the idea of "wear and tear" on the body and the emotional regulation of the mind. What is often loosely ascribed to "personality disorder" or "borderline behaviour" could usefully be reframed within a different narrative of attempting to process cumulative life stress. This makes a more workable framework to construct new ways of seeing what is going on, particularly with fathers and mothers involved in repetitive or protracted disputes around the care of their children, and children who have suffered these.

## A child's awareness of a father's upsetting effect on their mother: one influence in alienating processes

The way that alienating processes mutually influence one another and lead to negative escalations of misunderstanding is important to grasp before attempting any work on changing these. In the second example in Chapter Five, the child, Jalil, came to a conclusion that his father's judgement and behaviour were wrong, not only on the basis of his own experience but from his observations of his mother's upset; even though she also encouraged him to stay connected to his dad; "I didn't want to leave mum . . . [overnight]. She might be lonely. I don't really think she's got a reason why dad left either." His father's inability to understand his perceptions and descriptions or to respond to his concerns around these led to his moving further away from his father, because he could not find acknowledgement, let alone agreement, from him. In the third example, Alastair and Mark's family, the boys actively tried to change their father's ways of treating their mother, giving him clear options about how he should change his behaviour: "He's got to show he's nice to mum in two ways: he wouldn't drink beer and . . . if I could see him apologising through the door or hear him on the phone . . . if we could see it or hear it . . . then we could forgive him." Following an intervention that separated the couple from the intergenerational family influence, these parents were able to acknowledge, and the father accede to, the children's requests.

## A father's unwillingness to change: amplifying alienation

To access the goodwill of his child, a father necessarily needs to take into account the child's capacity to work out his own intentions towards, and understanding of, the child's mother, and become ready to change his behaviour within that awareness. Processes of negative influence are not overt and direct, but are co-constructed alongside what a child observes, and what he sees, hears, and feels himself. There are many moments when a child's views are open to change within a process of observing a parent responding to their concerns. What a child chooses to share with any professional attempting an assessment of the family and the wishes of the children on behalf of the family court will also be affected by a series of previous observations and decisions that a child has made internally.

## The single incident and partial truths

It is worth noting how the selection of a particular, often single, incident of negative behaviour by a father may be used and reused in repeated assertions about why he is a "bad person" by a family in opposition. In one family, it was the "garage door control" incident; in another, "he didn't look after me properly when I fell off my bike"; in a third, "he only had a towel round his bottom and he let it slip off"; in a fourth, "he read the papers instead of talking to me at breakfast"; in another, "he let the bath toy hurt my bottom". It is clear that some of these assertions contain more potential for harm than do others, but it is important to listen to the way the incident is used and brought into the narrative, often inappropriately to the conversation currently taking place. In a family life which is continuous over time, a child learns that inconsistencies of mother or father within different contexts still add up to a whole person, "that's just dad", but where a father is separated from his children, and the mood is hostile, some very small piece of inconsistency can be picked up and made into a total description of father as a "bad person". The narratives of children who are caught between parents after divorce are filled with such examples of fragmented and partial descriptions, delivered as "truths" about the totality of the out-of-house parent who is seeking contact. In some cases, a child might feel his mother's love for him has become contingent upon him joining her emotional "set" by rejecting his father. On the other hand, it has to be borne in mind that children themselves might have come to grossly dislike their own father in the context of long and acrimonious quarrelling preceding separation, often augmented by court processes following it. Children might then collaborate with each other as well as with their mother to ensure they no longer have to see "him". Small negative examples, such as those described above, might be part of the armamentarium the children hold on to for convincing others of their dislike of their father as a bad person. A third possibility is that a divorce might be so culturally unacceptable in some families that only framing a father in negative ways, including lying about aspects of his behaviour, such as depicting him as violent, can legitimise the divorce itself and, simultaneously valorise the mother for surviving the marriage.

When studying the nuances of alienated narratives, however, it might be possible to discriminate statements which evolve from the child's own difficulty in managing the complexity of the painful situation between their parents from those which are simply copying, or borrowed from, the narrative of an "alienating parent". While one is likely to be influenced by another, due to a child's vigilant observance of a parent's moods and feelings, strong personal grievance and a sense of injustice can emerge from discovering, for example, that a father has been lying to them as well as to their mother; "I used to have a very warm feeling inside and now I just feel disappointed", or "I hate that flat he's living in now and I am never going to go there again", or "do we have to take the rabbits just 'cos *she* [the father's new partner] gave them to us", are feelings that belong to the child, whereas to say, "You didn't pay us the money that you said you would" comes from another discourse that a child has either often heard repeated or has been required to pass on.

## Conflicts of attachment, economics, loyalty, and security: struggles over time

Liam had been "required" by his mother, Beth, who formed a family with a new partner, Jason, when he was seven years old, to place his commitment to his stepfather Jason above that to his father Hugh. In Hugh's report of alienating behaviours by Beth, she had always "diminished him", "scowling and hostile" even in front of Liam on contact handovers, so that her attitude to him was shown clearly to Liam: "she is often rude and abrupt to the extent that she slams the door in my face . . . she raises her voice against me in front of Liam . . . as Liam leaves the house she pulls him back, kissing and hugging him, increasing the pressure of him not to leave . . . she places all responsibility for contact on Liam's shoulders." Hugh did not realise how much Liam was picking up this hostility until Liam rang announcing that he did not wish to see him any more because he had been "mean about money", and that he now considered Jason to be his real father. He said he would kill Hugh if he took any action against his mother to prevent this. Beth dismissed this laughingly as the "kind of thing boys his age say", but went on to describe how Liam might have recognised certain unpleasant traits in his father's behaviour, "a bit of a bully . . . intimidating . . . makes me cry . . . makes me feel sick . . . I think Liam might sense my fear when Hugh and I meet." When she and Jason married, she thought Liam could relax, "feel more comfortable . . . he would feel he was protected from Hugh." While the feelings Beth described, of physical dislike, of anger, and of a sense of injustice towards Hugh were obviously authentic, she would not acknowledge any overt contributions she had made to Liam feeling alienated from him.

### *Involuntary influence and careless thinking, or deliberate influence*

Further work with this family offered evidence of other ways in which Beth's "neglect" of Hugh's contact with Liam could be framed as either deliberate, or as something too difficult for her to deal with at particular periods in her life. During a period of Liam refusing to meet with his father, Hugh had written to him on a regular basis, but Liam initially denied receiving or reading any of these letters. An interview with him and his father clarified that he had seen them, but decided not to read them, disqualifying them in front of his mother. Liam was able to acknowledge that he had chosen not to read them, which seemed to bring him some relief from maintaining his lie. Hugh withdrew attempts at contact through court procedures, feeling that the choice not to see him had been clarified, and that his son needed some space As part of the ending of two years of work with this family, I wrote an open letter to Liam and Hugh about the complexities of their relationship. I pointed out to Liam, "There is a difference between not remembering if you received a letter from your dad, or acknowledging that you received it but did not read it, and there is a further difference if you read it but chose to forget it . . . each is different from saying categorically to your dad 'you never wrote to me' [which is where we had started]. It's the same deal with phone calls and times he tried to make dates with you. These small details are the kind of truth that might be important in the longer-term story of you and your dad. It is important to know that your dad tried to be constant in the context of increasingly difficult circumstances." I related this to the ongoing financial disagreements poisoning the relationship between his father and his mother and stepfather, and pointed out how his position in the middle of the conflict could have affected his own ability to think about his father. "You were not only aware of this disagreement, but placed in the middle of it, which intensified your own conflict of loyalty . . . I believe that being in this position and hearing many negative views expressed about your father may have led to you misreading many of your father's actions . . . and to your relationship with him being muddied. I am afraid . . . that you will disqualify your father's affection for you in your mind when you think about him. As the outsider who has witnessed many aspects of this complicated process over the last year, I think it would be unfair to him and a pity for you. Even if you do not see him for a long time, I think you should have as a rock bottom principle for your growing up to know the fact that he loves you and is proud of your achievements."

For me, this piece of family work further raised profound questions about how a child's mind can become distorted by the process of the two quarrelling parents who have decided not to see anything of each other's point of view. Liam felt that to enjoy something with his dad was also to threaten his loyalty to his mum. ". . . anything you saw as threatening her you would instinctively turn against, whatever the logic your father tried to persuade you was behind his actions." Although this framing of his father's love within the letter was not one that he could make use of at the time, it contributed to a space in his mind in which he could hold on to a different idea about his father from that held by his mother. It also provided evidence, which he could look at, that he had a loving father. Over the next five years, when Liam lived on another continent, his father kept in regular communication, and when Liam was sixteen, he himself made a lengthy journey to seek his father out and start a new, more adult relationship that continued. (Information from a third party.)

### Involuntary influence and careless thinking

When working with families where alienating processes are being cited as part of legal proceedings, it is always important to distinguish involuntary processes from those that are malign or deliberately careless. However, in daily life, it is sometimes very hard to "catch" a careless habit that has, in fact, become an ongoing negative influence on a child's neutrality towards an absent father, or which curtails their freedom to think about him. In the example of Gary and Halima (Chapter Five), Halima is aware that Jalil might notice her own responses to Gary when she is upset or annoyed, "I can't change my face." This open recognition and acknowledgement of an involuntary response, however, is different in quality and strength to a mother's response which has become a habit in the presence of the father, as with Beth, above, or in a regular discourse about a father in the hearing of the child, or as part of her conversations with the child. For example, another mother, Nancy, gave repeated implicit disqualifications to Meg, her daughter, about her father, spoken in her presence: "It's never been a brilliant relationship because her dad isn't really child friendly", or "He isn't very competent and hasn't got a lot of common sense." This contributed a low but continuous level of negative influence which, during my visits, became expressed as a clear negative opinion, "I can't see what he's got to offer really." Daily talking of this kind provides a regular drip of disqualification. More emotionally and less cognitively, calibrated to the stress caused by a series of court processes, Rose's (see pp. 121–122) own emotional responses could raise the stakes in the contest for Cherry's emotional loyalty: "There will be such an upset, how will I get her to see him? [tears, and emotional utterances]. I've had it up to here with contact [stroking the child's head, clutching it to her breast] . . . we have had enough . . . her father's wish to see her is making us ill. It's been going on forever." She claimed that she could remember Cherry locking herself into the toilet when she was only six and saying, "I don't want to leave you, mummy." Such upset drew her daughter in so that they cried together.

### How does a child retain positive memories in the context of negative stories and their repetition?

The problem for very young children in alienating contexts is how to retain any of their own positive memories of their father. Where, in addition, a child has directly witnessed violent or verbally abusive behaviour from father to mother, the child will need a significantly different range of embodied personal experiences of his father inside himself in order to counteract the behaviours towards his mother which he has witnessed, and their subsequent emotional impacts on him. Whereas Jamie, aged seven, could hold on to memories of good things he had done with his dad, "making things in the shed together", which allowed him to retain the idea of his dad having good in him in spite of the current tough circumstances, Deanne, also aged seven, in another family, could not recollect any positive times she and her father had enjoyed. She even refused to look at photos of the two of them together, framing his image as one only of threat, following times when he had "burst in and flown at my mother". Her expressed belief was that he might try to kidnap her, a belief based on threats he had uttered in temper on previous occasions, fears which were consolidated by both her mother and her grandmother's fears that this might actually happen.

Once a father is positioned out of a child's life through "bad" behaviour or narrative, or both, his reintroduction is a complex task. The reintroduction of a mental picture of a father in the mind of a child, where the notion of father is either absent or taboo, requires a new commitment by a mother and her relatives on behalf of both the child and her father to reinstate him. Mimi, above, having rejected her father's gift of pens, asked her father later, "What's a man for . . . why do you need a man . . . I mean, there's nothing a man can do that a woman can't do . . . I don't want one." She was originally reported (by father's sister) to have "adored" him, but she had only known him through contact centre meetings since she was two years old. Her older sister, in a separate interview, had said "I used to think I had a father, but I don't want one any more," and the often narrated stories of father's "ill doing" (in this family, centred around financial wrongdoing) had spread down the all-female sibling group. Children's intersubjective understanding can work against a father. Dunn showed how young children in families where feelings are frequently discussed show more intersubjective understanding of others (Dunn et al., 1991). Her research was illustrated in positive family contexts. Unfortunately for fathers at odds with their families, the converse is also true. Where a father has committed acts which the children see as upsetting to their mother, as well as having perhaps committed a small act of behaviour to one of them which they interpret and narrate as offensive, a negative discourse about him between older siblings can influence any future potential relationship between him and a younger child. Loyalty to the sibling group with whom a younger child lives is likely to be a stronger impulse than loyalty to a parent who constantly receives negative press within that same family.

## Negative appraisals and feelings held in the body

Negative reflections about past experiences with a father, and poor expectations about what might take place in the future, evolve from a combination of personal experience and negatively tuned personal and extended family narratives about the past. These will inevitably fuel a child's reactions: "We feel sick when we have to get up to go and see him . . . mum has to pull the duvet off me . . . I'd rather not see him ever, ever again, it's upsetting." The emotional arousal created by demands for a child's time and attention from a parent who is not part of their daily lives, in addition to court processes around contact disputes, and the wider effects of these on the life of the family, can bring into play former negative representations of a father, rather than any positive ones being allowed to surface and develop. This can sometimes motivate a child to reduce their own emotional arousal, which can be stirred up by the imposed relationship of enforced contact, through avoidance strategies that help them cut off from painful feeling. This is shown in contact disputes as a refusal to engage on the child's part. Ongoing enforced contact can also re-trigger and refine earlier ambivalence into a clearer statement of dislike, in part as a way of a child relieving themselves of painful and ambivalent feeling.

## Not "parental alienation syndrome", but undeniable alienating processes

Ayres (2014) has pointed out that the risk of talking about a parental alienation syndrome is that the debate about what constitutes the syndrome itself becomes a red herring, which distracts people from the reality that parental alienation is all too common. (Child, 2016). The following characteristics, drawn from my own experience, have appeared in alienating narratives.

1.   The child views one parent as only good and the other parent as only bad (draws an image of "beautiful mum" and "ugly dad").

2.   The child expresses only negative feelings towards the parent they profess not to like, and the reasons they give are very trivial and in another family would be laughingly dismissed. "I can see you're giving me another rip-off present . . . I mean a rubbish present . . . a packet of pens . . . I mean, what kind of present is that . . . a packet of pens . . . pens aren't very exciting" (four-year-old girl).

3.   The child denies being influenced by the "good" parent and states that their views and utterances are all their own. ("Tell the judge I'm not going to see my dad ever again; that's what I say, it's not what my mum says".) The corollary danger is that a child's own truth might be lost in the loyalty to her parent's wish.

4.   Small instances of negative behaviour become a totalising negative description of the person of father (as in the previous descriptions).

5.   Economic narratives that a child would not normally be aware of can be thrown in a father's face, "You didn't give us the money that you should have", suggesting that financial irregularity has played a large part in family stories.

6.   Highly emotional outbursts in which it is clear the child is "standing on a parent's shoulders": "I can't call you daddy any more because you are not really my daddy any more; why did you do this to us? You have spoilt our lives. I hate you to death."

7.   Direct rudeness on behalf of a mother, "When I get married I'm going to have a husband that's way better than you . . . a saddo like you."

8.   Verbal threats: "I want to put you in a boat to China and it would sink down to the bottom very, very deep and you'd be eaten by a shark" (Mimi); "Unless your behaviour improves one hundred per cent I am not going to see you any more. I want to stay with mum and I will kill you if you try to stop me" (Liam).

9.   Texting threatening images, sending threatening messages, images related to lavatories and turds.

10.  Physical threats: attacking with a chair, threatening with sports equipment, a hockey stick, a bow and arrow, throwing things at a father.

*Using a higher morality or religious belief as
justification for not seeing a father*

For children, taking a high moral tone about not seeing their father can also be a way of them distancing themselves from distress and anger at the reality of parental loss, often a key underlying issue when a child chooses not to see his father. Where the children have been brought up with religious and "family" values, God might be invoked to authorise their choices: "Don't try and talk to me on the phone as that hooker may be listening . . . you may have gained a devil and turned into one yourself, but you have lost a daughter." An attempt by this father to have a reasoned discussion with his child, whom he had formerly brought up to value a shared religion, was met with rebuttal and resolute denial. This was escalated when he tried to justify his choices on the grounds of personal happiness. "I understand that you are hurt and disillusioned by me leaving mummy . . . but I hope you understand that this is a result of problems that have existed for a long time between us", is countered with, "Stop coming to our house. Do not talk to me or mum. I just want you out of our lives forever. I do not count you fit for fathering . . . God will look after us, not you."

## Keeping a presence alive in a child's mind

One of the major difficulties in working with children stuck in positions where they are seen to reject a parent is that any intervention from an outside person is likely to be long after these alienating processes have become established, both as an external process in the family and as internal and patterned processes within the children's minds. However, pursuing small inputs that keep a warm presence going, seeing how children respond, which, in turn, might influence the responses of their other parent in the long term, is, in my experience, always valuable A few examples of changing patterns through deliberate strategies are included below.

1.  Getting a father to write a letter to his children, laying out his understanding about those things he believes have gone wrong between him and their mother, which are currently affecting their

relationship with him. The letter should include an expression of sorrow and regret for any harm done to the children, both by him and by the ongoing disputes, as well as a continuing assurance of his love for them. (In this intervention, there has to be a genuine assurance by the father of his sorrow, as well as evidence that there will be no continuing harm arising from his actions, such as financial hardship on mother's part while he might be having a better standard of living.) This is best discussed with a sympathetic third person before being sent, to check for tone and any outrage and righteousness that may have crept in. (Violence as a component of wrongdoing is discussed in Chapters Nine and Eleven and might or might not be a component of alienation. Violence requires a different series of strategies that aim at bringing emotions under control before other work can be seriously attempted.)

2. Using photographs of good times the child/children spent together with him (their father) which they can hold on to as evidence that they enjoyed a good relationship in the past. This can include expressing an updated and current interest in how his children might be pursuing these interests or activities in their current lives. (It is very common that fathers estranged from their children become stuck in an earlier version of them, as well as a rhetoric of love that the children do not know how to manage. Updating these sentiments to mesh with the children's current development is much more likely to engage the children.) Even if these letters are rejected at the time, they provide an evidence base for a future possible relationship that might be less fraught.

3. Maintaining regularity and reliability around birthdays, acknowledgement of academic successes, and religious festivals where family goodwill greetings would be common.

4. Sending regular pocket money, allowances, and gifts as an assurance of ongoing fatherly interest.

5. Therapeutic work with the children's mother to help her to separate her own sense of outrage at the father's "wrongdoing" from her awareness that the children's needs, wishes, and feelings could allowably be different from her own.

This is usually a long term-procedure where smaller earlier interventions have failed to produce any change. Where a woman as wife or partner has felt the treatment she received from her former partner in life has deprived him of the right to have a further relationship with his children, this acutely painful feeling can take many years to set aside. Economic wrongdoing and infidelity, leading to irrecoverable low self-esteem, can lead to powerful hostility as a way of distancing overwhelming emotions. A former strong attachment that is seen to have been abused can lead to an extreme sense of internal dislocation. The rebuilding of a new life might partly depend on the perceived loyalty of the children. Until this is no longer felt to be a central need of the mother's, hostility may remain a barrier to a father's further relationship Mental illness in either partner further complicates relationships that are hostile, and acute depressive experience can follow a divorce, further contributing to an inability to change an alienating position.

# CHAPTER SEVEN

# Fathers, stepfathers, and complex families

"Well, I may be her stepfather, but as far as I'm concerned a father or a dad is someone who's there when you're crying, when you're happy, who picks you up when you fall down, who takes you to school, who feeds you, who fights with you, who cuddles you, who talks to you, who doesn't talk to you, who's there . . . this other man who gave birth to her through sperm is nowhere near her father . . . the only influence he must have on her is a genetic influence . . ."

(Eddie, 1997, personal communication)

T his chapter considers some of the ways that "reordered" families interrelate, both practically and emotionally, with families that have both preceded them and continue to develop alongside them, and the complex and often conflicting positions that men as fathers and stepfathers can find themselves in. My conversation with Eddie, nearly twenty years ago, raised questions not only about stepfathers, but also about contemporary expectations surrounding the role of father. What are fathers for at a time when economic, gendered, and generational roles are increasingly fluid. The wish for a strong father is often expressed by children experiencing change:

"Fathers are meant to be strong and solid people . . . a dad is meant to stay loyal and committed to his family no matter what, but when he goes, there is a break and other people are allowed to come in that call themselves father, and you might not like them" (Sukie, 2012, personal communication). The different positions for stepfathers, as repartnered fathers often separated from children by a former relationship, and concurrently positioned as social or "stepfathers" (often becoming second time biological fathers), offers unusual opportunities to talk about complex fatherhoods with fathers themselves. Open conversations that acknowledge uncertainty and complexity can facilitate the development of new approaches to negotiating hazards and facing conflicts of interests, exploration of a complex social identity aspects of which a man might not have thought about. The role of stepfather is both chosen and fallen into. Within a wider family, there will be separate subsystems, where different wishes and expectations of him will be held. These might not be chosen or recognised by him, but are, none the less, held on to and determined by other family members. Stress can be conceptualised within a context of conflicting demands from multiple perspectives at different generational levels.

## "Going under": failing as stepfather and father at the expense of a second partner

The Bennett–Simons network consisted of Susan Bennett and her three children, Matt, Seth, and Rose, in their late teens. They visited their father, John, every alternate weekend. John had remarried and had two small children under five. Susan had recently repartnered with Kevin, who had two teenage children, Romana and Miguel. Kevin's children initially lived with their mother, Clarissa, after she broke up with Kevin, and had a complicated relationship with her due, in part, to her drinking, as well as neglectful, highly irrational behaviour. There was often no food in their fridge, and their home deteriorated to a point where they suddenly decided to move out. Both children had become unused to parental supervision, having largely looked after themselves during their later childhood and early teens. Susan Bennett was unexpectedly faced with accommodating five teenagers rather than three in her household. She managed this by dividing two rooms into smaller sleeping cubicles and made house rules about what moving in would involve. Subsequently, she coached Kevin's children through their A-levels by insisting on a homework schedule as part of the condition of their living in the house. This caused resentment and rowing from all parties: from her children because they felt they lost out on time with her, when they also were doing exams, and from Kevin, her husband, because he believed she had succeeded with his children where he had not.

Kevin had been without work for over a year and worried continually both about his children and what he chose to frame as the different resources offered to the children who came from his side of the family. His own failure to provide economically, as a key construct of his definition of what a father should do, kept him in a state of irritable unavailability. This meant he did not provide other aspects of fathering, like emotional care, practical assistance, or help with planning their lives. His constant arguing with Susan over her "management style" escalated to angry rowing, most of which the children could hear. Kevin appeared to be trapped in a version of fatherhood in which he could not enjoy his partner's competence or thank her for all the daily work she put in. The Bennett children came to consult together, without their mother, to explain the distress these rows, and their stepfather's angry presence, were causing them: "We hate the fact that Kevin is so hostile . . . it's our house, too. Mum seems able to forget the rows once they are over, but we can't do that. We can hear every single word they say in the kitchen and out in the garden, their fights seem to be uncontrollable. I don't think he's nice to her anyway. She wants everything to be so much better: she wills it to be better but it's not." The boys amplified the story by reflecting on the effects on their mother of dealing with constant resentment from her partner: "She doesn't absorb enough *of our* distress. She takes our distress seriously for a bit, then there's an explosion and she can't think. She cries more and she tries to keep everyone happy, which is hopeless."

*Constructing a whole family meeting: airing grievances, making acknowledgements, and children gaining permission to tell their fathers what they need from them*

All members of the household agreed to a "whole two-family meeting" and each of the young people was given an opportunity to discuss their concerns about what was happening and to reposition themselves in the eyes of the others. Kevin's children were able to explain their stress in relation to concerns about their mother's mental health, a preoccupation which they carried at all times, and their fear that, due to the rowing they had witnessed in Kevin and Susan's household, *this* family might also break down. Susan's children explained more about their difficulty in going back and forth to their own father John's house and feeling that they had been "ousted" there by his new family of young children, and they now felt doubly "ousted" by Kevin's children coming to live with them in such a precipitant manner. Susan and Kevin were confronted about the effect their rowing as a couple was having on her own children, which took them by surprise. "We don't want Kevin going out of your life 'cos then you would be more upset, but we don't want him so much in our faces in his grumpy way." The meeting challenged them to take their marriage more seriously and to undertake major rethinking about how to structure parental time, household management, and shared responsibility.

Whole family meetings around issues of "unfairness", which can be both complex and raw, also make it possible for children to experience their step-siblings as real young people like themselves, negotiating or fighting for similar needs to be met. Such meetings, and sharing and highlighting direct ongoing troubled experience, can diminish persecutory ideas and fantasies about one another and construct more empathic understandings of what is going on. Step-siblings might not love one another, but they can develop understanding about each other's lives that enables them to get by in the context of the new family their parents have formed. Talking together in a therapeutic context, as well as talking with their parents in front of all the others, can help individual children manage the confusing emotionality devolving from loss, change, and the skewing of former relationship patterns. The sibling subsystem can also provide a protected space where the more "alien" aspects of adult behaviour can be put into a shared intergenerational perspective, without the children fearing being accused of disloyalty. Joint meetings allow each child to put his or her personal sense of unfairness in a wider context and can also free them to become more active in mobilising their own parent to meet their needs. Kevin remained a father who could not take initiative in mobilising his resources for his children, but he responded bit by bit to being told by them what they required of him. His own children felt more secure in organising him to recognise that they needed his ongoing attention and positive regard, even if he did not "do" anything active on their behalf without them prompting him to do so.

## Conflicts of role and expectation

Common expectations, simultaneously held in different relational groups in the family, can pose extreme conflicts for stepfathers unless openly faced and then mediated. Conflicts revolve around love, both romantic and paternal, family economics in more than one family, as well as fathering "jobs". Outer conflicts around what a father or a stepfather should be doing can be regularly voiced, and inner conflicts might also be held by a father himself at the level of personal guilt created by his own competing wishes and desires: what he should do with his own children, how they see him within his new coupledom, and how he should respond to the unhappiness or demands of a former wife. He might fail to recognise the conflicts of interests and role in the context he is living in, or to understand the confusion or depression he is experiencing. One man might have to carry out numerous paternal positions simultaneously and, in addition, be seen through various lenses: by the mother of his children as ex-husband or failed partner, and by second (or third) partners as current lover, potential husband, and future father of as yet unborn children. In many situations, a new partner already has children from a first relationship, and he will have to work out his part as stepfather from the start of the relationship. Children see "fathers" in diverse ways that also depend on the multiple narratives about fathers they hear in their families and schools ("mum's new boyfriend, friend, bloke", etc.) (Brannen & O' Brien, 1996, Gorell Barnes et al., 1998).

## Stepfathers' attunement to their stepchildren

The question of a stepfather's attunement to stepchildren is a difficult feature of step-family living, specially where maintaining good relationships with his children from a first relationship is his highest preoccupation. He might find his "paternal self" divided in ways that he cannot always sustain. Step-families who look for professional assistance are increasingly complex. They might involve three or more sets of relationships that need to be considered, and a father might have less clear expectations of which responsibilities belong to a current partnership and which belong to a former relationship. Subsystems could be collaborative or acutely competitive for his time and love. Expectations and wishes devolving from different partnerships, and any children born within them, might, at times, become irreconcilable. This can lead to further disruption or break-up. In clinical work, we can also explore richness in the development of family attachments across larger family groupings, with multiple relationship possibilities for children with half-siblings and step-siblings. The question of when "rich complexity" collapses into a disconnected "heap" with insufficient structures to support the children appropriately at their stages of development always has to be borne in mind. Flouri (2008), studying adolescent adjustment in relation to father involvement, children's residence, and biological fatherhood presence, found more conduct problems and hyperactivity in stepfather families. The aetiology of stress in step-family life requires further subtle understanding, as families form and reform across cultural and continental boundaries. These might, in themselves, bring new forms of emotional burden through factors such as civil war, violence, and migration trauma.

## Fathers and the Holy Grail of family life

For some fathers, patterns of gender-related expectations and roles derived from previous generations might also be playing a relevant part in current difficulties. These hidden "drivers" can often be bizarre and lead to strange requests of children. In one family, for example, a father expected his son to dress "like a gentleman" at all times and provided him with specific sets of "gentleman's clothes" to wear while on contact visits. Another father expected his nine-year-old daughter to host "literary soirées" for him while she visited. A further father in this more unusual group continued to try and run his "family" of four children aged from four to eighteen, by four different women, as though they were an intact first family and the children were all of primary school age. The search for the "Holy Grail" of a good family life in which a man can feel he is being a "proper father" is one that might be driven by inner longings or ideals of what a "proper family" should be that lead to abandoning one partnership and taking up another. While this "tribal" approach to serial monogamies is often simplified and ridiculed within the publicised domain of "trophy wives", there might be less obvious reasons why men "move on" and find it hard to settle within one relationship—reasons that they do not understand themselves and might be unwilling to explore unless some aspect of discord in the family forces this upon them.

### Threats to new partnerships: death, divorce, former wives, and children

In a complex step-family, where both parents bring children from former marriages, it might be the strength of the father's attachments to his biological children and their competition for his time and attention that threaten the new partnership. Step-parents support for the parenting efforts made on behalf of one another's children is central to making the new system work, but many step-parents are not understanding of their partner's children and the harmful effects of any current life experiences these children might be having.

### Davina, Imran, Dino, and Soraya

A young couple, originally from Iran, contacted me to sort out these conflicts between them. Each brought children from their first marriage: Davina, two daughters (nine and six) who were still living with their grandmother in Iran, and Imran a son, Dino, who was also six years old. Davina's husband had died in an unsolved killing a year before she and Imran got together, and her own children had lived in a close household with her mother since that time. Imran was the eldest of three brothers and was raised by a family of traders as the first university-educated boy in his family. He was a boy who always had to get 95% "or more" and met his family expectations by achieving a Master's in Business Studies. He had separated from his first wife, Soraya, saying it was because she was equally ambitious and he wanted more tenderness and less strife in his life at home. However, her volatile and unpredictable behaviour entered strongly into the conversations between Davina and Imran during our three consultations, suggesting that she would be an ongoing troubling presence.

Davina was anxious about the intermittent closeness Imran, Dino, and his mother Soraya maintained. Her own husband being dead, she stated that she found it "almost too much to manage at times . . . he is preoccupied with him more than he is with me and will talk to her about him all the time. He never says 'don't do this' to Dino, he calls it 'picking on him' and fears the child will not love him." Soraya had equal parental care of Dino and took him on business trips to many parts of the world, but would rarely look after him herself, hiring local helpers who spoke no English. Sometimes she would ring Imran and say, "I can't manage him, you take him."

It was clear that Dino's insecurity of attachment and his resulting attention-seeking behaviour was affected by all the changes and inconsistencies in his life. This had to be discussed with Davina, who found aspects of Dino's behaviour very threatening. Her mind had not previously been open to understanding the possible impact of the complex relationships and the multiple non-attached carers Dino had to manage She said of Dino, "He will come and stand beside his father and ask to be told what he should do; but then will often take no notice and continue to do what he wants himself. . . . sometimes he gets into a rage and throws things about because he doesn't know what to do of his own accord. If we are sitting and talking he comes and interrupts us . . . he should realise he can't get attention straight away. He also made suggestions to his dad that meant he could spend time with him on his own." In this joint conversation, Imran also noted that much of Dino's time was spent with non-English-speaking carers. He suggested that in those situations Dino often had to take care of the grown-ups in his life and take charge of what he wanted to do because the carers had not been helped to think about how to fill in the time in his mother's absence. He pointed out how Dino had had more than seven different carers in his life since the separation eighteen months before. Davina challenged this observation, giving it a different frame: "I think it is you who have taught him to take charge, not these girls . . . you want him to grow up and run the family business." Imran concurred with this, saying, "You are right to say I am training him right from the start to think for himself and to take charge of situations, but I am also right in what I say." Being right was very important to each of them.

Setting up a structured plan for exploring both points of view and then introducing a framework for incorporating these through discussion and negotiation, their preferred problem solving approach, moved forward the development of a shared plan about how to integrate two different sets of children, and their experiences, into their lives.

### Marrying into the extended family: further variations on too many commentaries—Asad and Samirah

In Chapter Three, the impact of wider family relationships on a father's freedom to construct a relationship with his partner and new baby, as variables a father has to take into account, was discussed. In a second partnership, where a prior family of elders travels with one of the partners, the vigilance of a kinship network might be further heightened by anxiety, resulting from the failure of a first marriage: "will she make it this time". Patterns of elders can exacerbate tensions in the couple already managing each other's children. In a complex step-family from Pakistan, with a history of high emotionality and mental illness in the grandparental generation on mother's side, each parent brought their own parents home on a weekly basis. Asad, the father, described the mother, Samirah's, relatives "sitting about like a huge committee meeting where nothing gets decided". His daughter from his first marriage, Reena, was living with them while she completed her university education, and she became particularly incensed at the "relatives gang", feeling herself vulnerable and over-scrutinised by her stepmother's side of the family. Feeling that they intruded into any possible intimacy that might develop in the family, she had several extremely angry outbursts, expressing to her father fears that she would never be allowed to find her own place. Reena explained to her father, Samirah, and myself, "I feel a little tired trying to keep everyone together . . . daddy hates your mummy, Samirah, your mummy hates my daddy when he hates her, and then you and daddy don't get on . . . I could get to love you, Samirah, but if it isn't the little children, then they [the elders] are always in the way". Asad also became exhausted by Samirah's elders, described them as watching him vigilantly as the "second husband" to make sure he did not commit offences like the first—"so busy that they forget to look after their grandchildren". The emotional tone of Samirah's family was high and intense, and the effect of their criticism on her was volcanic, in that she would flare up very quickly and decide to leave the marriage. Her parents and aunties would be terrified of a second marriage break-down and for a while would be nice to the couple, and then the cycle would start again.

In the face of so many different concerns, it was hard to know where best to develop new thinking. Samirah and Asad decided to work on some typical interactions between them, and take charge of themselves before addressing the issue of the grandparental presence. Reena reminded them of an episode that had taken place the previous week. Samirah was "trying to be a good mother" by bathing her baby, and Asad was trying to "be a good stepfather" by getting his stepchildren their tea. While he wished to "be seen as good" in Samirah's eyes, the activity of tea making was in conflict with an "important" presentation he had to prepare for the morning. He reconciled his inner tension with the mantra "it will only take a minute", but he was unable to find the agreed-upon fish fingers in the fridge and shouted up the stairs to ask where the packet was, thus disturbing Samirah and the baby. She shouted back, "It's in the fridge as I already told you" (the first trigger). He suggested something else to the children, which they rejected, saying, "Mum says it's bad for you to eat too many samosas." This was a meaningful reference to his waistline, which he and Samirah were in conflict over as she said him putting on weight was ruining their sex life. When he asked her again, she added, "Why can't you ever find anything?" (second trigger). One of his stepchildren found the hidden "tea" in the fridge at the bottom where he "had not bothered to bend to find it" (third trigger). At this point the granny rang to ask how the baby was and Asad heard Samirah saying, "I've only asked Asad to do the tea this once and he's making a hash of it." Asad gave up and roped Reena in to take over the tea duty, while he went to do his presentation, now feeling discredited by both the younger and the older generations as well as by the voices of women in his life.

For this couple the humour generated by this detailed discussion enabled them to overcome the tension. Careful analysis of their communications and the meanings embedded in the minute zones of high emotional tension, the moments when the "fog of unreason" overcame the clarity they were struggling for, were entry points they accepted for taking back their lives from their elders. They made a contract with each other to limit the number of weekends on which grandparents were allowed to visit. They asked for a "take-home ther-apist" in the form of a letter spelling out the intentions they were aiming to achieve, and they included Reena as the "third person" who had permission to point out any potential escalation of rows if she was present. Although this gave her too much responsibility in the family as a whole (reversing the notion that it was her father's job to look after her as his daughter), she was already carrying this responsibility and was pleased to move towards having her role as peacemaker and mediator given a formal status while the attempted changes consoli-dated.

### The deterioration of relationships with one's own children in the context of a new partner

When an older father has left his wife and teenage children to live with a younger woman and her children, becoming an instant step-father, the transition might not be the wished-for romantic life he envisaged. Managing the social and emotional adaptations such a transition requires, without acknowledging and discussing the pain caused to his older children who find themselves only a few years younger than his new partner, might also expose a younger child on overnight visits to an experience of a father reconstructing his life unsuccessfully. This experience of "failing father" can become a signif-icant emotional burden to the child who is going between two house-holds.

*Example:* Posy, aged eleven, who was going through the double transition of her father, Norman, and then her mother, Maggie, repart-nering, had not spoken aloud for a year. Her mother explained to her father that Posy found it hard to be in his house as she felt a constant atmosphere of hate expressed toward her mum by Marina, her father's new partner. When I met her on her own, Posy explained that she felt "very unsafe". In a tiny whisper, with me sitting up close to her on the sofa, she explained that she had thought her parents might get back together because she had seen them hugging each other (a year before) and neither of them had actually told her they were not getting back together. She said that dad is "now living with Marina, and her two little kids", and mum has just had Luke move into the house: "... my eyes feel tight all the time, as though I am about to cry, I don't feel safe out of the house and actually I don't feel safe in the house either, except with my sisters or with mum. I don't really feel safe with Luke, though he's nice to mum. Everything has changed." She did not want to go to dad's house because dad sits on her bed and talks for hours about how unhappy he is with Marina's children ... "sometimes it's better just to stay quiet".

In a meeting with her father, Posy, and her older sisters, they told him about the difficulties they were all experiencing spending any time with him alone now he was "being a dad" in another family. This made Posy feel bolder. All the girls felt Marina (only five years older than Norman's eldest daughter) had hijacked any intimacy in their relationship with their father, stealing him away "to look after her own kids". "We don't want to be forced into the wrong family." Norman was fearful of how Marina would take it, but he agreed to construct some special "father times" with his children rather than ignoring their feelings. While he was furious at being "told" things by his children, he had to hear the fact that the new "instant" family did not feel as perfect to them as he had wanted to believe. This opened a more realistic way in which his daughters felt they could get to know Marina very slowly and at their own distance.

### Generational difference in couple relationships: changes for fathers and their internal equilibrium

There are numerous complexities in fathering when a mother moves in with a younger man or a father's second partner is only a few years older than his oldest child. The parent from the first marriage might find themselves disapproving strongly of changes that the other parent is making. What is "normal" in a step-family has diversified since step-families became a subject for wider research, with new models of parent partnership upsetting biological, generational, and gendered roles, as described thirty years ago (Gorell Barnes et al., 1998; Hetherington, 1989). Where an older woman repartners with a younger man, children might dislike the "younger mother" who emerges, and their father might have no way of responding to her either. Her new partner is more like "bad brother", one teenage son reported. His father said, "I am seeing devastation in our family; she's out every night, they smoke dope together, it's back to a teenage lifestyle." The generational shifts in perspective this induces might then lead a father to choose a second partner who is closer to the "conventionality" of his own inner family style. Contrary to stereotypes that fathers marry younger and more beautiful women the older they get is an alternative systemic pattern where a father seeks to rebalance an internal family equilibrium that he has held on to all his life, but now experiences going out of control in the wake of his ex-wife's post-divorce behaviour. A new partner, chosen to "rebalance stability in his life", in turn has to deal with the disturbances brought about through the children's conflicted experience of parenting style and household expectations, in terms of which standards they are expected to adopt and live by. As one stepmother said angrily, "The boys show no respect, he won't condemn them because he doesn't want to lose them and I am driven mad." Expectations of what a stepmother *should* be can produce unrealistic ways of living, to the extent that new partners who hold high expectations of themselves about what they can achieve where an earlier wife "failed" become frustrated, angry, and feel they are failing in turn.

### Father holding many roles: conflicts of belief and lived experience

Concurrent relationships, in which a father commits to a second partner and any children he has with her before ending a prior relationship, have always been with us. Adults who have grown up in hidden families, who felt they were "disallowed" in the public eye, have borne witness to the injustice of not being acknowledged (in biography as well as in therapy). Despite the way he is living in two households, a father might still hold on to the value systems supporting monogamy and the ideal of one family and household.

### Dot, David, Flo, and Roxie: wife or mistress— whose children are the "real thing"?

Dot, who had been in a "secret" relationship with David for several years and had two children by him, was determined, now the children were three and one years old, respectively, to make sure David did, in fact, divorce his wife, Flo, and marry her. She had two children by her first marriage, whose father was failing to maintain a strong relationship with them and they looked to David as their social father. David continued to care for Flo in what Dot experienced as too committed a manner. In David's mind, Dot was well supported, whereas he feared that Flo, who still had three teenage children living at home, would collapse unless he continued to be a strong presence in family life. To prevent collapse, he would have supper with his first family twice a week and go to all the family birthdays and festivities (without Dot). He would spend much of the time over weekends, Christmas, and New Year phoning Flo as well as his children to make sure they were all right. Flo's daughter, Roxie, aged fourteen, became her emissary and brought the troubled feelings from her mother's household into the second home.

It took David a couple of meetings with Dot to be able to think consciously about his behaviour without "sliding away" and to verbalise to Dot, who was furious with Roxie, the idea that he was, in fact, still the father to Roxie and his older children as much as he was a father to his young children with her. David recognised that Roxie's jealousy of Dot was not only on behalf of her mother, but was also her own, Whereas Dot, not Roxie or Flo, was now the primary love relationship in his life, none the less Roxie remained his *child*. This seemed to allow him to separate the two families in his mind and allow more thought about his own responsibility as father and partner in each case. David noted, "Since we have been thinking about getting married, Roxie barely speaks to Dot." Flo had told her children, "When Dad has a baby with Dot he won't have time for you any more," but three years on she changed the warning to "Once they are married he won't have time for you any more." Flo's words continued to act as a powerful controlling higher "moral" order in David's mind, organising his behaviour and preventing him thinking things through for himself .

When provoked by Dot to take a position that put their own children first, David always feared that, if he gave his second family more time, his older children would turn on Dot and their household as '"driving their mother, Flo, mad": "She's the bad woman who enticed dad away . . . got nothing to do with us . . . *we are the real thing* . . . the rest is background." When overwhelmed by the complexity of his life, David would fall back on the dramatic rhetoric of "dedicated fatherhood" in relation to his first set of children to stabilise himself: "I'll walk over hot coals to see my children even if it means having dinner with Flo. I will still be there for them . . . everything else has gone 'boom' in their lives."

### Constructing a developmental frame with David

The paradox for David, and other fathers in unclear partnership definitions for a second time, is that they have simultaneously positioned themselves as "successful lovers and potential husbands" as well as "good enough" social fathers, in distinction from uncomfortable positions as "failed" husbands or fathers. In realising the degree to which they remain rooted in their original family life, where their strong attachments to their older children lie, the necessity of embracing both families as different aspects of themselves is key to their longer-term emotional survival. Finding that Dot was able to explicitly recognise his commitment to his older children while facing him simultaneously with his responsibility to his younger ones moved him to focus more strongly on the future rather than his failures of commitment in the past. Over two years, he moved towards seeing the two parts of his life as "family", within which he had different commitments. He moved towards a legalised commitment to Dot and the smaller children and worked out a new balance with Roxie, in which he acted more as her father and less as though she was her mother's "twin".

## Mediating behaviour between fathers and social fathers: "Who is my 'real' dad?"

A major accommodation that has to be made within many larger second family systems is the relationship between a biological or "first-time father" and a social or stepfather.

The larger commentaries on good and bad social behaviour offered by television, comedy, and film have sensitised many parents to the foolishness of continued "bad behaviour" in front of their children. However, other parents remain unable to contain themselves, and children as young adults have to choose how they will "manage" these events. One father, now in a second relationship with small children, reported of his older daughter at her school graduation, "Suki is used to being in the middle of family rows now . . . the only way she can escape from the madness of her family when we are all together is to bring her loyal friends along." The effect of such troubled patterns in all families who have experienced adversarial divorce can be an important component of inner disturbance in an adult individual later presenting for therapeutic help. Young adults might experience relief in subsequently reviewing these childhood experiences in the light of their own maturity, or at the point where they experience relationship difficulties with a partner of their own.

In families where a biological father has had an "out-of-house" relationship with his child during the larger part of the child's lifetime, a mother's decision to repartner might lead to unexpected difficulties in a child continuing his former visiting relationship, especially if he feels their mother is now being "protected" in a new relationship. Saul, aged twelve, asked his father why he had been unable to adapt to his mother remarrying so that he had a second father, a stepfather. He said, "When mum and Julian got married, I said to you 'I have got two dads now' and you said, 'No you haven't, you've only got one' and you could have said 'Yes, but I am your *real* dad'." Fathers and stepfathers might be actively competitive, rather than co-operative. Suki said about her social father, Paul, " I might like Paul . . . I didn't want to choose him *over* dad but just wanted some time where I didn't have to choose at all. It's always one 'father' person or another. Dad pretends he doesn't care about Paul, but he really does care and he's always checking out, and I don't know which of them I should belong to. Dad says 'when I decide to forgive mum things will be better' but I don't know when that will be, and the worst thing for me is that mum and dad are not together and they don't talk."

## Sorting out "fatherhood"

The most difficult questions for Suki at that time were who was her *real* father, and was she really loved for herself. The family work with Suki and her competitive fathers involved all the intimate members of her three family network and had three related aims:

1.  To improve the negative interaction between her mother and biological father to diminish the quarrelling in her life (which was making her feel suicidal).
2.  To establish an agreed idea about "family life" that her "multi-parent group" and her "social" father could subscribe to, so that

Suki could see she had a loving family, even if it was not what she called a "proper family".

3.    To work on diminishing her anxiety about her mother's relationship with her second long-term partner, which Suki feared might undermine her own relationship with her preferred "dad" if it became a solid, long-term relationship. In all this, the goal was to help Suki keep a clearer head, not a head that was full of quarrelling adult voices.

I worked with her father, Ted, on the phone as he "didn't want to travel". I had a long conversation with his partner ("sort of step-mum"), at Suki's request, to talk about the arrangements and dynamics of Suki's visits. I met with "*quasi*-stepdad" in a joint interview with Suki's mother to review the conflicts, including his openly competitive relationship with her "bio-dad" around his "lifestyle and inadequate provision for his daughter" (his words). The main body of work was with Suki and her mother, as well as Suki alone. Her constant concern, based on astute observation, was whether the caring that she was being shown was, in fact, care through love for her, or "performances of competitive care" to show each other who was being the "better parent". Suki feared, in particular, that Paul was only "acting concerned" to make her mother like him more.

## Negotiating healing conversations: responsibility vs. happiness

Working with an alienated two- or three-household family system involves careful work with both individuals and subsystems. It might never involve bringing the wider family system together. Bringing the original parental couple and their children together on behalf of a suffering child might become possible if other parts of the family are rebalanced in their post-separation lives and there is some sort of equal emotional tone between them. Conversations between older children and their fathers about the effects of his choice of second partner on the rest of the family can be hard for a father to listen to. They are likely to bring about greater closeness between parent and child only when there is a willingness on both sides to talk from the heart and not from positions of recrimination and justification.

*Example.* A thoughtful teenage boy, Ramon, who acted as a carer to a mother who had become deeply depressed when his father left, refused to see his father and his new partner and her children for a year. Following the birth of their joint baby, his half brother, he agreed to a meeting with his father with me as "witness" to his thinking. He engaged his father in a profound conversation about the meaning of "responsibility *vs.* happiness", which left his father, normally a quick-witted thinker, perplexed but impressed. "You broke her heart, you know. It's three years on and mum still comes home in the evening and cries: it's quite shredding for us children . . . for me it's easier not to see you, not to be part of a re-created family . . . even talking on the phone feels wrong . . . for me thinking with your emotions is bad: a lot of what goes wrong in the world stems from this . . . it's better to live with less contact and fewer emotions." His father, struggling to engage at the right level, said, "It's something I have to work on, putting myself in your shoes . . . moving your point of view alongside my point of view. I can understand it, but I have to work out how to live with it." His son continued trying to work out the balance of justice, including me as clarifier of points he was struggling with, but finding the fluency of his own thoughts which had obviously been distilled over a long period: "Of course, I don't know how unhappy you were before . . . it seems as though the happiness of one person has been traded for the unhappiness of four people. I'm struggling with [contrasting ideas] 'live as happily as you can' *vs.* the question of being responsible, 'living as conscientiously as possible'."

His father, racing along to keep up with the speed of his son's thinking, answered from the heart: "I did put myself first, but I had spent months trying to make things work . . . my unhappiness and dissatisfaction would have led to breakdown." His son replied, "It may have been the right choice for you but I can't entirely come to terms with the consequences. Over the summer I have been able to separate my emotions from mum's emotions . . . I think I was feeling hers too much. I have had to detach myself from lots of emotions 'cos it's easier to live my life like that . . . others say it's not good to put emotions in a box labelled 'do not touch', but for the moment that's where I am going to keep them." Following these conversations where he had aired his moral dilemmas and had them seriously respected by his father, he began to visit his father, see the new baby, and "take a turn around the block". His father reported, "He has warmed up from not talking to being pretty mature and insightful and agreed to continue to visit but not to stay over . . . not make plans but take it step by step."

*Abusive legacies from earlier family experience:*
*fathers who are no longer present and*
*stepfathers who manage the legacies of violence*

Two brief examples follow of ways violence experienced in an earlier part of a boy's life can become distorted attachment legacies for a stepfather to manage when he enters the emotionally charged union of mother and son. Each of the boys below had a close relationship with his mother in the context of violent or inappropriately authoritarian relationships with their fathers. The resources that second partners can bring to address disturbances shown in the context of the step or social father relationship might not always be capable of encompassing and standing up to these. Social fathers, chosen for calmness or relative stability by partners to mitigate their own earlier disturbed experience, often explain that they do not believe they have the strength, authority, or problem solving skills to work with troubled adolescents.

### *Jo, Lana, and Rory: confusions of role—father, son, or rival partner?*

Jo was less than a year old when Lana left her husband, Rory, who had been in and out of prison for selling drugs. The closest relationship in his life was with his mother. Jo got into trouble in school, but Lana described them both as "muddling along" until she met a very "good", straight man, Robert, an accountant, who wanted to live with her but did not want to live with Jo, who was now fifteen. He felt he shared no social values with him and was also a little bit scared. Jo was highly rivalrous to Robert and showed openly that he believed his mother belonged to him. Jo lived in a tiny room at the top of Robert's house where he spent a lot of time being depressed, failing to go to school, and smoking dope. When Lana tried to help him, he would shout at her until she cried. He would then try to provoke Robert to hit him so he could say to Lana "Look what he's done; are you going to stay with a man like that?" A redeeming feature for Lana was Jo's apparent love for the baby she was expecting to have with Robert, but it seemed probable that Jo and Robert would not be able to compromise. Jo displayed a belief that if he got a job, he and Lana could live together without Robert and look after the baby—"I'd like to be on my own at home with mum." Jo could not see that it might not be in his own best interests if such a dream were fulfilled. As his mother pointed out, "I want you to be a brother to this baby, not his father." His rivalry with his "stepdad" was accentuated by the intimacy that the coming baby produced in the relationship between Robert and his mother. Jo felt doubly excluded from this intimacy, both as a rejected partner and as the less preferred child. "I don't want Robert's child to be better treated than how he's been treating me; it's no good saying I'm not old enough to think like its dad, I'm the same age now that mum was when she had me. Robert 'made it', like [the baby], but, I mean, any idiot can do that." Robert did choose not to manage the challenges posed by Jo, and Lana had to face a choice between her coming baby being able to live with his father and continuing to offer a home to her older child.

### Longer-term effects of civil war: Julian, Roberta, and Marek

In the second family, longer-term shadows of former civil war ampli-fied the fears of violence experienced by a stepfather, Julian, on behalf of his stepson, Marek. Marek was self-harming and often threatened to kill himself. In Marek's country of origin, his biological father had beaten him and his mother, Roberta, until, in the confusion of the war, she escaped to England, her home country. Julian was a stepfather who wanted to offer his new family peace and financial security, but the family Roberta had recruited him into was beyond his normal emotional threshold in every dimension. Roberta had strong views about women's independence and not being a financial burden, and worked extremely hard, often until her teenage son's bedtime every night, leaving Julian with a stepson who did not wish to do his home-work, was depressed about his lack of achievement, and obviously needed his mother. The degree to which Roberta, in the context of her first marriage, had become alienated from the possibility that a father or husband could be a resource for her as well as for her son, but that he needed her support, was the beginning of a new conversation.

### Coming out as gay: father and stepfather dilemmas

It is only in the second half of my lifetime that gay men have openly had their children living with them. Golombok and Tasker, in review-ing the research on gay fatherhood in the first decade of the twenty-first century, conclude that it is still the case that most gay fathers who no longer live with the mothers of their children do not have their children living with them (Golombok & Tasker, 2010). As the number of children raised in gay father families has increased—through adoption, co-parenting with lesbian couples, and surrogacy arrangements—so patterns of living in gay families have diversified, as have the notions of "fatherhood" within them. However, gay fathers who come for consultation to think about their children might still hold rigid ideas about performances of fatherhood, just as heterosexual fathers do, sometimes bewildering their more flexible new partners with their ideas about discipline and nurture in what it takes to bring up a "man".

In the minds of many people in different societies and different religious groups, gay relationships continue to be seen as a threat to "normative", heterosexually constructed family life. "Some people are gay: get over it": an NHS equal opportunities poster displayed in many NHS facilities carries a positive injunction that cannot always be applied to the former wives of fathers who come out as gay. For a deeper understanding of this, we have to look to the domains of both loss and conflict of interests, as we would with any couple divorcing where one of them has already found a second partner, as well as considering the aspects of "seeing dad as gay" that children go through. The largest group of gay fathers researched in the UK are those who had children in the context of former heterosexual relationships. The decision to "come out" remains stressful and, at the start of the new millennium, was associated with increased risk to mental health. Whereas most fathers move out of the marital home, some continue their fathering relationship in-house, with the mothers of their children acting as a front to the sexual preference of the fathers. Some gay fathers formerly in heterosexual marriages still fear that disclosure might cause rejection from their child, or that their child might suffer by association with their father's new open identity.

### Freedoms and constraints in post- divorce parenting

How flexible a society is about incorporating different models of sexual relationships and new structures for family life still varies greatly. Despite this, the passing of laws on civil partnership, and now marriage, and the much wider discussion of family created by these changes in law, will, over time and between generations, change the way that couples can consider their own freedoms. All professionals need to be aware that life in gay families offers the same possibilities for healthy child development: models of intimacy that attend to the attachment needs of adults for mature peer-based relationship, models that attend to the attachment needs of children, the ability to offer secure loving bonds and responsive relationships to children, and adult minds that consider a developing infant. The reflections developed in these new contexts will further dissolve prejudice in future generations as children themselves challenge former ideas about "proper family" and the role of father.

The decision to come out by a father who has been in a heterosexual marriage none the less still remains more fraught for the family members concerned than a father who leaves for a heterosexual relationship. The downgrading of gay relationships in the minds of society in earlier generations has inevitably contributed to the internal downgrading of self within a father who has been concealing a gay identity in a heterosexual marriage. It has contributed to precarious self-esteem and terror about what might happen if a father reveals his true sexual identity. At the time of deciding to come out, this is often positioned against a tremendous rush to show the new identity as well as to integrate into the gay world. The tension between what is received wisdom about sexual relationships and the higher organising rules within a society will also affect the inner space of all adults concerned. Coming out acts as a perturbation to a particular society's sense of cohesiveness: the image of "normal" itself becomes elaborated, as is happening in the UK in this decade.

*For a former wife, how might the experience of being left for a man be qualitatively different to being left for a woman?*

In addition to the shock of parental separation, mothers who have been passed over for a man have described the rejection in complex ways affecting her view of her own sexuality. In changing the frame of the relationship to accommodate a new social partner to her children's father who is gay, there are also issues of "telling and timing" deriving from her own readiness. How soon does the husband, now he is "out", expect everyone, wife and new partner, to be friends? How quickly does he want his children to meet him in the context of a new partnership or lifestyle? Fathers can be very keen for children to meet a new partner or reconcile to a new lifestyle and might be torn about whether to place their new love or their child as the higher emotional priority. Hinting at meanings the child cannot comprehend can create new anxieties unless an explanation is on hand that the child is ready to hear; for example, exposure to new groups of gay friends too soon without a clear introduction or letting a child know about desires: "Bob and I sleep together". In turn, a child's readiness to hear will be affected by the degree of upset a mother is feeling and showing. Whereas some of these anxieties equally take place when a father leaves for a younger woman, the additional change is about the unknown quality of the other lifestyle a father is moving into.

*How does a mother's positioning, with regard to the new relationship, affect the child's readiness to accept it?*

A mother's web of upset and concern can include some of the following: a double rejection experienced by her body being set aside for that of a man; rage at being used for the production of children before being set aside for "true love"; concern about the health risks a man has been bringing into the family through "cruising" prior to choice of a committed relationship, "Why is his desire more important than the health of his family?", and the mourning for the loss of the marriage compounded with the question of whether its love was ever "real". Fears for the children include questions about whether they will be bullied at school due to prejudice, fears about a teenage son's identity, and a concern that there might be risks through a son's future involvement in a homosexual world, including that the son could himself become solicited into relationships with men: "It is important that they know their father, but do they have to know his friends?"

Some of the above preoccupations also relate to the degree to which a man has brought his alternative sexual identity into the marital home and his wife's mind: "Soft porn: images that really upset me infiltrating the safety of my home . . . a website where, at the click of a mouse you could enlarge the penis of your imaginary lover 'do you want a bigger one . . . just click here'." Seeing this "turned me against him and his sexual practices . . . I want to remain friends but feel I am being tricked into something I do not agree with . . . I do not want the boys staying with them." The fear of father's new partner as a sexual being can be in conflict with the social experience of getting to know another adult parent figure. Alongside coming to terms with her repositioning in the life of her husband, a woman might experience herself angrily as being repositioned as "mother to the relationship" ("best friend to the boys"). It is not uncommon to be told about the husband's love of his new partner: "He tells me about his dependence on Juan and his need for him . . . 'I yearn for the sound of his voice on my voice mail' . . . I don't need to know that." It is important to remember that many of these feelings are also experienced by women whose husbands leave for another woman. However, some of the more subtle differences that may interfere with the father's subsequent relationship with his children can be heard in the nuances of the difficulty a mother is struggling with, which is associated with the degree of difference she can process while also dealing with her own loss.

Children, in my experience, also go through different stages of acceptance. Often, there is an avoidance of telling anyone followed by a selection of key "safe" others to tell. There might be a request to the father not to perform "gay" around the school and often not to come to school with his new partner. There might be a temporary loss of trust in the parent's love, "he is not what he seemed to be", a rewriting of the family past, and increased attempts to control parents' behaviour in different contexts. Some of these are similar to any child hearing of his or her parents' divorce, but the added uncertainty is around the quality of relationship with his or her father and the new partner. Questions to a father from a child include: how do you know you are gay? When did you decide? Can't you try harder? Does that mean you don't love mummy any more? Does that mean you won't love me any more? [from a girl] Will you love Dean more because he is a boy? Does that mean I will be gay? [from a boy].

## Monitoring with the sense, not the brain alone

In trying to specify the quality of difference a child experiences, I have drawn again upon on the idea of inner working models carried from childhood in which a parent and their interactions with others have been represented at varying levels of specificity in the mind. An attachment–behavioural system is initially maintained through an infant's continuous monitoring of the proximity of the attachment figure. In contexts of unpredictability and insecurity, this monitoring can redevelop or intensify. Behaviour in their parents that children have accepted/adapted to when very young might no longer be considered acceptable by them as their critical faculties develop. Following a father's news of change of identity, in addition to the loss of role as formerly constructed, a child's perceptions are heightened and they might dislike subtle changes that they experience—a father's hair, the way he carries his hands, his smell, the way he walks, and his "new" voice being some changes that pre-adolescent children have mentioned.

If we understand that the transformation of the inner representation of "father" suffers a fracture, and confuses the child's representation both of family and of gender role at the point of coming out, acceptance by them in turn requires time, patience, and commitment by a father as well as understanding from his new partner. Things that fathers do without thinking, like hugging their partner (now in potential role as step-parent) can accidentally create new fears in a young child who has not yet processed the idea that their father now "belongs to Bob" and not to mum.

## Normal post-divorce processes

Following separation, unpredictability and unacceptable behaviour are often cited by children as reasons for not wanting to pursue contact with a parent. Where a dad has come out, the absent father, when he is present (on visits or shared events), might be experienced as too different from the "wished-for" parent in a child's mind to be tolerated at a time when a mother is still suffering from this experience herself. A mother can be unwilling to help her child process her own new experiences. As in all contact dilemmas, the child acts as a loop in the process connecting parents' post-divorce adjustment to one another, when they are likely to be at different stages of developing new lives. Bringing back observations, comments, or complaints can retrigger high emotional arousal and the desire to protect the child from feelings similar to those the mother herself is experiencing. However, all the principles of a "good divorce"— telling the children together once an acceptable formula has been worked out, joint planning about the care arrangements for the children, management of the future, minimising children's disruption and pain, co-parenting, his house, her house, and "we can still be a family"—seem to have worked in couples I have seen where goodwill has prevailed over pain and anger. I have found imagining scenarios to be helpful: what hazards might trigger you away from goodwill and co-operative parenting?

### The new couple want their own child

Issues might later present to a family therapist around the differential longing in a couple to have a child of their own. One partner, possibly the man who does not have a child from a former relationship, might want it more than their partner. The "magic" of assisted fertilisation and surrogacy in childbearing has created the possibility of children for all family arrangements, which was previously unimagined. However, the tensions of different couples, and threesomes or foursomes, in relation to negotiating shared parenting issues around children, require therapists to attune their ears to the particular differences that each new construction of family involves. A further issue raised in the context of therapy has concerned the question of openness about insemination: the possibility of discussion with all the children currently involved, and how a model of family that fits children's understanding will be developed in the family. (With older children, this is usually redundant as they will be ahead of the couple.) While it adds further complexity to the life of a half-brother or half-sister, if they are participants in the new baby's construction, to my mind it can only lead to more open thinking in the future.

### "A stepfather can make you feel safe: but Brett, not Zak"

Mel's parents, Flora and Abe, had co-habited for the first two years of her life before Abe came out and went to live with Zak. Mel said she always felt closer to her mum than her dad but had continued to visit him most weeks during her childhood. In recounting her earlier childhood, she found herself crying unexpectedly and her own tears surprised her. She said, "I don't like having a divided life, you miss things out. His house is really different. It's confusing, and strange." She made the point that she regarded Abe and Zak more as friends than as family, distinguishing the kind of warm emotional feelings she felt for her mother, the dog, and her mother's new husband, Brett, whom she had now known for two years, from the feelings that she felt for Abe, whom she had known since she was born, and Zak. After her mum married Brett, she stayed at home much more. Mel said, "When they got married it was really settling ... it was absolutely wonderful to feel settled", and that made her think she did not want to have to be in the other household.

Mel also did not think her father appreciated her own developing outlook as a girl of twelve years old: "He loved me as the six-year-old that I wasn't any more." She became very tearful describing the experience that she named as her dad trying to interfere too much with her new life with Brett. She said, "It felt as if I might have to actually choose my Mum against my Dad." Sometimes I would have to say to him, "I'm not living with you, so just leave me alone." She thought that she had also become more attached to Brett and described him as extremely kind and thoughtful. She said, "Just because I'm living with him I got closer and closer", and "Mum is the one who brought me up, who taught me how to behave. I could always talk to Mum and she'd always make it all right." She explained, "It was really hard to take the decision about not being divided, not going to Abe and Zak, but it was easier than going backwards and forwards." She said several times that this was a very happy time in her life, saying, "Brett's happy, Mum's happy, and I'm happy."

Mel made Abe a list of how future arrangements might be better managed: "I don't want to stay the night with him ... at least not for now ... I'd like to go on my own and not take a friend ... I want to keep friends separate from this ... I'd like to do some sort of planned activity, so that we went out for the day and did something together ... I think maybe twice or three times a year." She also told me that although Abe was her biological father, "He has never really acted as a dad". She added, "I really want to settle down and have local roots and friends, and not have so many different parts to hold in my mind."

It seemed clear that the advent of Brett into Flora's life, and the settling down through marriage, had created a sense of security greater than Mel had previously experienced. Brett, recognising Abe's upset, met up with him and talked it through so it was clear that, although "put second" for the time being, he was not excluded from the mind of the family in the other household as Mel's father. Abe said, "I will try to understand and deal with her as a teenage girl."

Recalibrating his daughter's difference in terms of her teenage development allowed him not to feel ostracised on the basis of being gay, but more on the basis of not being her mum's partner.

# CHAPTER EIGHT

# Violence in couple and family systems: anxious attachment and disorganised love, power, and control

Violence in intimate relationships operates in predominantly unthinking and reactive ways. It is, therefore, hard to conceptualise and work alongside. Multiple lenses need to be maintained, both for ourselves and on behalf of a family in any piece of work. In addition to former childhood factors and resulting internalised patterns of violent feeling deriving from these, this chapter considers violence within wider social and institutional systems of which a father might have been, or continues to be, a part.

Violence can become an unthinking response that clicks in automatically in a father, as a way of taking and maintaining power. When a man has "reached the end of his tether", an expression of helplessness men have sometimes used when describing themselves trapped in a situation seen to them to have no solution at that moment, violent feelings can move out of the control of barely regulated responses. In many families, the upbringing of boys, with its emphasis on suppressing, rather than expressing, emotions, might provide no mediating outlet for the management of arousal through words and understanding. The absence of these mediating processes leads more swiftly to physical expression (see Fonagy, p. 170, below) and possible violent actions. If violent action succeeds in its goal, it could then become a habit through the reinforcement of its use by reward, desired results including subordination of others as well as a thrill or rush of power. It might be used repeatedly as a solution: "They go on and on at you and you say 'OK, it's enough' and they go on and on and they follow you about . . . you walk out of the room and they follow and say do this and do this and you just lose your rag and push them . . . that is domestic violence."

The origins of violence in any father can be tracked back to different sources, often developing initially as a series of emotional responses in infancy and childhood to unthinking states of mind in his own parents, as well as to wider disorder in his family environment as a child (Bowlby, 1984). Extreme stress experienced at a very young age and which remains unprocessed is likely to limit a man's range of emotional options. Rage becomes a dissociated part of himself—split off, and liable to recur in similar contexts where high emotions are generated. There is also a social learning dimension for preverbal children witnessing violent behaviour, as preverbal infants often mirror adult behaviour and later try it out in peer situations (Sroufe, 2005; Sroufe & Fleeson, 1995). Violence offers a confusing role model of authority for children, in which a person who commits violent acts can also be perceived to be the person in charge, demonstrating to a child that force can be used to get your way between people in intimate and dependent relationships. Many men present with forms of behaviour which can include failure to connect to others' feelings, and a lack of awareness about themselves, but what moves an individual from extreme emotional distress towards violence remains open to scrutiny in each family. As one aspect of a boy's attempts to find solutions to his insecure wishes for love and connection, the same boy, later in life as man, might find a range of ways of managing anxiety through intimidating and subjugating other people in intimate relationship with him to keep them close. The term domestic violence is defined by CAFCASS as

> including any incident or pattern of incidents of controlling, coercive or threatening behaviour, violence or abuse between those aged 16 and over who are, or have been, intimate partners or family members regardless of gender or sexuality. This can encompass but is not limited to psychological, physical, sexual, financial or emotional abuse. (CAP, 2014, Practice Direction 12J, 2014, para 3)

Controlling behaviour is, therefore, defined as a pattern of acts designed to make another person subordinate and/or dependent, by isolating them from sources of support, exploiting their resources and capacities for personal gain, depriving them of the means needed for independence, resistance, and escape, and regulating their everyday behaviour.

## Violence in socio-political contexts

Violence arises in multiple different contexts in the socio-political world, in which violent actions and thoughts are carried out and replayed at different levels. Some of the effects of civil wars on family life might include ideological beliefs imposed through physical violence. People who have witnessed, as well as been forced to experience, violence will have longer-term legacies to manage inside themselves. The rage and upset equally held by women and men in response to the stress of war can loop back into family life and escalate division between people in intimate relationship. It is an aspect of family violence to which we might also have to attend in our work with some fathers and families. Although domestic violence is banned in law, it continues in secret. In social situations where men are still accorded traditional authorities, the intersections of gendered beliefs about dominance and submission can reignite patriarchal rights and behaviours within a family, within a larger context of social and civil helplessness.

In working with families longer term, a three-generational model for looking at violence in the family now and how it connects to earlier gendered expectations around power, helplessness, and anger can link current violence directly to wider contexts of violence. Earlier stories of family violence challenge the façade of "civilised family now". For example, Georgiou, who could not control the onsets of rage that affected his heart and his sons, returned in his mind to the Greek civil war of the 1940s and 1950s when invited to make associations to his anger. The civil war had affected his family in multiple ways, involving the destruction of his family village and stories of his grandmother walking through the snow "with bleeding feet" to flee from one village to another. Her son, Georgiou's father, beat him, Georgiou, ritually throughout his growing up. The message was, "do not become too 'soft' in case you ever have to deal with such events in the future". Such discoveries of the line of violence do not take away its pain, but allow a different framework of thought to develop between family members from which new premises for managing strong emotion in the present can be devised.

### Punitive parenting and ongoing acrimonious interactions between couples in adult life: effects on children

In the 1970s and 1980s, studies of violent men showed that there is an intergenerational effect on their children. In a powerful study of multi-level family processes in the 1980s, which continued over forty years, Patterson and his colleagues analysed levels of stress and violence affecting individuals that make up a violent family system, a multi-level family process model which included, for fathers, economic hardship, irritable discipline, and anti-social behaviour, and for mothers, in addition, social isolation (Patterson, 1982; Patterson & Dishion, 1988). They found that when both mothers and fathers had experienced punitive parenting and/or ongoing acrimonious interactions as a child, the likelihood of this model being passed on to their own children was over eighty per cent. Where only one parent had this experience as a child, it dropped to below sixty per cent. What also made a difference was the way in which the punishment was remembered: the more punishing, distant and negative the home environment recalled . . . the more likely the children were to be anti-social. In a separate one-year prospective study, men who had been exposed to interparental physical assaults were found to be three and a half times more likely to hit their own wives (Straus et al., 1980) and many other studies testify to the increase of violence among fathers exposed to violence as children.

Cummings and co-authors (Cummings & Davies, 2002; Cummings et al., 2010) have demonstrated that exposure to persistent heightened negative emotion in the family weakens children's resilience, compromises their emotional development, and connects to increased conduct disorders. It weakens children's relationships with fathers more than with mothers (Harold et al., 2013). Nearly thirty years ago, Emde (1988), thinking about the relevance of research to clinical intervention, addressed the ways in which experience that is lived directly, as well as witnessed in the behaviour of others, might become transformed into represented relationships in children's minds, inner working models of how relationships are, which, in turn, influence their relationships with other social systems with which the family interacts; we do not know at which points children's ways of viewing the world become relatively inflexible and self-perpetuating. The question of how and when a learning system becomes closed continues a quarter of a century on: a review of attachment among adolescents asks

> at which point does attachment shift from a primarily behavioural and relational construct where children may display different attachment with different caregivers . . . to one that is more cognitive in nature and more like a generalised style or "state of mind". (Fearon et al., 2014b, p. 1044)

Equally, we need to consider the effect of violence on children's own emotional range and potential depressive disorders (Moutsiana, et al., 2011; Wilkinson & Goodyer, 2011).

## There is no one model of the outcome of family violence and the narrative is rarely closed altogether

As part of reviewing her own clinical work in a community mental health team in the UK, Priest (2013) considered research focusing on the long-term effects of violence in childhood on fathers' own behaviours. She noted that factors mediating abuse as a child and becoming abusive as an adult include many variables: individual, family, and environmental characteristics such as depression, intelligence, socioeconomic status, social support, and stress. Powerful sequelae of childhood abuse include anxiety, depression, irritability, avoidance and dissociation, substance abuse, and mental health problems, but not necessarily violence. In one longer-term follow-up study, it was found that men's relationships with their partners and children was widely varied. This replicated Priest's clinical experience, as it has done in my own. Hawkins and Haskett (2014) found that children who are violently abused exhibit clinically relevant individual differences in their internal working models, demonstrated in their adjustment in the school setting, some children internalising stress and others externalising stress, or "acting it out".

*Dominant behaviour, a man's definition of himself, and the development of a toddler observing the interactions*

The more dominance develops as central to a man's definition of himself, the more he might inadvertently use violence as unthinking communication in all his intimate interactions. For a father who is, in his mind, the boss, the more vulnerable family members can be internally framed as "subordinates" who constitute his internal identity and who, in everyday life, are positioned to "assist" his fantasies about his patriarchal role and the associated rights. The range of freedoms around such ideas within a family can become more tightly controlled, so that, over time, the threat of violence becomes as powerful as the overt behaviour. Cross-culturally, family violence includes rituals designed to constrain, to inhibit, and to keep women and children within boundaries. In the UK alone, we know of multiple ways of punishing children "for the child's own good", some of which are further discussed below. Fifteen per cent of women and less than ten per cent of men report being subjected to domestic violence, and some examples of mother to father violence follow later in the chapter. However, of those who are most severely attacked (four or more incidents of domestic violence) women are the most victimised.

*A further attempt at developing an understanding on the deep-rooted nature of violence taking place in a family*

How does violence come about? Bowlby recognised that anger is the natural response of a child whose access to the attachment figure is jeopardised. Fonagy has taken this recognition of "anger in relation to threat" forward in valuable ways. Fonagy's speculation included a consideration of the powerful ways that anger is programmed by the person on the receiving end in order to maintain his or her own sense of themselves. Anger in an infant thus threatened serves to maintain his own sense of who he is: *"How dare you do this to me!"*. A threatened toddler who is simultaneously angry is developing a self-protective response in which anger and aggression towards the person who is the threat are internally twinned (Fonagy et al., 1993). While an infant's anger is normally responded to with a soothing or loving response by a parent, this is less probable in families who are not thinking about emotions and their effects, and a response is more likely to be reactive and angry. A child's oppositional response to threat then becomes integrated with his developing self-structure. Assertion becomes permanently twinned with aggression. Fonagy brilliantly relates violence to the absence of thought on the part of carers, an absence which subsequently leads violent perpetrators to act on bodies rather than minds, as they have little or no experience of a mind thinking about them. As a consequence, they, in turn, might not develop a mind that thinks about themselves in relation to another, but only responds in relation to protecting themselves. They are more likely to act rather than think or hold on to a violent impulse.

### Thinking about work with fathers who are violent to partners: keeping children in mind

As Child (2016) has put it, domestic violence, as a poison to be continually addressed by those who work with families, divides men and women into gendered opponents. Gender-rights thinking and policy moves to protect each side, rather than each side struggling to think about the other. The result is that women's rights groups and men's rights groups become opposed to the original feminist aims of equality between genders. Although gendered debates and the realities of what is possible for women have moved on since Goldner and colleagues (1990) suggested that the vision of all relationships between men and women were inseparable from larger contexts of power and violence, violence in many cases has moved contexts rather than disappeared. With fathers working from home on the increase, and senior jobs for women also becoming more normal, different specificities for understanding violence beyond the debates of twenty-five years ago are essential. What exactly is going on in any family where a man still resorts to violence in spite of wider gendered changes of opportunity and attitude, and how, in each instance, can we assist him to become different?

Goldner and colleagues' (1990) classic paper on love, intimacy, and violence included in their work with couples the following notions: violence as a choice of action not a "helpless" response (which might only be a reality in a percentage of cases), violence to be viewed within a wider perspective of social control of women, and, central to clinical intervention, the importance of deconstructing the "interior of the violent episode". Their thinking also held the balance between violence and the warm, and often passionate, attachment each partner in the couples they described felt for the other. In working with violence in families of changing cultures throughout my working life, I have always focused on violence towards *children* as well as the *effects on children of witnessing violence between adults*. In these larger systemic family frames for addressing violence, passionate attachment between couples is often absent. In my own thinking, I have focused on the effects of negative interactions between parents—that is, anxious, insecure, and sometimes disorganised attachments—as well as the longer-term effects of anger, irritability, and general violent behaviour on children and their development. This clinical approach intersected with two long-term streams of research, referred to throughout the book, that were emerging in parallel during each decade—Jenkins and colleagues (2005, 2008), and Cummings and colleagues (1993, 2010)—each showing the negative effects of anger, discord, and violent interactions between adults on children. Enlarging the systemic frame to include patterns between couples and children derived from the childhood of one or both parents opens up multiple perspectives on violent behaviour beyond the couple alone and different specificities emerge.

### Separating the violence from the person: systemic lenses

In considering violence through systemic lenses, practitioners have continued to adopt a number of different frames, which range through psychodynamic understanding, attachment theory, and communication theory. Working with coercive power and the abuse of women and children highlights the tensions between attempting to hold a non-blaming position at the level of family, while retaining anger at the recognition of how such imbalances continue to become built in and reinforced at wider and more powerfully institutionalised levels of society. I have found Karl Tomm's analysis of Michael White's approach a useful mantra when working with men who have used, or continue to use, violence to "carefully direct the protest against problematic beliefs and practices, rather than against the persons who hold these beliefs and enact these practices" (Tomm, 1993, p. 63). Burck and Daniel's elegant separation of the wider systemic implications of violence, cited here, is also useful in retaining a more neutral concep-tual focus than I have often been able to achieve when in the emotional heat of the job,

> we try to hold a position that allows us to take sides against violence, but at the same time, use an understanding of the constraining and brutalising nature of a violent interaction to help men own responsi-bility for their violence, and to expect them to stop. (Burck & Daniel, 1995)

An understanding of a man's own history enables me to take an empathic stance in painful and violent circumstances (see Brian, Chapter Ten) and leads me to de-construct with him, in as much detail as he can manage, the processes by which he believes he arrived at recourse to violence. In a useful article that enhances former feminist perspectives on intimate partner violence, George and Stith (2014) update and enlarge an earlier definition of men's violence towards women as "caused by patriarchy" to include the co-occurrence of psychiatric disorder, substance and alcohol use, and attachment issues. I have found each of these important to recognise and consider as part of my own work with fathers and the adaptation of my own input in situations of emotional and physical violence and children's exposure to this.

As already discussed in Chapter Two, aggression and violence in current family life are often aspects of a survivor of violence's own experience in childhood. A father can be emotionally bound by inner patterns of traumatised experience which have become encapsulated and can be re-aroused in the ongoing dramas and extremities of his own adult life, as well as by any threat of family separation, with its attendant burden of loss and disorientation. Earlier personal vulnera-bilities might have become emotionally locked in subsequently, making them hard to access or relate to in a therapeutic way. We know from multiple different research paths that ongoing parental conflict can violate children's core development and their lifelong self- esteem (Cummings & Davies, 2002; Jenkins & Curwen, 2008; McIntosh, 2001). Some fathers and mothers know this themselves but, none the less, involve the children, both as provocation and self-protection: "It didn't begin to happen in front of the children ... I think by drag-ging them out of the bedroom and screaming and raging in front of them . . . what she was trying to do was put me in situations where I would jump" (Roy, personal communication, 2015). Many of the limitations of capacity a child develops through constant exposure to domestic violence can show in adulthood, and the difficulty in working with these is that they could be linked with damaged early neural patterning, which changes the capacity of an individual who has suffered in such ways to think "outside the box" emotionally.

### Small but useful approaches to regulating violent emotions in the family in short term work: emotional and behavioural sticking plasters

Cognitive work that identifies, describes, and names a range of feelings and responses in parents contributes to more conscious management of unregulated emotions. It can lead to damage limitation, but not necessarily provide long-term repair. Giving words and categories to feeling states allows thinking about them to develop, and rehearsing better options for managing them is a valuable first step in regulating them. With hope, time and space to change the vocabulary of emotional expression, verbalised and better processed feeling in the family will have significant value for the children (Lieberman et al., 2005, 2011). Ways of effectively changing violent patterns that endure remain one of the most challenging concerns for a family or a professional to face. The reality of time accorded within current child and adolescent mental health service, or social service schedules, as well as the structures of court work (see Chapter Eleven), is likely to mean that the most we might be able to achieve in a family troubled by violence is small changes in the over-tight patterning of the daily systems in which violence has become embedded and which trigger its recurrence.

Some sticking plasters follow: first, the identification and conscious naming of new structures for dealing with and managing violent sequences when they occur creates the idea both of a safety net and taking charge of something frightening. Second, helping individual family members find ways of moving to another position by either (a) physically removing themselves, or (b) mentally taking up a rehearsed response likely to be protective at times of highly unregulated emotion. Third, spotting and naming sequences connected with rising tension, enabling these to be marked, and the situation defused, before things get out of control. Partners and children who have been subjected to violence are likely to be highly sensitive to facial expressions and minute physical expressions of rising aggression. As victims of patterning through intimidation, they can often read what is coming in potentially violent situations. However, they are likely to need permission from someone with a fresh viewpoint outside the family to change what they do about it. For a violent father, even small deviations from what he has come to expect of others' responses can be seen as major threats to his self-image. Therefore, working on small changes to his own expectations and the responses of others can enlarge the circle of less tension-laden circuits of family interaction. Working on this, each person in the session is required to note and take responsibility for patterns of their own behaviour that amplify rising tension. Parents are asked to do all they can to avoid these on behalf of any younger children.

Over the years, approaches to taking self-regulating interventions home have changed in my work. Twenty years ago, a family with teenagers would accept interventions that required them to shout key words of their choosing as tokens of back-down from conflict, accepting the value of a physical interruption with each other. Many families and teenagers now would accept mindfulness techniques aimed at "stop and reflect". In mindfulness strategies, each member of the parental couple are invited to stop their habitual pattern of escalating tension and focus on their bodily feelings in that moment (moving from reactivity to reflection. Older teenagers can also value doing this. Such techniques are unlikely to work with repetitive unmentalized angry behaviour, however, as they will not be sufficiently intensive. Fourth, developing a meta-perspective, or a cognitive restructuring schema, for thinking about what is going on within the family allows further discussion in their home milieu. The family members work this out themselves, and any member of the family can initiate the conversation: "Why are we lot [the Greens] as [angry, loud, emotional, or a chosen family word] as we are and what can we do to make it better [in which contexts in the family, at home] now . . .". Mothers and fathers can each contribute to a joined-up schematic understanding on behalf of protecting their children, since fathers often identify children as the precipitators of their own anger and wish to stop being triggered into angry states: "I see his behaviour as a problem to be eradicated and he [the little boy, aged five] just gets blown apart with it", can move to "My son is an angry little boy a lot of the time", and can become connected to, "I was, and still am, angry a lot of the time myself". Also valuable is the identification of positive, often protective, pathways that men have attempted to build up for their children, based on their own experiences of earlier resistance and survival. "I would say to him 'get lost now while I calm down and we'll kick a ball around later." To achieve schema for taking a hold on violence with parents that is conscious and maintained is to achieve much, since more optimistic frameworks for addressing the context of a father's behaviour towards children can subsequently be built on, whether a couple stay together or separate.

Parents describing to their older children the effects of their own childhood experiences of rowing and violence, and reflecting on them out loud with them (usually following individual and couple sessions to become comfortable discussing this and giving words to painful emotions), can also be highly effective in changing the family mood at home. This can be particularly useful if a parent allows a child or children to make their own comments about what they have heard, and what it has made them think and feel themselves, a kind of reflecting team of children

All these possible approaches to change are dependent on the degree of damage carried by a father himself, as well as the extent to which a partner is willing to remain in the family context to work at modified ways of being together. Even if ongoing regular sessions are not possible, follow-up appointments are, as these maintain the idea of the third person—the professional—as a concerned person in the mind of the parents and older children.

A core experience for men and women who resort to violence, as discussed above, is the experience of not having been thought about protectively in their childhoods, and, consequently, finding it hard to develop protective thinking of their own either about themselves or about others (Bowlby, 1984; Prior & Glaser, 2006). To discover, with the assistance of a third person, that they have cognitive resources that they can hold on to can be a protection of both self and of others. As one father said of family work addressing family violence, "By us knowing you are having us in your mind, it helped us to manage things better." In my own experience, to continue to be available to review with a family how their own management is going might be the most valuable asset, even if the review is only every few months. As the Early Steps multi-site intervention programme in the USA put it, one purpose of their annual review visit to families participating in their study is to show ongoing concern: "such thinking has value, because families see it as someone watching psychologically over them and this in itself makes a difference" (Shaw, 2013).

### Fathers and therapeutic work on anger in everyday life: action replay on failures of mentalization

I have had the unusual and privileged experience of working long-term with fathers who have decided to work on themselves and their current intimate relationships where their own tempers have taken them by surprise. In these scenarios, they want to learn how not to "lose it", and I have consistently used one valuable clinical idea with them in a number of different ways. This shared idea is the exploration of the gap between the specific and idiosyncratic ways in which they themselves were brought up as children, the ways they were disciplined or punished, and the different experience they are now attempting to offer their own children. The apparent lack of recognition from their children of the good things they are being offered can elicit unexpected anger in a father, usually in the context of particular action replay sequences. When a father's attempts to give his children a better life do not seem to be recognised or appreciated, this can usefully be linked to anger that was formerly not dealt with in isomorphic (sequences that are similar in pattern and form) earlier contexts. The specificities of these anger provoking sequences need to be identified in a father's contemporary family life now, and brought out into the open for conscious exploration. This is likely to require one or more sessions with a father on his own to allow him to explore freely his own emotionality in the situation. Internal representations of himself as a child in subordinated positions in relation to others in his childhood, can, over time, have constructed unworkable emotional premises for managing parallel situations in adulthood.

For many fathers, earlier compliant ways of organising internal experience and conforming to the requirements of their parents are often likely to have supressed hard to handle emotions. The same emotional experiences can happen in both care and school experience if a boy has been sent away from home at too early an age, around seven or eight years old. These areas of emotion are usually around competition for love or scarce emotional resources, and sometimes around authority. The challenging of father's authority by children can become a challenge in the ongoing course of family life. In suppressing important emotional aspects of his own experience in childhood, alongside suppressing rage at injustice done to him and others, such as siblings, or peers at school, a boy might have taken on an alien reality and inauthentic mode of being and relating in certain contexts. This false self can be challenged by the behaviour of his own children. At the intersection of key moments of present with past experience, a father might re-experience earlier unprocessed anger that amplifies current anger; a failure of mentalization in the father's childhood breaks through as unexplained or disproportionate anger, and sometimes as violence, in the current situation. For example, a father's longing for games of "rough and tumble" in his own childhood might mean he makes sure to offer them to his own son now. However, his son might reject these (in one instance, by stopping in the middle and withdrawing because he sensed too great an urgency on the part of his father). The father, driven by an unfulfilled need of his own, "loses it" through disappointment at not having his efforts at "play" enjoyed, instead of recalibrating his own behaviour.

As therapists, we might individually have relatively little experience in how to stop patterns of recurrent violence. It is both complex and, sometimes, frightening when the degree of violence expressed in a family meeting is apparently disconnected from the current relational context. It can be so disproportionate to the current precipitating event that family members and we ourselves have no understanding of where it came from. Over the years, however, some therapeutic bits of process I have relied on have worked better with some fathers than others in making relevant connections in the room and, subsequently, for father and the family in the longer term. These combine, first, a spoken recognition from me that there are leftovers from former life events troubling a father now, with my own professional acknowledgement that the original trauma or upsets might not be available to us to do more than acknowledge, name, and mourn on behalf of the child who experienced these. Second, when relevant, letting a father know that for us to re-arouse trauma on the premise that re-experiencing it will free him from it is not necessarily functional for the work of maintaining a calmer presence in family life now, but that I can offer him a space to explore it further if he would like to. Third, focusing on work in the current family context that takes account of earlier experience but emphasises change in the here and now, building conscious and deliberate processes of control that can be aimed at in family life.

## Institutionally sanctioned violence: bearing witness—boys becoming men

The main thrust of our work within the NHS is more likely to be with men from more socially disadvantaged backgrounds than professional men. Working in independent practice, as well as within the context of the family court, has, however, allowed me to work alongside violent behaviours in family life throughout the social strata of the UK today This includes colleagues within psychotherapy, doctors, psychiatrists, and men in the longest established professional traditions, such as the law and the church. Men from booming economies overseas may equally raise issues of wider institutionalised violence in different societies today (not in the UK alone). Many distressed fathers describe systematised experiences of violence in schools, which they describe as having scarred them. Contemporary boys from all cultures in the grip of industrialisation (such as India, the USA, Russia, and China) have been pushed into educational aspirations which are seen by their own parents as a pathway to safety in the contemporary world. They have also suffered the unsafe realities of educational institutions. Stories of success might, one hopes, outweigh stories of failure as a result of contemporary public school educations, but fathers who seek therapy in adult life usually bring a sense of low self-esteem, often resulting in long-term depression, amplified within establishments where they were bullied and abused and where, in addition, some of them suffered racial stigmatisation and insults. One father described how, facing the line of boys waiting to be beaten at his Catholic educational institution, was a "tender picture of the Virgin Mary cradling baby Jesus in her arms, torture I think it was." In many educational establishments and religious institutions, performances of violence were ritualised in the service of "character formation" as recently as the 1990s and were accepted aspects of what education has to address if a boy is to become a man. "Whenever you hear about a new flogging it reminds you of the last one you had and you wonder when the next ritual will be called for you" (Montagu, 2014, p. 179; see also Duffell, 2000). These experiences of repeated imposed violence are still active, therefore, among men who are fathers today.

Ritualised punishment in schools frequently carries an additional sexual charge. This goes unacknowledged at the time. It also conveys a message that violence is inevitable among men. Sexual charge, which can play a part in the administering and receiving of punishment, was usually legitimised within educational or religious institutions by inauthentic reasons which a child can see through without being allowed to voice his own perception and understanding of the experience. The sexual element comes through in descriptions fathers have given of ritualised requirements preceding beatings: the requirement to wear certain kinds of pants for the beating, the stroking of the cane, the tears of the perpetrator (the legitimised executor of violence within the guise of discipline), and sometimes the hugs afterwards. "You are beaten to a point where you can no longer take charge of anything, but at the same time you desperately feel that you should be able to take charge of this person who is doing it to you" (George, 2015, personal communication). Abuse can destabilise not only the brain, but also the psychobiological systems (van der Kolk, 1994; van der Kolk & Fisler, 1994), and maltreatment can be a source of developmental alterations in biological, psychobiological, and interpersonal regulatory systems. Adult survivors of childhood abuse, sexual abuse, and physical abuse are at risk not only of stress disorder in greater or lesser degrees, but also for other affective addictive and personality disorders as well as alcohol addiction and addictions of all kinds as cover-ups for early brutalising experience. See, for example, St Aubyn's powerful autobiographical account of growing up following a sexually abusive childhood (St Aubyn, 1992).

The concept of significant harm is now used to describe experiences of violent behaviour that could lead to removal of children from their families to be taken care of by the state. The significant harm to boys who have been sent away from home to a boarding school at too early an age has been less often publicly considered, although many of the same emotional family variables, prior to being sent away, might be common in both social contexts: emotional neglect, mental ill health, parents who themselves were institutionalised at an early age and remained emotionally frozen in aspects of their family behaviour, parents who were violent, or parents who were sexually abusive. Aspects of mental illness and emotional disturbance can be cushioned by money, but depriving emotional experience and parental antipathy may, none the less, be similar for a child across social classes (Bowlby, 1984). The impact of negative emotional experience on a father's mental health is often found in depression, violent behaviours, and absence of a sense of being lovable, accompanied by a fear of being unable to give enough love to their own children. As spoken by one father, the additional pain recurring in the present day is that his own parents "never saw the pain I was in . . . they are fucking stupid not to see it and if they did they would meet this need now, immediately . . . it is the fucking malevolent withholding of what's needed that leads me to those violent places . . . I want to hurt the other person is the bottom line" (Stuart, 2015, personal communication).

Fathers who, in many other respects, hold their lives together can reach trigger points in their relationships with their own sons, the power of which makes them lose control. A historical family tradition of sending boys away to be made into men, which a family might have favoured for several generations, can leave legacies of vulnerability and dysregulated emotion on young minds which often resurface when boys leave the institutionalised worlds of school and enter the emotional maelstrom of family life. As one father reflected about his school, "School makes you prepared for anything in life . . . the punitive structures give you constant practice at keeping your place, not slipping backwards and aspiring upwards." A number of men facing their own violent impulses have asked in therapy of their parents (who were not in the room, but in their minds), "Were you aware of the level of brutality going on? Was this part of the preparation for life you wanted to put me through?"

### Bateson and the "dominator culture"

In 1942, Bateson reflected on public schools and the systemic nature of bullying and abuse in an essay titled "Morale and national character". He commented,

> The boy on whom an English public school education does not take, is . . . nonetheless . . . reacting to the public school system. The behavioural habits which he acquires may not follow the norms which the school intended to implant, but they are acquired in reaction to those very norms. He may acquire patterns the exact opposite of the normal but he cannot conceivably acquire irrelevant patterns . . . his deviant characteristics will still be systematically related to the norms which he is resisting . . . the motifs and patterns of relationship in the society in which he lives. (Bateson, 1973a, p. 66)

This recognition of the power and the ways by which the contemporary ruling class established and maintained its domination came to be known as hegemonic masculinity, and has been widely discussed by men seeking to think in other ways (Smith, 2011).

In the three generations of men I have seen during my fifty years of practice, the assumptive model of the "dominating father" has lessened in the public domain, but fathers with internalised models of abusive power developed in institutions, where such models have been conserved for over a century, themselves take a longer time to modernise the belief of male as dominator. Communities, both religious and purportedly spiritual, and even therapeutic, have also contained the seeds of dominator culture, however much the founders might have been attempting to weed them out. In some instances, these have paradoxically become places where, in the attempt to forgo old structures of abusive power, new ones have replaced them. Boundaries that are to be respected, like the power differences between adults and children, were lost. Encounter groups set up to mitigate abusive child experience under the aegis of therapy (in other countries, where social norms upheld by law were less stringent) have led to attacks and sexual abuse on under-age children as part of their "therapeutic journey", suggesting the ongoing power of internalised violent and abusive experience for those whose overt aim was to heal.

*Dissociation and older voices: consequences of childhood trauma for adults in the therapy room*

The degree to which former abusive childhood experience might carry forward into subsequent poor adult behaviour, and the new thinking and practices within the family patterns of interactions a therapist can facilitate that might modify such encapsulated behaviours resulting from earlier abuse, needs to be continually debated and challenged in working alongside a family. Violent emotion or expression breaking through in the session in the room needs to be recognised and named as a current showing of a much older practice: "We know this voice from what you have told us but didn't think it would join us in here". The reality of such dissociated voices is that they come into the room raw, simply because they are cut off and, therefore, unprocessed: "You are such a fucking wimp; I can see why I used to bully you!", one eminent father yelled at his twenty-something son, in effect bringing in the voice of his own father, who used to beat him to "break his spirit".

Where it has become clear how violence in a current context relates to earlier violent experience suffered by a father himself, either in a family or in the context of political persecution, multiple conversations that include some recognition of his former suffering and his dignity in that context have to be maintained alongside the recognition that violence is not acceptable in the current family context, and is against the law. It is essential for therapists to monitor any ongoing violence in the family actively in their work, and to make violent activities an open matter of discussion with the family itself.

*Working with violence in a family with young children through father and mother together. Jamie and Kirsty: the repeat of earlier affective episodes and the combined effects of violence at home and at school*

Jamie, a medical research scientist, who suffered from "mood disorder", a recent categorisation of a much longer-term deep emotional distress which had first shown itself when he was in a long, dark depression in his teenage years, had not found a way of accommodating or discussing either his violence or its effects on his family life, either with his wife or anyone else, until the month before he and his wife came to see me. He had broken down for the first time since he had children, who were now five and seven years old, and felt unable to function. He ascribed this first severe breakdown to his estrangement from his wife in the context of her primary preoccupation with the children. She, in turn, was angry with his "emotional absence". He described his intense jealousy of his children in graphic terms: "I just

could not believe the impact on our time, our love. It was a nightmare
. . . the resentment that built up has never left me. At times I would
yell 'our relationship is over' . . . I am very emotional to anything
that's just not right in the family . . . I throw my toys out of the pram
big time. She won't give me any time . . . she's either with the kids or
she's working. There's no space to play." Jamie would escalate quickly
from irritation to "exploding". "If my mood disordered behaviour
pushes them away, I find it very hard to take responsibility for that
and tend to always blame them and would react in such disproportionate ways that Kirsty was glad to have me out of the house." Kirsty
said that she was terrified of him when in these moods. He would
indulge in verbal mocking and denigrating comments so his words
alone were hard to bear, and she feared he might hurt one of the children, but his physical temper had always limited itself to breaking
objects and to kicking the dog, rather than hurting her or the children.
The injury to the dog had frightened them all. Sometimes he would
leave for a few days and return when he had "got over himself".

Kirsty, who also worked full-time, stated that she had thought
parenting would be a joint project but that she had ended up organising everything to do with the children. She was highly critical of
Jamie's current fathering, and had never recognised his jealousy as an
expression of his own need, but her main concern was that she had
never been able to convey to him how terrifying she found him when
he was "ranting". She went into a frozen watchful mode (her words)
and would try and calm herself by saying repeatedly to herself "It's
not a big deal", or "Chill . . . it will all work out if the brakes are in
James's head." She kept herself physically as far from him as possible
in these times, though he would be yearning for "closeness and more
chat" to correct his sense of isolation. "I seek endless demonstration
of unqualified love or I will die . . . when I go right down I just say to
myself 'keep going for today and I can always kill myself tomorrow'."
His intense need led to her further distance, but his desperate desire
for sex—"If we can't talk we have got to communicate somehow", in
turn was met by her black anger "that he could behave like that and
expect sex as well."

The effect of these respective manoeuvres was that neither of them
had dared tackle the narrative of his violence, which was opened up
for the first time in our conversations together. In talking about the
black hole he went into during his very low periods, Jamie associated

his own negative self-esteem with aspects of his childhood. He had been beaten by his father "for his own good" to encourage him to learn, and had his childhood destroyed in ways he remembered: "Burning my comics, removing my toys to make me work harder, giving me cold baths every morning to make a man of me." He had then been sent away to boarding school at nine years old, ostensibly to have a better education than his father.

Over three months, and with medication for his depression, as well as fortnightly couple meetings, Jamie was becoming better at letting Kirsty know when he needed space and respect for his "quiet times" when his brain simply had to calm itself down before he could enter the arena of family life. He was also getting better at letting her know what had upset him. I encouraged them to embrace criticism without feeling attacked, and to try to talk about it in neutral ways: "What are you trying to tell me there?'; "How would you like me to be different?" In each relating to the other's fear of them they became able to recognise and respond to each other's vulnerability. "At moments of losing it, can you, Jamie, bring the more vulnerable Kirsty into play and not the ruthless fascist organiser . . . and can you, Kirsty, bring the lonely boy into the room and not the raging father of your own teenage years."

*Growing emotionally alongside children: shedding negativity and developing mutual positive reinforcement between fathers, mothers, and children*

Developing emotional regulation skills will be easier for a father to undertake alongside his own children when they are small if he has someone calm at his side to help him monitor new courses of action. Self-soothing is difficult if the person on whom reliance has been placed to provide soothing withholds this love, leaving a void. A combination of the provision of a more available other person (Kirsty) as well as the spontaneous warmth of the children alongside a neutral therapeutic space in which to deconstruct the violent sequences and the meanings that lay behind them, meant that James became able to anticipate more positive responses to him from other family members, which soothed his mood and helped regulate his emotions. Simultaneously, we labelled many of his strong emotions towards his children positively, to move towards changing his negative identity as a father.

Depressed mood has to be taken into account in work with violent behaviours since, for many people, irritability and a negative outlook go hand-in-hand with depressed mood. Fathers in these states, as Jamie himself said, might regard children as rivals for the emotional warmth available and many outbursts relate to this sense of being excluded by the children in a mother's eyes. More valuable in this case is to work with mother as partner, on behalf of the children, and to let the deprived child image of himself go. "I kicked it down the garden with the green football, but I'll have to keep practising . . ."

### From disconnection to connection

As well as needing a father's care and thought, rather than rivalry, children also offer parents a second chance for reliving and reworking the inner working model of family through the deep emotional connection they can bring forth in their parents, and, for many fathers, this comes as a surprise as it had done for Jamie: "A moment of pure love when I first held them in my arms." Internal working models (according to Bowlby's own theorising) are open to change if current positive life experience can mitigate former emotional disturbance and different opportunities for how to relate and respond to new storylines developed. While it is important not to compromise a child's development by his or her becoming "healer" of the parent, the recognition with a father of the importance of different kinds of non-verbal emotional connection with his own damaged emotional self is an important idea to keep alive, particularly when words have become used by him as dangerous tools: "In my mind when I am in these states, I can cut them all to pieces with my words . . . to cook together is more soothing." The children listed other things they could do to together where daddy felt like a safe person: playing football with Rob, his son, or helping Meg, his daughter, with her rabbits, or simply watching one of their television programmes with them without his own constant negative critical commentary.

### Violence and depression self-marking and self-monitoring

Depression does not have to determine all the parameters of family life and connectedness to others, but conscious effort may have to be made by both parents to allow a father who is depressed to make better choices than to "cut off" within the relational domain. A systemic approach connecting the different relationships and their potential for soothing or further provocation is valuable for all parties where a family want to stay together. Different emotional responses and behavioural sequences, different contexts along the way, can modulate former negative experience (Steele & Steele, 2005). It is always important, therefore, to help parents to mark positive moments, positive inputs, and positive relational experience with their children, as well as moments of self-change. This is particularly so for a father whose poor childhood memories crowd in on him to organise all the potential in his current family life. Positive experiences of events in current family life can develop a fresh template in which, as a parent, a father can experience and note positive differences to set alongside negative memories. In therapeutic conversations, it is important to help clients to note the discontinuities between their lives as adults and their earlier childhood experience, their powers as an adult in relation to experiences their children are living and they are reliving, and their capacity to change something they do not like. The use of their adult voices to speak out against any injustice they see children suffering that they could formerly only suffer themselves can be a significant growth trajectory. Continually marking their adult capacity to behave in a different manner stands against the still present critical self-diminishing voices. Jamie gained in stature in his own mind the week he was able to tell another "football father" not to shout at his son in a particular way because it might make him think badly of himself for the rest of his life.

# CHAPTER NINE

# Working with couples: developing skills in managing unregulated emotion

I n this chapter, some of the small details of working with highly unregulated emotion associated with violence, past and present, are discussed. It is important to repeat that nothing is easy in working with emotional dysregulation and violence. There are a lot of stop–start processes during which thoughts are regrouped following extreme outbursts, and it might be important for people to be able to leave the room and do some deep breathing for a few minutes before resuming work with a partner. The therapists also have to have familiar recovery paths to hand, since they, too, might become emotionally aroused by the work.

### Developing language around emotional experience

Changing the interactional context of violence between a couple while it is still a hot issue and interrupting escalation is something a therapist has to practise in order to manage it with confidence. Stopping mindless process is necessary to allow the creation of a more reflective space that might otherwise be obliterated. Spelling out what is happening once greater calm is created in the room is more effective in changing violent sequences than listening patiently to ranting. Following this up to ensure that any new and better patterns instigated have lasted is an important part of the work, as well as instilling a focus on changing violent interactional patterns before they become part of the mental representations of the children (depending on the age of the children. Teenage children can usefully become involved in sessions later, as discussed later in this chapter). Working with the recognition of internalised trauma or violence from the past as it relates to current distress requires ongoing calm and patience on the part of the therapist.

As discussed in Chapter Two, changes in right-brain function, the area that regulates affective experience, are associated with abusive experience in childhood. It is suggested that trauma or overwhelming affect, suffered at a time when the infant or developing brain was unable to sustain or process the experience, contributes to a state of being temporarily unable to function "feeling caught in the headlights, unable to move", as more than one father has put it. Schore (2001) notes that individuals with right-brain impairment are compromised in their ability to reflect, and can become overwhelmed by aroused affect, shown, for example, in both driven outbursts or dissociative withdrawal. Both of these ways of responding are common when working in contexts of high emotionality, where a key goal is to lower the potential for violent response. The implications from research are that self-regulation has to be learnt as a new skill and then continually practised so that it is not lost as a new behaviour within the changing system of response to upset. I have taken account of "indelibly printed traumatic memory" (Renn, 2012) and I discuss this as a recognition of what we are all up against: the difficulties in changing behaviour, but without allowing it to become a reason for not attempting new behaviour which has to be learnt and worked with. I also recognise that ongoing maladaptive behaviour can further contribute to intergenerational transmission of trauma, and share this with parents on behalf of their children.

It is always important to consider how future triggers for violence will remain in the family system, internalised differently in each member's inner working models of emotionally charged patterns of provocation and response. Certain sequences, whether of words or actions, can, almost without fail, retrigger or stimulate violent responses. It is valuable to a couple to identify these as precisely as possible and find ways of challenging them with each other as they occur. A person outside the system (the therapist, or any family or professional other who has been brought in) who has identified and named the triggers and any subsequent escalating sequences might allow a different marking of triggers when they occur at home. The goal is for this to lead to a checking of escalation levels. I use the concept of hardwiring as a metaphor with fathers, facing them with the challenge, "Are you saying this behaviour is hardwired and can never change?" If the answer is "Yes", there are different implications for everyone involved, and a father might need to engage in additional help through a domestic violence programme if he wants to remain living with his partner and children. This could involve a determinedly confrontational approach. One father in a family where ongoing violence had occurred throughout the children's lives said, "You [i.e., himself] get so stuck in your point of view and in backing your own position that you forget how you are also contributing to it going on." However, in order for him to make this more reflective observation, I had to forcibly (with my voice) intervene in the shouting rhetorical exchange between him and his wife to stop the hypnotic rhythmic patterns of tone and voice that were preventing either of them moving from reacting to thinking: "You are just doing more of the same . . . this is only helping us by showing how reacting stops you two thinking in the room . . . Farrah [their daughter] was yelling at you about this last week . . . Let's move to what you need to be different from one another, not get stuck again in your rage at not getting it."

## Considering why violence is privileged over other potential ways of handling events

Frameworks for considering why the violence pathway is being privileged over other possible responses in any particular family subsystem are more safely approached by a cognitive and curious framework from the therapist (rather than by confrontation, as in the example above where I knew the family well). Treading cautiously and with an open mind is safest and best in deconstructing pathways into violent states within a particular family group with a particular culture and history. Wetherell and Potter (1990) analysed the "selves" that speak in the justification of violence, and one fatherhood model that has recurred over the years, independent of culture, is the self in which violent behaviour is naturalised and universalised. The argument put forward by a father can take blaming away from individual responsibility, and it is often accompanied by a rhetorical question: "Well, what would you do in my place?", or "Anyone in my position would do the same" (the "honest soul, violent self" discourse). Violence is objectified as a neutral activity to be done, rather than something harmful carried out by one person upon another. I have worked with fathers to move them away from objectification to breaking down their own violent behaviours into specific descriptions, and recognising hurt, blood, bruises, and tears. This is useful only once a father decides to face what he is doing to a partner or a child, and when both people involved are able to work at this level of particularity, taking into account awareness of differing power and understanding. If guilt at recognising the damage caused becomes too high as a response to that recognition, and overrides empathic exploration, it is also better to wait until a father has moved from the emotionality of self-blame to a readiness to think about responsibility.

One positive way forward I have found is using prepared questions from a mother or a child to a father about his use of violence (not because I believe the questions can be answered, but because they give a guide to what needs further exploration and provide space for him to think). For example, from Leyla to Yiannis, "What does it mean for you to say 'I love you' . . . this way of showing your love [beating her] is not fulfilling for me, why not look for something better? You do not understand how desperate it makes me feel . . .". I explore a father's actions as part of the reply, which usually leads to questions of his own: "I now see this is not love . . . it is the behaviour of the worst man I knew [his father, who used to give him ritual beatings whenever he came home from long business trips] . . . I am copying him . . . how come his violence is getting played out with us . . . how come my mother would let it happen to me? Why didn't she stop it?" A larger discussion about "woman as controller of man" then entered the discourse (from his mother withholding her power to rage when his wife withholds her love). When men want to know specifically what they can do to change their own participation in a historical action replay, I invite them to keep notes and prepare lists between sessions as discussed later in this chapter. "Identify what Leyla does that makes you become angry, not just irritated, but so angry that you lose it." I then ask a father to read these notes in the session, sharing aloud thoughts that were previously not talked about so we can deconstruct them further together. Sometimes, a man will say, "To make the notes is enough to stop me . . . I don't need to bring it here." I also use letters with specific narratives of love, damage, remorse, and apology, written from both partners to one another as further deconstruction between meetings.

In the comparative calm and safety of a clinical interview with a third person, a couple might be able to move from expressing reactive anger into a more reflective tenderness, but it is crucial to remember that the habitual reactive responses of anger can be swiftly re-provoked in the crucible of family life, so that rehearsal of alternative ways of responding to sequences that trigger violent emotion also need to be a regular part of changing therapeutic work with emotional arousal. Families read each other's signals with great care, and their reading guides their responses. The amygdala, at the core of the emotional brain, has been shown to be particularly attentive and reactive to subliminal facial expressions of fear and anger (van der Kolk, 1994). Certain facial expressions preceding violent emotion can be accompanied or followed by automatic behaviours that partners and children might abhor, but which the person who is acting seems to be unable to change: "Dad's ranting again". Once in these high emotional states, a father could become dissociated, cut off from feedback, and unable to listen, functioning until he cools down only within the range permitted by the angry maladaptive self. Ranting as a phenomenon has been described as what fathers do when angry in many families, "as though he's just wound up and can't stop". The therapist's tone of voice is, therefore, very important in working with high and dissociated emotional states. It can make the significant difference between a father staying in the room and slowly becoming able to listen and their not being able to hear words at all, often finding words themselves unbearable (as with Jamie in Chapter Eight). A relatively emotionally stable partner can provide a containing element that balances out the behaviour of an insecure individual who "loses it", but this cannot necessarily be relied on. The pairing of two different insecurities can construct a highly volatile partnership in which a request for intimacy and reassurance by a husband (who may fear abandonment) is met by disdain or withdrawal by his partner (who might have difficulties with intimacy: see André and Joanne, below).

*Interfering with repetitive patterns of aroused emotion*

Helping a couple to become aware of their own physical indicators of the onset of emotional arousal is a valuable first step in enabling them to break escalating sequences following arousal before these become too high and block their capacity to self-regulate completely (see "runaway" Chapter Eleven, p. 227). The capacity to imagine what others are feeling, or to make sense of your own feelings, is lost when either or both parents have had traumatising childhood experiences that keep repeating through emotional triggers, switching off any capacity for reflective thought about the relationship. For a father (man), his wife (woman/mother) who is "behaving badly" in the current context, might become compounded with the original traumatic relationship experience of childhood "bad mother". In intimate adult relationships, anxious attachment and some of the associated behaviours mirror an infant's tendency to monitor the carer and her availability and responsiveness, which helps him to regulate his own anxious affect and feel more secure. If a partner is not available, anxiety can mount, emotional arousal can set in, and the pathway to an unregulated and possibly violent state can fall into place. Although most adults can generally articulate their needs for care, where this is not the case many couples become conflicted because of a mutual lack of understanding developed around these needs.

In all interventions designed to identify triggers, and then to gentle down rhythms of angry response, specificity and developing a collaborative approach to managing change are key. It is worth spending time, therefore, allowing couples to develop and ponder on strategies they both agree might work, since they will be the experts on what does not work. In addition, imagining the space in which self-regulation at home is likely to take place is valuable as part of rehearsing future planned changes. Emotional coaching and encouraging parents to stick to more consistent and affectionate approaches, rather than yelling or threatening, are obvious changes to aim for with fathers and mothers, but for some parents such reactive changes are difficult and often take many months or years to achieve. Aiming at one or two changes at a time is, therefore, more realistic and achievable. The focus on the self-regulation of emotion is a skill that can be honed during a lifetime, so the principles of finding ways of dealing with more extreme behaviours, both self-change and more enduring interactional change, can be started in a robust way with this knowledge. When focusing on transforming chaotic and reactive emotional responses based on unmet childhood needs, people need to give time to learn to tolerate their own painful emotions, to soothe and make sense of them rather than simply blast the feelings out on an available other, whether partner or child. With determination, adults can also become able to internalise loving and supportive aspects of one another's presence, so that they can feel soothing effects through thoughts about each other without the other actually being present. However, following confused childhoods, where the absent figure might have been irrational, dysregulated, or mentally ill, such reliable internal figures are much harder to visualise and might not be held on to for long without constant reinforcement. Tokens of reliability can also be usefully exchanged with each other as reminders of good faith.

## Working with suffering evolving from the context of civil wars

In civil society, we are faced with issues arising from war-torn countries. Enforced migration, violence, antipathy from a new host society, poor living conditions and unemployment, are only a few of the urgent changes affecting lives which can translate into mental health or illness concerns. There are longer-term aspects of survival that might enter family work long after a family is repositioned safely in a new country. The impacts of civil war on families and individuals who have escaped it might continue into future generations. As with the long-term effects of the Holocaust on families in the UK, the painful legacies of other world tragedies now affect civilian life and aspects of family development. It is respectful to enquire into, and attempt to understand, the meanings and contemporary effects of both war and migration for any troubled family situation affected. Tempestuous behaviours in current family contexts might also be understood as a partial legacy from childhoods of social upheaval and civil unrest. It is important, in situations of high emotion, to keep a mindful eye on whether the re-arousal factor in telling these stories is playing a destructive part in current interactions. An analysis of what went wrong at earlier times in the life of the family in the room can be used as a working guide to what needs to change in the current maladaptive family scenario. This is likely to be of more value than dwelling on often unrightable wrongs from a previous generation. Similarly, painful fights in the present can be talked about in relation to ongoing cultural dissonance between the partners of a couple. Warring about who has the better culture or religion can take precedence over the future life of the family in this country and the possibilities ahead for the children, and can amplify disturbance arising from family factors. "The tyrant is coming out in you" might be experienced by both parties at a personal and political level: "You mirror my mother, you are sarcastic, turn everything around, drive me mad inside my head" (the tyrant mother and the tyrant dictator).

In certain contexts, where vigilance has previously been an essential part of living, encouraging too much mind reading can also be dreaded as intrusive experience (mentalization gone wrong, like being spied on). As one mother described, "Any kind of tension, one of us must go into another space . . . proactively remove ourselves." While complete understanding was also yearned for, she warned her partner to "keep a physical distance unless I invite you to hug me" and he had to learn to go along with this. The invitation to look into the future, the question "five years from now", can be pronounced unthinkable: "The future does what it wants from you" [civil war]; "Tragedy after tragedy in my life"; and "I will live a month at a time, thank you."

## Venetia and Jorgen—violence and neglect earlier in life breaking through into the present: fathers cannot do it right

In the first of a series of four consultations, a young couple with their first baby, who both worked full-time, are arguing about whether to set up a baby webcam in the flat they live in. The ferocity of the argument had previously led to physical violence, which frightened them both. Venetia talked about her fears of the new baby minder, "She might be a violent psychopath", and, in the face of her extreme anxiety, her partner, Jorgen, became defensive: "You think that about me too . . . the moment the baby cries you jump up right away and have to see to everything right away . . . and in my mind this triggers the reaction of the baby . . . makes the baby cry more but if I try and hold him you say I am not doing it right . . . it's hard when you always blame me, it's always made my problem." Venetia, now in tears, accuses him, "You're a man, you don't care, you would leave your child with just anyone . . . I want to have a hidden camera up, so we can be sure she is not smothering him."

In making a jump to the experiences I know Venetia had on the way to the UK, spending a year in a UNHCR camp without her mother and being responsible for her two younger brothers, I bring other, earlier relationships into the conversation: "I am thinking about all the anxieties Venetia went through before she got to England", and (to her), "There was no one there for you when your father went off to fight. Can you explain to Jorgen something about how that affected you? Do you think he understands how worried you might be about leaving your baby now?" Venetia: "Well, everybody [referring to her childbirth trust group] knew it would be stressful, everybody but him; he understands nothing." I say, "Well, I don't think he understands nothing . . . just not the power of your feelings" and, to Jorgen, "Can you imagine the way in which it was for Venetia?" Jorgen responds, "Well, to be abandoned, maybe to be left behind . . . not to be taken care of . . ." Venetia (crying), "I would do everything to protect that baby even if he thinks I am crazy." Jorgen says, more tenderly, "Now that she explains it like that I can see the schema behind it."

I invite him to say more about the "schema" that he can now see. "How do you imagine those experiences affected her?" Jorgen: "She probably had to grow up real fast. She had to leave; the Serb soldiers had threatened to kill her brothers and rape her. They were in the camp for over a year . . . it was a hostile environment, her mother wasn't there . . . there were maggots in the food and stuff, and there were threats. Her mother finally got a permit to get them out to the United Kingdom." I risk linking past and present anxieties around the baby: "She has made a very successful work life here, but inside there is still a frightened young girl that didn't know if she could manage, and having her baby has brought all these vulnerabilities out into the open." Jorgen: "Yes, I understand" (takes her hand, she weeps, they cuddle).

However, there was a second layer of earlier vulnerability and misperception that influenced Venetia's view of fathers. This was coming between them and now emerged: "My father was OK, I suppose, strict but weak; he beat my mother and my brothers because that was the way of things in our town. He was weak because he left us alone to do everything ourselves to help us survive." So how did she think this might relate to her need to supervise everything Jorgen tried to do for the baby? "She wants me to do everything only her way." They puzzle it out together. Venetia agreed to self-correct, to take a hands-off approach in relation to seeing Jorgen as a potentially responsible father (not as weak, abandoning, or abusive) and letting him work out how to do it his way as much as she could. He agreed to try to be understanding: "She is a temperamental person: now I just try to step back, I could have torn her head off many times but I didn't." The talking itself released tensions between them that amplified into further warmer conversations and then having more fun, including resuming sex. They were able to take up the reins of their life together, including the baby.

### André and Joanne: too much responsibility too young— migrating in childhood from war-torn countries

André and Joanne came to address the violence in their couple and family interactions, which had aroused the concern of their general practitioner. They had three children, all boys, which aroused Joanne's historical desire to reform the men in her life. We used ideas of attachment and loss, since both of them had talked early in our meetings about anxiety in relation to the absence of closeness with their own parents, both in their childhoods and in the present. It seemed that their parents all remained fully preoccupied with managing their own lives and each had different migration stories regarding self-survival and "making it" in a new country. They each described their own inability to be soothed in any way by a parent in either family of origin. Joanne had been beaten by her father regularly, not for her own good, but because he wanted to remind his children who was the boss. Joanne said of herself, "My emotions are very close to the surface, rage, panic, and terrible grief. I want André to look after me, to be available and to be close. I cannot bear it when he is so distant and gets so frustrated, I lose it with him and I take it out on the children."

André was a child of Polish parents whose mother went out to work full time when he was six weeks old. He had various carers, some of whom he still remembered as actively unkind. By the age of five, he was packing his own school lunch box, and a key memory for him of loss of his own control was "crying at school because I had forgotten to put my school books in my bag". As the eldest of three brothers, there were always very high expectations of him to be a good role model and to look after them. He picked up on the smallest negative comment from Joanne: "I push her further all the time to know if she approves of me." Joanne was of South East Asian origin and had looked after her siblings in two countries and six homes in the context of her own mother's parental breakdown during civil war. She showed seemingly endless energy and determination in relation to the future success of both her husband and her children. Her resolve would frequently transform itself into rage when either husband or children did not achieve the standard she thought they should, and she would often attack them physically. In moments of reflection during our later conversations, she worried that she had taken after her father, identifying with him rather than her mother because his strength had been in contrast to her mother's dependence and weakness over many years (her parents had subsequently separated when they arrived in America). While she was very remorseful about her violent behaviour, she could not always control her need to hit when in a state of high emotionality, and André's response of "quiet and frozen" drove her further out of control: "I beat him to get a response, I want him to be man to my woman." At these moments, all sense of the real André as a gentle, caring husband disappeared and was replaced by "schema" or intense desires that he would be what she wanted him to be.

The longer-term goals we agreed were for them to become more able to tolerate their own needs for dependency, and to expand the restriction of their lives with three young children. In the following extract, we are exploring the use of a "stop and reflect" practice. I have found that this can help a couple change gear between performing reactive behaviour and stopping to reflect on what they are doing.

*Stop and reflect 1*

Joanne was very aware of André's hyper-alertness: "You are easily startled." [To me] "He has actual anxious watchfulness . . . I can tell you that. I learnt that in my psychology lessons in school. I have to temper my outbursts because he is very sensitive. I know his anxiety stems from very early fears about his mum never being there." However, she got fed up with making up for his mum: "Get over it!" He believed she found losing her temper energising. "You get a charge out of losing your temper . . . learn to be spontaneous without being mean . . . I don't want unexpected outbursts, I can tell you that. I have lived all my life in a state of heightened alertness. It's the unexpected-ness that makes me anxious, the change of tone, a sudden shift from friendly to hostile in a nanosecond. It's not the message; it's the manner of the message."

Now that they were talking with each other, rather than "at" each other, I asked them to change places so that he was facing her. André asked her, "I've been treated like shit, how did I allow this to happen?", and Joanne replies that he misunderstood her style: "In my family, we screamed at each other, we yelled at each other all the time . . . we were teased and picked on and mean to each other. I've learnt a lot from you, André, about how to moderate it, but shouting is just 'family' to me still."

In the continuing discussion about family rows, I stop them again a few minutes later as, following a number of generous things she says about André's family and how she has tried to change her style to accommodate his, he picks up only on the negative things. I ask, "How come you filter out all the positive things and only 'rise' to the one negative one? Is this a common pattern? Have you heard how she has been trying to support you? How would you like her to take that support forward?" (Focusing on positive alternative behaviours.)

## Stop and reflect 2

André talked about an earlier depressive breakdown of his own: "Before, I often did not feel loved at home . . . she expected me to be showing high levels of care as her husband, as father of the children . . . if I filled ninety per cent of the basket of care I felt exhausted, but she would be saying 'where's that other damn ten per cent?'" Joanne replied in a more wistful tone, "There is a lack of romance crucial to what a husband should be . . . fulfilling therapeutic services, husband, father, lover." André said, "I did try to live up to those expectations . . . just didn't know how to do it."

Goldman and Greenberg (2013) suggest that the emphasis on accessing underlying vulnerable feeling should follow the attempt to change interactions.

1.  The therapist identifies the cycle and its features, placing emphasis on the cycle as the problem rather than the individuals.
2.  The therapist begins to focus on underlying emotions and core sensitivities (family of origin stories or earlier life experiences where a person has felt vulnerable and at risk).
3.  Core to success is the display of vulnerable emotions and to help partners learn how to identify blocks to, and interruptions of, underlying feelings and how overcome these blocks.

In my experience, no particular order organises the clinical experience of emotional change. The most important component of a therapist's input is to keep the couple feeling safe enough to manage high volatility and new experiences of each other concurrently. If the couple are ever to move beyond talking about feelings, to feeling them fully and sharing those feelings, they have to feel safe enough with both partner and therapist to overcome their usual avoidance patterns (Minuchin, 1974).

## Neurobiology, violence, and splitting

Neuroimaging suggests that specific cognitive processes play a role in escalating arousal in emotional interactions that feed on earlier stressful unregulated emotional experience. Siegel (2013) and Renn (2012), summarising earlier and ongoing research, suggest that splitting, flooding, and rumination all work to activate and reactivate memories that have the power to exacerbate current emotional distress. Splitting causes upsetting negative events to be experienced in an extreme form so that an event of high emotional content in which both partners participated is viewed as "all bad", the other participant often being denied altogether, "I just want to obliterate her". At these times, all positive memories and contact with the other person are lost. Instead, memories of similar events are activated according to the psychic equivalence of their emotional content in relation to the current situation (emotional valence).

Neuroscience research on emotional memories suggests that positive and negative emotional memories are retained in different neural networks and, when revived, add intensity to the current emotional experience. In principle, as memory networks are stimulated, similar negative experiences from the past are remembered and flood the emotional field in ways that complicate further the distinction between past and present. This illuminates the experience observed and struggled with in couple debates, when neither person is able to remember anything good about the other in the relationship earlier, despite this being discussed in the same session. Such extremities of position are sometimes very hard to come back from, and might require long, slow, recovery times before anything further can be usefully discussed. Additional important aspects of splitting, gleaned from psychoanalytic understanding, is that wished for emotional experiences, those that a child may have glimpsed but never really experienced, are idealised (Sandler & Sandler, 1978). Studies of women who are frequently hit (Siegel, 2013), as well as clinical experience, show that women cling on to the ideal of love in the same relationship. It might help the understanding of why some women who are repeatedly ill-treated return to the men who "love" but abuse them, since the divisions of memory and emotional experience in their minds might not allow them to make balanced assessments of the probability of harm happening again. Clinical work also suggests that this capacity might not change, even if the relationship is let go, and might repeat in other relationships without cognitive recognition playing any significant modifying part. In the following chapter, I consider two such violent family situations from widely different economic and social systems in which repetitions of earlier childhood negative experience play a part.

# CHAPTER TEN

# Working with fathers within family court proceedings: disorganised attachments and violent outcomes

T he majority of the fathers that I have worked with in the context of the family court have been men who also suffered from mental and emotional disorders that, in turn, could be considered through the lens of anxious and disorganised attachment. The therapeutic work I have attempted in a legal context has been first in the framework of alternative dispute resolution agreed by both parties as an attempted way forward, and second as "expert witness" (someone defined as having special skills or knowledge), sought and agreed by the parties and solicitors concerned and recommended to the court. The primary goal of all this work has been to provide an opinion relating to specific questions regarding future care of the children.

*The clinical setting and the court assessment process:*
*some differences and similarities between them*
*in direct work with families*

In families where violence has played an ongoing part, the court process itself—the observing eye and the controlling functions of the court—can often elicit a more thoughtful and sustained consideration of what needs to change in a parental relationship than work in non-legal settings. Family court work evolved within a legal framework that, under the 1989 Children Act, gave primacy to human rights in the best interests of the child. This meant that both parents had to consider a future working relationship on behalf of a child that is within a higher order framework of a national protective concern in relation to children as developing and dependent beings. The emphasis placed by the Act on the child's best interests can be directly placed before each parent as an alternative position to their own, strengthening the focus on the child but also acting as a freestanding meta-position that is neutral to the parents disagreement. Using the idea of a higher national concern for children embodied in law has facilitated changes in parental attitudes, even in very difficult situations. The consequent ability of parents to set aside their own grievances and consider the different position of their child in relation to any witnessed violence, as well as the possible effects on the child of any ongoing disputes, is always a useful indicator of likely success in making parental care plans.

A common therapeutic goal is to facilitate a parent's move from a reactive to a more reflective narrative about self and other, in which a balance between hostility and some recognition of the good qualities of a former partner could be included. In addition, I have found it useful to focus on the grasp a father has, or can develop, on the effects of his violent behaviours on those towards whom the violence is directed. In minor ways, this has included aggressive responses towards me during interviews: observed levels of arousal and threatening behaviour (clenching of the jaw, dilated staring eyes, tightening of body in the chair). I write these down as they occur and then discuss them with him when the threat is no longer active. Fathers who want to continue a parental relationship with their children are usually surprised to receive such feedback (that they have usually not received in other circumstances), additionally, at times, expressing amazement that their behaviour can be understood as threatening. When this happens, they often express shock, which can then potentially lead to some new thinking.

A state which could be defined as mental disturbance can frequently be triggered as one aspect of deeply felt loss at separation, and should always be part of our awareness in relational breakdown contexts, especially where a fragility in one person has been held together in the context of the strength of another (as for Patrick and his wife, Anna, below). The co-occurrence of psychiatric disorder, as well as substance and alcohol use, alongside attachment issues are important to recognise and consider as part of work with fathers in situations of emotional and physical violence. CAFCASS recognises that drug and alcohol abuse and/or mental illness are likely to prevent couples from making safe use of mediation or similar services to sort out post-separation arrangements for children. Official Home Office figures indicate that the dangers of rape and murder of former partners are intensified in the context of a childcare dispute (Humphreys, 2006). Her analysis suggested that a quarter of all contact applications (at that time 16,000, so about 4000 cases) featured violence, where issues of possible significant harm to children were at the forefront of professional concerns.

To describe any therapeutic work with fathers in the context of separation of a father and his children following family violence inevitably can only represent a tiny fragment of the overall field. Many parental relationships might not be available to be addressed through direct family work because of the fear by family members of provoking further violence. These cases are likely to be better served for fathers through ongoing group work on violent behaviour, with ongoing supervision of any contact with children.

## Thinking about responsibility for violent behaviour

Violence towards a partner with whom a man has been sexually and emotionally intimate, and also brought up young children, can be seen to demonstrate an impaired capacity to "mentalize" at the times such acts take place. McIntosh (2001) has used the phrase "a profound web of 'unthinkingness' within which violence is propagated", to refer to this impaired capacity. She suggests dual exploration, first of the quality of thought and reflection on what the child has experienced within the immediate family and helping system, and second, an assessment of the personal resources and capacities within this system towards the emotional recovery of the child.

Fear of losing the future possibility of "growing through your child" (a craving or fantasy many separated fathers are surprised to find themselves consumed by) and how this is affecting a father's mind is important in the assessment of the security of future contact. "When you lose an adult you love the experience gets better over time;

when you lose a child, it gets worse" expressed one father. The desperation engendered by loss, or potential loss, often creates a narrative for a father in which the reality of the child and the child's own emotional experience is obliterated by the personal pain and rage experienced and expressed by the father. This has been part of the emotional force behind abductions I have worked with. I have found that time spent with a father listening to his narrative, and the repetitions embedded within it, helps to understand factors that are likely to trigger future violent actions. (See Brian and Suzie, below.) These repetitions of his own definitions of events have become embedded in his management of the world and his journey through it. Difficulties impeding a recognition of his own responsibility can include any or all of the following ways of blaming others, externalising responsibility rather than taking it on himself:

1. Holding the world around him as the instigator of violence, and constantly expressing indignation at the way the world has treated him.
2. Blaming the behaviours of a wife or partner for his own violent actions, which are then framed as self-protective: "she pushed me to the limit . . . she wanted to turn me into a bastard".
3. Blaming the extended family: "why didn't they do something if they could see it coming".
4. Blaming social agencies for not taking action earlier.
5. Relating violence to earlier childhood bad experience but using this as a rhetoric justifying punitive corrective action to a partner, rather than a basis for thinking about taking a different responsibility towards children.
6. Slipperiness around any attempt by a third person to relate his violent actions to his own responsibility for it. For example, the habit of not answering a question, asking for the question to be repeated, then accusing the speaker of bullying or nagging for repeating it.

### Is it possible to change the behaviour of a father towards a mother without a mother being committed to the process?

Within the constraints of work undertaken for the family courts, working on changing violent behaviour is primarily regarded by fathers as a route to holding on to, or getting back to, their children. For these fathers, certain common emotional characteristics include: first, feeling they have little control over events within their family; second, a dislocation of personal responsibility (no sense that they can be in charge of their own emotions); third, a lack of recognition of the individual needs of others (partners and children); fourth, feeling upset about not being able to offer their children positive lives. In my own involvement with fathers, their wish to change behaviour in order to have the possibility of a better relationship with their children and, therefore, offer them better lives themselves, has always been expressed *before* any work begins. Where fathers are not able to make such agreements, attempting work with the family is contra-indicated in my opinion. If one takes attachment processes within the family as being constructed in relation to affect regulation in the future, including the development of interpersonal understanding and the provision of comfort within intimate relationships (as cited earlier in Hill et al., 2003), it is likely that domestic violence is typically a part of the behaviour of a man who has not experienced these qualities in his own childhood, or has experienced them in distorted ways so that he cannot return to these in his own mind as a concept to aim for. The introduction of such concepts on behalf of his children, therefore, requires both work in the present and monitoring over time.

Dysfunctional anger expressed towards a loved partner weakens rather than strengthens the attachment bond, and, therefore, works against the wished-for goal, which is to keep the loved person in greater proximity. Children witnessing ongoing violence between their parents often partially understand this paradox. They are aware that one parent cannot protect themselves from the other, and become troubled by their identifications both with the parent who is being bullied and with the aggressor. They wish that the "victim" parent would take charge of the violence, but also feel fury that that parent does not (as with Paul, below). Children can also become "triangulated", taking sides with first one and then the other parent, often feeling it is their job to sort it out and blaming themselves when they cannot. Such feelings of combined powerlessness and anger might then continue into adult life and replay in different adult contexts.

Divorce in violence-related circumstances is likely to bring complex relief for a mother. As well as taking charge of her own life and her own relationship with her children, a mother, when she has been able to distance herself from the hurt and rage that the partner's violence left her with, can decide whether to work on reconstructing the ways a father and his children can be together safely. The construction of shared frames for recognising harmful emotions, thoughts, and behaviours as they affect the children can slowly evolve alongside changing family structures so that joint, more limited, parental narratives focused on the care of children and the importance of both parents having a part in the child's life can then be developed. All this depends on a mother having both somewhere to live and her own ability to earn money, so that she does not have to remain economically dependent on her violent partner. The work described below was in this context.

### Patrick and Anna: anger, abuse, divorce, and the involvement of the children in violent experience

In Anna's marriage to Patrick, violence had occurred sporadically over a long period, and the axis of love and intimacy *vs.* power and control between them had swung too far towards the latter for her to wish to repair the marriage. To counteract his increasing feelings of being "worthless" as Anna's career progressed, Patrick had constructed a narrative of neglect attributed to Anna. He found ways of ritualising displays of power which drove out from his mind the alternative realities of being financed and cared for by Anna. His obsession was around food: "She hasn't fed the kids properly . . . women are all the same."

Patrick suffered from acute attachment anxiety stemming from a childhood where he had been ignored by his father, and neglected in specific physical ways by his mother, who had often withheld food from him. In his marriage to Anna, he described himself as lonely because she was too wrapped up in her job. The secure attachment he had believed he had with her was initially challenged by the birth of their son, Paul, who then became his own primary object of attachment. He became increasingly preoccupied and conflicted over his attachment to Anna. Early in Paul's life, the violence of Patrick's feelings of jealousy had overcome his loving intentions, leading him to force Anna to have sex while she was breastfeeding Paul.

Following the birth of a second child, a daughter, and Anna's subsequent return to work, his sense of exclusion was intensified. His increased aggression towards Anna found him playing a part very close to that of the part of his own former aggressor, his mother, who had consistently frightened him as a child.

Dissociating from aggression in early childhood (discussed in Chapter Nine) leaves it unmonitored in a person's mind. Subtle processes of taking control over the other in subsequent relationships carrying both love and fear can creep in. A partner on the receiving end might fail to recognise what is happening to them or try to placate anger through submissive behaviour that fails to contain the ongoing dynamic of aggression. In such contexts, neither parent provides the function of protection and thought on behalf of the children, even though the children themselves might not be being hurt. Patrick had forced Anna into rituals where she was required to kneel in front of him and their children and apologise for neglecting them while he "punished" her, and she submitted to this for many years to "keep the peace". Through this, he sought both to control Anna's success as a journalist and, through her, symbolically punish the sins of his mother who had treated him as worthless in his childhood while pursuing her own career. When Anna eventually sought a divorce on the grounds of unreasonable behaviour, Patrick showed no understanding of her wish to leave: "Why can't you give me another chance/live with me/show me respect?" This pleading alternated with violent threats about what he might do to her if she carried through the divorce, and he told his best friend, "It's my job to make every day of her life a misery from now on." This extreme negative behaviour was a difficult place from which to begin thinking about developing some mutual respect as a basis for co-parenting the children in the future following the separation, but they did both agree to do this.

Working jointly, earlier positive aspects of the relationship were brought back into the arena as part of rebuilding stories of parental co-operation and resilience that could be shared with the boys. Anna talked about their early love: "Before we became parents . . . we were good doing things together, but once the kids arrived he criticised every aspect of my mothering as though from the start it was his job to protect the children against me. I supported him both financially and emotionally. I became his mummy as well as the children's mummy, but he hated me for it."

When discussing the meanings associated with his mother and food in his own childhood, Patrick told a long story of neglect and torment. His mother had been "beautiful and distant", more wedded to her career as an actor than to her children: "the pain of neglect . . . and everything that reminds me of it." He remembered her leaving her children for long periods of time on their own, when they were dependent on finding their food as best they could. Thus, for him, almost as a matter of principle, Anna, as a mother, was suspect every time she went away to work. It became his inner mission that he should countermand anything she said to the children. Anna said, "I think Patrick's projections are so strong that he has turned me into the abusing mother of his own, and at the same time he is turning Paul into a replica of himself in his mind."

In Patrick's own inner working models, the disorganised patterning of relationships in his mind became expressed as "mummies are to be severely controlled, punished, and denigrated". He would team up with his son, saying to Anna, "We don't want you here, do we Paul?" They agreed on incidents when he had failed to find a certain food in the fridge or a particular cereal he liked in the cupboard and how he had "gone mad". He had sworn his children to silence and woke Paul up one night to make him promise never to reveal what he had seen him do to his mother: "Don't tell anyone outside the family what I did to mum or I will get put in a mental institute."

Over a year, we named and talked openly about the power of these experiences, but also focused on questions relating more to Patrick's good intentions as a father than to his intimidation of his wife as mother. Anna recognised his ability to look after his children, noting his strengths as a parent, rather than his powerlessness as a child, and these were listed and repeated many times. Seeing that his wife corroborated most of his own childcare values (though not the distorted extremes to which they had carried him) allowed a basis for arrangements for the children to be agreed between them. A key feature in reducing violent feelings in Patrick involved him hearing the expression of his loving and protective feelings towards his son being validated out loud by Anna, from the two positions of wife and mother. "I do see you as really loving your children and doing your best by them, in spite of what you did to me."

However, Patrick's habitual verbal abuse of Anna still continued for many months following the separation in spite of individual work attempting to change his rhetorical attributions and "badmouthing". As with other fathers who have themselves been emotionally unregulated to such a high degree in childhood, new habits were hard to stick to. During a period of recalibrating the post-separation family arrangements for the children, abusive phone calls, emails, and other forms of harassment continued to take place. These decreased as the new patterns of being with the children were consolidated, and Patrick experienced directly that he was not going to lose them.

## Working to undo the child's entanglement in the mental construction of punitive violence

Ongoing disturbance in a parent, formerly expressed in violent behaviour (which may have been contained within the marital relationship), will not necessarily dissipate. In a post-divorce situation, a child might become temporarily annexed to form the "other person" for a parent whose own self-definition as "good" or "capable" has formerly required, and might still require, a couple in his or her mind. The other person in this inner working model of relationships is assigned the part of "bad" or "incapable", someone who has to be punished or shaped correctively. Where a parent has resigned from this ascribed role through divorce, the child might take up the understudy position in the parent's mind. This can put the child at additional risk if they go against their parent's point of view, and would be an important reason for recommending supervision until it can be established that a parent is not likely to behave in this way.

### Children absorbing and mirroring violent behaviour

A dissociated splitting mechanism (described on p. 202) was exemplified by the way Patrick could suddenly return to making the children all good and their mother all bad, despite many months of work. The problems are great for a child, like Paul, who has to co-exist in two separate households with two psychological modalities following such a divorce. Due to the child's loyalty, each parent carries emotional power and his own experience has given him evidence of how power can be used. He could remain uncertain as to whether this is good or bad. Although Paul himself was not, and had never been, at risk of physical harm, as the target of suspicion and fear was mother, there were signs that he was imitating his father's role of controlling

Anna as a result of the actions he had witnessed over time; for example, by being drawn into becoming father's partner in punishing crime. In the words of the 2002 Adoption and Children Act, Paul was experiencing "impairment suffered from seeing or hearing the ill treatment of another". Music has drawn attention to the power of mimicking, even in very small children, and the function of mirror neurons (Gallese, 2009), the ways children learn through empathic observation and identification with the person observed doing a task: "I am willing you to succeed and corresponding neurons will be firing in my brain" (Music, 2014). Children learn through reading the intentions of others and might then replicate the actions. Two years later, Anna said of her son, then aged seven, "He regards me as a pushover ... he criticises me for going out to work ... sometimes now he is winding me up ... and he says, 'I'm going to do this like daddy did to you'." She added, "In my house, Paul sometimes wants protection at night from the vision of his father saying 'never tell anyone or I will be put in the bin'." Paul's vigilance and control with regard to his mother continued, and he remained intermittently wary and watchful of Anna throughout his childhood. However, the parental couple continued their mutually agreed arrangements for the children in spite of anxiety on both sides.

## What neurobiology tells us about trauma that is important for clinical work

There is an extensive research literature considering how early experience can affect brain development, which has been drawn on throughout this book. Early trauma-influenced difficulties with emotional regulation can show itself in a wide range of highly emotional parental behaviour. Clinically, it can manifest in behaviours shown in various domains; disorganised attachment in relationships, including violence, as well as in mental illness. Renn (2012) has summarised the current research in relation to the practice of psychotherapy. The amygdala (a mid-brain nucleus) is at the centre of the fear regulation system and involved in the implicit learning of intense, emotionally charged experiences (LeDoux, 1996). Because affective and frightening experience, initially processed in the right brain, is inefficiently transmitted to the left hemisphere for semantic processing, the individual is left more likely to behave impulsively and aggressively in situations of stress and arousal (Fonagy, 1999; Schore, 2001). The way that any of us subjectively experience and interpret traumatic and abusive experience is central to the modulation of affective arousal, and to the development of symptoms and disorders (van der Kolk & Fisler, 1994, 1995). This finding offers frameworks for many aspects of behaviour that seem inexplicable within the context in which they occur. "It is recognised that traumatic early life events predispose individuals to later psychiatric disturbance when they are re-challenged with a matching event" (Moutsiana et al., 2011). Emotional dysregulation in infants and in adults requires a clinician to recognise the possible underlying neural impairment in many clients. Trauma-influenced difficulties with emotional regulation can show themselves in a spectrum of symptoms and behaviours that can be hard to name or classify. Some of these features have been categorised under, for example, borderline personality disorder. However, this term or construct might be most useful to help other family members in relation to the confusion and distress they experience. The definition could help them to distance themselves from the emotional effects of often unpredictable sets of extreme behaviours, so that they can begin to think how their own more appropriate ways of behaving and responding can be developed.

### Father kills mother and seeks residence with his daughter: the risks and value of future contact between them. Recognising attachment but limiting connection: Brian and Suzie

Where a father has been excluded from the life of his child owing to harm caused to the child's mother by the father, powerful issues come into play that can determine whether a successful relationship can be re-established. These are likely to involve all participants in any alternative system of foster care that has been set up for the child. It is also likely to include the extended family, outside agencies, and agents of the family court. Where a father has killed a mother and been held in custody, the caring system has to help the child deal with the simultaneous loss of both parents at the same time as managing their own shock and horror. Assessing the nature and integrity of a father's wish to see his children becomes a complex, multi-level process.

Hendrick Harris and colleagues (2000) urged contact between father and children in these circumstances. They concluded that crisis intervention with skilled help to uncover what had been witnessed minimised the risk of disorder in the future and recommended visiting father in prison at least once a year to "cut him down to size" in children's minds. It is most likely that children will receive help through their schools and social worker, but many children affected by shock and loss of this extreme nature are subsequently fostered (Hendrick Harris, et al., 2000). In Suzie's case, she was now looked after by long-term foster parents who had many questions of their own. Suzie's foster mother in particular needed support in relation to understanding the value of a future relationship between Suzie and her father, Brian, since she was horrified at the experience Suzie had been through, regarding the parent who had killed as a "monster". In considering any future relationship between Suzie and her father, and as part of the assessment of Brian's acceptance of responsibility for his actions, the degree to which this was contingent in his own mind on forgiveness by Suzie was initially hard to formulate. Would accepting responsibility enable his child to see him in a way that took his violence into account, but also enable her to recover and acknowledge other qualities of attachment he had always carried for her, and that continued in different ways in both of their minds? Was it important for her to come to terms with these contradictions in him for her own future life?

The wider social system, the care workers involved as well as her foster parents, had taken great care to protect her from negative narratives about her father. She had been encouraged to mourn the loss of her mother and developed a storybook around her death. All adults involved had found it very hard to believe she might have any wish to connect to her father again and did nothing to further this goal. However, Brian's solicitor had sought leave from the court to assess whether the development of the relationship might be in Suzie's best interests, and I was contracted to assess this question. It was clear to Suzie's foster parents, Jean and Mike, that there were many unanswered questions in Suzie's mind about the death itself, what had led to it, what her father's intentions had been, and whether, in her own mind, she herself was in some way to blame.

The question of future contact for a child whose father has killed her mother might not be easily resolved and could remain uncertain over time. Access to a parent is the right of the child and may be granted to a father upon the determination of the court. If a child refuses access, they are generally supposed to have a clear idea of why they are choosing this route. However, many will have been too young at the time of death to know what their own wishes might be based upon. Memories of connection to a parent are held in the child's body as well as in his mind. In my view, contact is often in a child's best interests for a cognitive working knowledge of the father when he is older, so as to have a picture of his strengths and faults as a whole human being. This is likely to be of particular importance where a father has formerly been a primary carer, as was the case with Suzie. In the killing of her mother by her father, she had suffered the double loss of both parents and both attachment relationships. However, as in this case, the success of future contact hinges on a parent's ability to show that they can think about and accept the child's experience of anger and fear and think from the child's point of view, not only from their own (discussed below).

### *What do foster carers and key workers need in the way of evidence to feel they have done the right thing by the child?*

As well as a necessary preoccupation with the future safety of a child, professionals involved in caring for, and bringing up, a young child often develop strong protective bonds with them. These bonds can sometimes compromise the professional's ability to recognise that a child's earlier attachment to a father still has meaning and possible future value for the child, despite the harm he has committed. The following questions are among those for which Suzie's "professional family" sought answers.

1. Is the father's mental illness a threat to Suzie?
2. Has anyone found out whether the father is able to recognise the potential risks to the child of his own parental wishes for close connection? Who is talking to him about this and making an assessment?
3. Will this assessment take into account the future as well as the present? Will it relate to Suzie's own perception of threat or is it on behalf of something that has not yet (developmentally) occurred to her?

4. How does Suzie understand her own position in relation to both her dead mother and the father who was responsible for her death? Who will help her sort out what she does not understand?
5. How will this be monitored over time?
6. Who else can usefully be involved in a protective network around the child?

The presence of larger family and kin networks have regularly been shown in clinical work to offer a potential protective forum in which a child and an ill parent can continue to have safe contact, in the context of warm but relatively non-involved adults. However, family networks can also themselves be unsafe and contain conflict and disturbance that might have contributed over time to the feelings and behaviours of the parent who acted out violence. While it can be useful to engage relatives as potential participants in the child's developing understanding of themselves in multiple contexts, of which family is one, a family will not necessarily be a safe base for future contact. This was the case in Suzie's family.

In a key judgement by Dame Elizabeth Butler-Sloss in the Court of Appeal (Sturge & Glaser, 2000), principles were laid out on which the restoration of contact in cases where children had been affected by exposure to violence would be based. It included specific reference to the promotion of the child's mental health and stated that the purpose of contact must have potential benefit for the child. It pointed out that the risks of promoting direct contact included promoting a climate of violence around the child, which could then undermine the child's general stability and sense of emotional wellbeing. The court would look for a history of meaningful attachment and a good relationship, which could once again be brought into play between parent and child. This key indicator of a history of meaningful attachment in both directions has been the most useful in allowing the development of therapeutic work in a court context (Sturge & Glaser, 2000).

### Interviews with Brian: relating narratives of a father's attachment to a daughter's future safety.

In the course of our eight hours of conversation over five prison visits, Brian linked past and present, the earlier deprivations and failed relationships in his life with his mother, stepfather, and brothers which were interwoven with the meaning of incidents between him and his partner leading up to her killing. Initially, I found the evasive and paranoid nature of his thinking in relation to his past and present relationships hard to follow. Brian had received a number of psychiatric assessments but not been offered any ongoing treatment. These assessments did all raise questions about the nature and safety of a future relationship with his daughter (for whom he was seeking a Residence Order at that time). He held the world around him to blame and showed indignation, rigidity of thought, and irrational contemplation of the facts of his life leading to the death of his partner. The prison psychiatrist assessed him as having Asperger's syndrome, described by him as "a form of personality/processing disorder". This was less apparent in our conversations than his sudden mood changes and blame of the wife's behaviour for his "self-protective" actions: "She wanted to turn me into a bastard."

Of the killing, he said, "I thought, what a fucker, what have I been doing? I sat down in a sort of shock. It's not fun having arguments, it's fucking exhausting for a start . . . and I've got to worry about my heart . . . all this stress, another thing going through my mind is she's trying to cause all this stress and windup so I have a fucking heart attack or something . . . I felt she had turned against me like the rest of the family." In another part of the conversation, he reminisced, "My mother turned against me . . . she would sit there with a blank look, just like Julia. It was a deep bitterness; it was their way of killing me." With more apparent understanding, he said, "I hit her because I was ill and she was ill. We had no help from Social Services." While this was untrue at a practical level, the seriousness of their situation had not been recognised by any service, including the school.

Of his wife's death, he said, "I don't believe she is dead. She could have killed me you know . . . it says so in the psychiatrist's report. I was bigger and stronger, but you can destroy someone with silence and emotional blackmail . . . because I was not getting through to her verbally she looked at me as if to say 'you are silly', as if to say 'big kid'. I then started to hit out and during that argument she looked at me, even as I tried my best to get through to her."

*Working with Brian: repetitions of mental experience*

In working with Brian, I paid very close attention to the minutiae of what he was telling me about his misunderstanding of communications.

Therefore, I focused on how my own responses might affect his ability to utilise my being there to think about his future relationship with his child. I was aware that he did not like "blank looks" and that if I said too little I could be perceived as "destroying him with silence". I was also aware that he was very angry that Suzie had not been to visit him, and that he might well blame me for withholding her. Thus, I made my input very child centred, emphasising Suzie's own vulnerability in the context of the loss of both her parents, and tried to engage Brian in thinking about what would make it easier for her to be in touch with him.

In a prison report, it had been observed that Brian claimed he had received no psychological support from anybody, ". . . the only thing that kept me going was the thought of Suzie". This made the relationship with Suzie both very precious and very vulnerable. He said of the killing of her mother, "I wanted to get a response" and, from his own explanations at different times in the interview, "The hitting was both an attempt to get a response and a punishment for the response that was wanted and not being given."

Suzie also did not give the "right response". In the first letter she had written to him after two years, Suzie said she was angry with him for killing her mother. Brian's thinking about this suggested some complexity in his understanding of whether Suzie should know more about his own mental difficulties: "Obviously a child does not understand the reasons . . . if I have difficulty explaining to her why her mother died, that would give her a feeling of my sincerity and that would be better for her than believing that I have things clear in my head . . ." Of the death of his wife in relation to his separation from his daughter, he said, "I resent the whole situation, that because it happened I should have lost my daughter. I should be sitting at home waiting for her to come home from school." More worryingly, he asserted, "I don't feel she really cares" (something he had formerly said about his wife and also about his mother).

Suzie herself had complex learning difficulties. She had separated from her father before her reading and writing skills were developed, and had not started writing to him until she was ten. His own guilty and troubled feelings about the death of Suzie's mother had also made him uncertain about writing to her, and it had taken much encouragement from the prison chaplain to get him engaged with the task, rather than just the idea. From a developmental perspective, allowing thoughts about her father to re-enter Suzie's mind in ways that could be assimilated rather than re-evoke trauma was important. Her letter to Brian mixed brief details of her own life with an expression of her anger: "Thank you for the lovely letter you sent me. I still feel cross when I killed my mum. . . . I have been on holiday to the seaside". This released her to formulate questions for and about her father, "Why did you kill her?" and to me, "When is dad going to come out of prison? Is dad going to get another wife? Can I send a Father's Day card to him?", and the comment, "I am still worried that he might come and get me."

Suzie's own memory of events was disconnected, but she had a narrative of living with her parents that she could hold on to. She had been seven years old at the time of her mother's death, but her own response at the time had been hampered by her parents' apparent wish to keep her as young as possible and hold back her development. She behaved, and was, in turn, treated by others, more like a child of three. What she found most difficult was locating her own feelings in relation to the experience. In her second long attempt to talk about it (following a number of more neutral visits from me), she cried and was able to describe something of her fear for her mother at the time. This led her to formulate some questions she wanted to put to her father. Her very positive attachment to her foster parents had strengthened her ability to talk clearly and recall earlier experience without feeling further threatened. Jean and Mike promoted independence of thought and expression, and although her foster mother was scared by the story of Suzie's father, she was not overwhelmed by this fear. She had enabled Suzie to gain some distance in perspective from which to revisit and talk about the traumatic experience with me present, as she, Jean, did not want to do it on her own.

## The family and professional network
### meeting when Suzie was eleven

Brian, his brother, sister-in-law, and key members of Suzie's professional network met with Suzie, her foster parents, and myself, as the safekeeping system that had held the relationship between Suzie and her father in their minds over the three years since her mother's death. Each person introduced themselves to the others by saying who they were in relation to Suzie, and how they had been part of her life for the past four years. All professionals were emotional and this was expressed by her foster father, Mike, directly to Brian: "We want you to know that she is happy, safe . . . time has not stood still, and she has grown up into a remarkable young lady. We want you to see she has been well looked after and that we all just want the best for her. I imagine it's every parent's fear that she might not have been as well looked after as she could have been, but we want you to know we always have her best interests at heart." They were invited by me to say more and encouraged to turn their concern into questions that Brian could contribute to. Mike asked Brian how it was to see the changes in Suzie, who had turned from a little girl to an attractive pre-teenager. Brian said, "I can't talk yet, I just need to look at her." I commented that they should not rush, that they each needed to have their own pace. Brian told Suzie "they looked after me in prison" and described some of the courses he had done, and asked her in turn about her own learning. She told him about her after-school clubs and they chatted. Suzie started to cry and Brian said that was good, she should not hold it in. We all commented on how it was difficult to process four years of not seeing each other. Brian kept saying in wonderment, "She looks like her mum." Suzie said, "When I first saw you I didn't recognise you, but it's all right now." (Brian, like Suzie, had changed his hairstyle.) He said, "You're older now, you make your own decisions, don't you?"

## Why did you kill my mum?

Suzie had previously told me she was uncertain whether she could mention mum when she met dad, and I had answered her, "As it's the first time you will meet since you parted, she will be in the room with you whether we name it or not, and I think it's important to do it." Suzie remembered how her dad used to "go on and on about things", and asked "if he starts being cross in the room shall I let him go on or stop?" I let her know that I would intervene if she was getting upset. In the room, she said to Brian, "I want to talk about mum but I don't want to upset you" and he replied, "You can ask me anything, talk about anything, shout at me if you want . . ." She asked him, "Why did you kill my mum?" and he replied, "It was an accident, my mind sometimes told me to do things I didn't want to do . . . it's called a mental illness . . . it's hard for all of us to understand." Whereas "I didn't mean to kill your mother" was a speech that Brian had rehearsed a number of times during my visits with him, the words that actually came out seemed more genuine. His earlier rehearsed answer had included the idea that Suzie should know that he had a mental illness: "It's good for her to know I am muddled. Better for her to understand really . . . I get voices in my head telling me to do things." However, in his confusion, he also understood that it was necessary for his relationship with Suzie, and for her inner relationship with the family who had brought her up for the first seven years of her life, to know that there was no intention in his actions: "Better if she knows how confused I am." (Suzie said later to her foster parents, "I needed to hear this from Dad.") He asked her, "Does that feel better?" and she said, "Really, really better." The tone of the talking between them then became more connected, and Brian was able to restrain his emotion in relation to his awareness of what Suzie could manage. They settled down for a few minutes into an interactional rhythm, picking up each other's tone and pace, which was important to recognise and respect. They reverted to hair as a safe topic. Brian recognised that Suzie was now old enough to do her hair the way she wanted, and she was pleased that he was not angry about her hairstyle.

Suzie's foster father, Mike, wanted to share an empathic thought with Brian before the meeting ended and said, with feeling, "We try to be next best things, but I can't ever be 'dad'." He and Brian exchanged some ideas of what each one imagined the other thought about them. Mike added, "We wanted to say, since Suzie came to us we have never pushed her in any direction and always kept an open mind, we never judged Julia or yourself." Later, Suzie reported, "It was quite good to see dad after three years . . . I think dad enjoyed seeing me. It was good that dad could say what he has wanted to say these three years. It was good that it was an accident and it was good that it was not my fault." She said that the difficult things were "When dad said I could shout at him I didn't want to. I stopped being angry with him after about a year and a half. I didn't want him to touch my hand or my head. I didn't want to give him a kiss goodbye although he expected it . . . I really just didn't want to."

*Brian and Suzie: the subsequent years*

Brian's inability to grasp fully the changed nature of the relationship was shown in his belief, expressed later, that he and Suzie would once again be able to live together in the future. He said, "A gap has been filled after three years; we should never have been parted." He made an application for parental responsibility to the court, which I opposed on two main counts. First, when his mood was disturbed he would not be likely to be capable of providing for Suzie's needs, or of determining her best interests. Whereas he had once been partially able to provide for her as a father with a young child (with the help of his partner), he would have no understanding of how to provide for her as a young woman. Second, while he had been able to show remorse in her presence, this response was often interfered with by less child focused thoughts, ones where Suzie herself could become the failing "woman" in his mind, mother or wife rather than daughter. I also had to take note of the more informed opinions of other women working closely with him when he moved to a hostel, and of his probation officer, all of whom reported hostility from him towards them as women.

My fear was that as Suzie grew older, and more assertive in her views, she would provoke disagreement or even aggression from her father. She herself would not understand how she had provoked such behaviour in him, or know how to handle it. In addition, it might remind her of the upsets and quarrels between her father and her mother, which were still close to the surface of her memory. While I believed that it was important for Brian and Suzie to maintain a relationship, this was not the same as putting him in a position where he would have authority in relation to her. Through her foster parents, she had learnt about the value of a more equal relationship between men and women and of the importance for women to be able to speak their minds. This would be likely to place her outside a range of emotions that her father could manage successfully.

It also seemed to me that Brian's continued, albeit intermittent, inability to accept responsibility for Julia's death remained very problematic in terms of how Suzie could construct an idea of him as a responsible parent. My view was that although she wanted to know him as someone who was familiar to her, she did not want to know him as someone with responsibility in relation to her own life. Responsibility now belonged to her foster family. The issues of a parental relationship, and the concept of responsibility, remained complicated by what could not be said in relation to the death of Suzie's own mother. In addition, the unpredictability of Brian's behaviour, which I myself had experienced directly on a number of occasions, meant that contact needed to remain on a supervised basis.

None the less, in my thinking, the familiarity and knowledge of one another remained an important component of Suzie's development. She had been positioned in a visiting relationship over which she had control, and had been provided with opportunities to think about her former relationship with her father and the good things she might have taken from it, as well as a recognition that he might not be able to provide for her in the future. What they could offer one another throughout her teens, and maybe young adult development, would form part of the foundation of a more secure adult identity for Suzie (in that she would not have a part of herself split off and denied). In reality, she continued to see her father throughout her teens on a three times a year basis. She expressed importantly that, as a young adult, she now knew what her dad was like, and could get in touch with him when she wanted to, but that she knew they had different ideas about a lot of things.

# CHAPTER ELEVEN

# Mental illness, fathers, and families

## A theoretical approach to the understanding of mental illness

This chapter focuses on different ways that mental illness can interfere both with a father's working relationship with his children, and with their attachment to him. In the 1960s, when I first studied theories about the social construction of mental illness, there were many disputes about how illness itself should be framed (Laing, 1960; Laing & Esterson, 1964; Scheff, 1999; Szasz, 1984). Systemic thinking attempted to bypass polarisations in the prevailing dichotomies between biological origin *vs.* socially determined in the framing of illness, proposing that the behaviour of an individual with mental illness should be seen in the context of interactional and interpersonal events mutually influencing one another. Cooklin, p. 226 below, has suggested a model of a wheel with multiple inputs, based on six factors that might lead a person to experience his life as going out of control. These inputs are genetics, epigenetics (or non-genetic intergenerational transmissions of environmental impacts from one generation), past events that organised the individual's response patterns, past family pattern, current family relationship pattern, and external events (such as loss of job, migration, relationship break-up). Up to a point, the individual is able to accommodate the confluence of these factors in what could be described as an error-controlled system, one in which the individual can adapt to changes by actions and behaviours that relatively neutralise their impact. For example, a father reacting to loss of an intimate relationship, such as break-up with a partner, might increase participation in peer relationships, football, social clubs, or sports groups, spending more time with "pub" friends, etc.

The factors are represented as a wheel (Figure 1) in order to express their relationship to each other, not as simple factors which can be summated, but as a set of mutually influencing and potentiating impacts on a person's life which can accelerate quite suddenly into an out of control state. A body has the capacity to adapt (to changes in temperature, bio-chemical states, etc.), but can only accommodate change up to a certain limit. Analogously, as the pressure of these six factors increases, at a certain point the strategies of accommodation break down. As a result, the individual's internal control of his mental processes can become dislocated from the coping mechanisms he uses to manage stress. The result can mean that the anxiety an individual might experience in the early phases of, say, a hypomanic state, ceases to be a warning of loss of control. Instead, it is itself transformed into the excitement, which further feeds the hypomanic state. Having a drink with friends can become an alcoholic binge: enjoying the company of women friends can tip into becoming a series of promiscuous

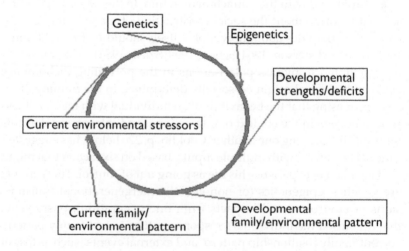

*Figure 1.* Six factors that might lead to the experience of feeling that life is going out of control.

affairs with their own destabilising emotional demands. The individual's responses can then flip from an error-controlled system to a system in which errors or destabilising changes actually amplify themselves, an error- or distress-enhancing system that could eventually lead the individual to feeling totally out of control. The resultant symptoms then can arise either as the result of losing control, and of feeling he can no longer manage his thoughts or feelings which have now taken on a life of their own, or through attempts to control the out of control situation

As an example of the former, Mark, in attempting to maintain a pattern of overnight visits from his children, who were familiar with his changing moods, would, when he felt himself 'slipping", draw on the companionship of his girlfriend, Nan, a close neighbour. His teenage son, Nick, was also given permission to call her if he believed his father was showing signs of "ranting" and was about to become more unstable. Nick chose not to call his mother, as her antagonism and concern about the perceived risks in overnight stays would lead her to rush to collect the children, when, in fact, they wanted to remain and be a loving presence and a stabilising influence for their father's emotional state. However, when Mark quarrelled with Nan, over a small piece of advice she had given Nick, the precariously balanced family arrangement went beyond its usual manageable parameters. Mark's ranting increased to a degree that Nick and his sister Mimi could no longer stabilise, and Mimi became frightened, texting her mum. Mark had to accept that a "runaway" had created a new level of anxiety in the children and, therefore, their mother, that meant he had to temporarily give up having his children overnight. In the tension between responsibility and mutual caring, the balance had swung too far in the direction of the children being the carers of their father.

Alternatively, as with Amir, below, symptoms resulted from an attempt to control the out of control situation, eventually culminating in obsessional compulsive behaviour. In situations in which an individual experiences hyper-arousal, he might feel he has no compass with which to differentiate intimacy from threat. The mental process which follows, as an attempt to control an internal state (controlling the internal environment) includes a suspiciousness which can morph into the imposition of a definition of threat to close others, such as partners and children. Once they are primarily defined as threatening, in extreme forms, this can become a paranoid stance. These are responses to the individual having little control over what is happening to him or to his mind.

## Research, mental illness, family factors, and implications for intervention

Lyman Wynne studied the interaction between systemic factors in the family and schizophrenia over a thirty-five-year period (Wynne, 1984). In a paper celebrating his work, Sluzki (2007) highlights two domains where family intervention has been shown to make a useful difference:

1.  Resilience-orientated intervention promoting family and envi-
    ronmental factors, which buffer against the development of ill-
    ness in a high risk child or young adult (see Steve, described
    below, whose family involvement gave a context to his suicidal
    ideas, and which also, when altered, improved his resilience).
2.  Addressing the specificities of both provocation (triggering
    uncontrollable emotion) and of recovery. Both of these include
    the levels of communication at which the traits of risk are
    expressed, for example, through distorted or conflicting demands
    and requirements.

I would add, vigilance for the small positive and negative details that enhance the functioning of a father, who is otherwise predominantly framed as "ill", so that trajectories of strength and positive relationship can be fostered. One contribution that clinical work can make to research is to increase the store of practice-based evidence for work with families with mental illness (Walters, 2011). Cooklin and colleagues (Cooklin, 2004, 2013; Cooklin et al., 2012) have added a wide range of interventions to work with parents with major mental illness, including a key focus on promoting the child's understanding and resilience, as well as working with the functioning strengths in the parent on behalf of their children (Masten & Cicchetti, 2012).

## Social factors as concomitants of mental illness: some effects talked about by fathers

For many people, as represented in Figure 1, structural associations with mental illness will include social deprivation factors, such as poverty, and job insecurity or unemployment, as well as homelessness and being dependent on state benefit. Any of these, or combinations of any of these, increase precariousness in couple and family life and can create their own strands of discord. Social disadvantages can intensify an illness experience in ways that make the maintenance of family life unmanageable. Researched factors, which are shown to amplify the adverse effects of mental illness on fathers, include loss of role and status associated with being the wage earner. Being unable to support the family due to illness is usually expressed by a father as shameful, however much a partner seeks to give reassurance. As one father put it, "For what most fathers go through if they are not in a job like I am fortunate to be in, they will start to say 'OK leave it . . . it is more difficult because I am going through this problem [of mental illness in his wife] . . .' and if you lose your job you will choose to kill yourself because there is nothing there for you to look up to . . . your self-esteem, because that one job that would give you daily bread is gone. Your family that is there for you to sustain will be gone" (Jonah, personal communication, Gorell Barnes & Bratley, 2000).

Many families in Europe currently live within a framework of relative poverty, and the number has increased rather than diminished over the past ten years. The toxic stress of intergenerational adversity as a result of acute poverty has been mitigated in Europe within the last half-century by the development of different welfare state frameworks. However, these are now under threat in many European Union countries as well as in the UK, and several countries are further addressing huge unassessed needs from North Africa and the Middle East as a result of brutal civil wars. Studies in countries outside the UK might, therefore, at times throw more light on the adverse effects of toxic stress-creating cycles of mental health disorders, and could also throw a light on nets of resilience and ways of incorporating these in daily work in more detail. One example of this has been the provision of mobile phones to refugees so they can call their families remaining in their home country (Denborough, 2016; Shonkoff & Garner, 2012; Yoshikawa et al., 2012). The relationship between stress and suffering is always mediated through a range of variables, some idiosyncratic to the individual and his family, some to communities, some contextualised within particular sets of religious beliefs, some with commonalities belonging to cultural ideas both past and present. We lack detailed information on how mental illness is currently experienced and categorised within families even in the UK. The ways different family structures mediate experiences of disempowerment positively or negatively within different cultures needs continuous ongoing exploration and further description and understanding (Maitra & Krause, 2015).

### What can mitigate out of control "illness experience" for fathers as well as for their children?

When assessing protective factors for children in relation to parental mental illness, most children cite another parent as the best protective factor. However, in many families, there is no other parent. A professional can assist in identifying which aspects of family routine can be maintained in the ongoing context of a father's illness, which other kin can be called in, what needs to be handled in a different way on behalf of both father and children, and by whom this can be done (Place et al., 2002). We know that contact with a reliable adult outside the home whom the child can talk to, ongoing peer groups through school or sport, and a reliable and continuing social life, which includes the opportunity to play and maintain a child's world away from the home milieu, are all important factors in mitigating the effects of parental mental illness for children (Cooklin, 2006, 2010, 2013; Gorell Barnes et al., 1998; Rutter, 1966). In addition, a clear explanation also meets the specific need that children have to make sense of the parent's illness, "to help the child associate the illness with a set of neurophysiological processes rather than just the parent's emotional responses" (Streeting, 2015).

However, we know less about what can help a father remain on track as a parent alongside such changes in their brain and mental processes. Fathers managing mental illness, both in their intact families and in a context of separation from the children's mothers, can usually manage looking after their children for short periods of time, but then need respite. As in other situations described in earlier chapters, a significant factor in whether they can achieve this will be how well they looked after their children over time from their early days. (The example of Mark, above, is one example of a father who was securely attached to his children in spite of ongoing bipolar disorder.) Being able to work in spite of illness, as many of the fathers featured in this book were able to do, can be a major support and the improvements in medication make this more possible than was the case in former generations. However, this might only be possible if the illness does not totally dominate the mind of a father, or lead to changes that undermine his caring abilities and sense of appropriate responsibility.

Where a father is not able to work, being able to retain even minimal aspects of daily routine is important for both him and his children, who are likely to derive comfort in seeing his continued competence, albeit in limited areas. Medication can support this process, although the unwanted side effects (such as weight gain and changes of speed in processing thought and emotional responsiveness) might undermine a child's confidence. Families themselves can juggle positions to retain some of the functional roles of a father in a household in spite of his illness, and in spite of separations in living arrangements. Demonstrating recognition of the whole person can include offering formal respect for his position as "head of house", in cultures where this is seen as a given, by honouring his different relational positions within the family, as well as maintaining his status (as father, grandfather, uncle, etc.) in spite of his illness. If there are other adults to maintain the structures around an ill father, the distinctions between the illness and the man can be subtly maintained: he can still be included in formal meals, his blessing sought for children and grandchildren, his participation in family outings be factored in to planning. In some families, however, the constant requirements of an ill father who still sees himself primarily as the holder of authority and power, particularly if he uses this for his own purposes rather than for the care of his family, will have become intimidating.

*Involving services*

A family member might be hesitant to call on health services to assist in managing a husband or father, not only through concern about letting him down or showing disrespect, but also having little knowledge of what his likely reception by health services will be, and what his treatment might entail. In talking with a family, the exacerbation of illness factors caused by inappropriate or unpleasant mental hospital experiences are only likely to be brought into the open if the ill member and the family are specifically asked about these. "Have you had any hospital experience in the family before, and what was it like?" can be important questions. Working with fathers who have suffered from mental illness should also involve exploring their recollections of their experiences of various treatments offered within, for example, the National Health Service in the UK. Of treatments offered, medication and cognitive behavioural therapy are the most common, including hospitalisation in more severe instances, and sometimes electro-convulsive therapy. Psychodynamic or systemic psychotherapies are less common, although still funded on a minimal basis in most regions. It is, nevertheless, rare in the UK for couple or family therapy to have formed part of their treatment experience. It is always useful to find out which aspects of treatments or interventions that might have been offered before have been found useful, and may be again incorporated into couple or family work. For example, I have often found that cognitive behaviour therapy has provided a base on which to build or further expand a father's thinking about his family (see Amir, below).

### Depression, fatherhood, and other competing preoccupations

Depression studies in the past twenty years indicate that there has been a rise in the diagnosis of depression in men (between three and five per cent), although the rates are still half those for women (Ramchandani et al., 2009; Woolgar & Murray, 2010). The authors cite changes in gender roles, a decrease in the number of men in full-time work, and the increase in opportunities for women as possible contributors. They associate these with men's uncertainties about losing social status as they lose the former security of the financial provider role. Two additional but unrelated factors that deeply affect fathers' emotional health, revealed to therapists more than to researchers, are loss of a lover and giving up the passion of an extramarital relationship to preserve family life. Loss of children following separation is also a major contributor to depression. Walters (2011) has provided a scholarly and thoughtful discussion around men's difficulties in seeking help for depression, making a plea for men to be specifically addressed about their perspectives on family life. She found that the emotional voices of men are often subjugated to those of women. Therapists could fall into the common social trap of defining a father as man who finds it hard to express himself, rather than a man who is overwhelmed by feelings for which he has as yet learnt no words. This could also be seen as another example of an error-controlled system turning into an error-enhancing system: his avoidance of emotional expression, originally a self-protection against not knowing how to express himself, becomes amplified as a trait by professional misunderstanding.

## Is there value for the family in a diagnosis for a parent?

Recognising and feeling permitted to categorise sets of behaviours as belonging to an "illness" can partially free a partner or a child from feeling personally responsible for it, and incapacitated by it (Hill, 2002). Descriptions of illness for children that lead to an understanding of what is happening to a parent might also be useful to the patient, or to those who live with him or her. Having "the demon recognised" is a relief, a sentiment that I have heard iterated by many parental couples. A diagnosis provides an externalisation that can be worked with and against in various ways. It is only the beginning of multiple possible conversations with a family, including the question, "How does it help you to think/do/feel things differently?" Children can feel freer to say, for example, "Oh here comes dad's ranting again . . . it must be time to (a) soothe him, (b) make sure he's taken his pills, or (c) remind him that it's upsetting us, which we agreed at the last meeting he wouldn't do." It legitimises the involvement of an outside agency. A child can feel empowered to call in another adult or the mental health team because they recognise that a serious illness state is coming on, and they will be able to cite an appropriate diagnostic "label" to alert professionals to the seriousness of their request, an expression of need that anticipates a positive response. As a daughter who cared for her parent with long-term mental illness shared with another group of children who were acting as carers: "You can call them at any time of the day or night and they will come to your aid" (Cooklin & Njoku, 2009). A diagnosis, in addition to an explanation, has both positive and negative attributes for a child: positive in giving a child a "ticket" with which they can summon services and resources, alerting the wider network that the family is unable to manage alone, and negative if it leads to the total categorisation within the family of a parent as a "psychotic" or a "depressive" while subjugating his or her other qualities. The cultural significance of psychotic behaviours hold discrete and distinct meanings in different communities, and these should always be enquired about (Maitra & Krause, 2015). In most families, there are multiple meanings associated with a major illness, both those idiosyncratic to the family view of the ill person and those that might derive from meanings held in the extended family, previous generations, or wider cultural settings. A diagnosis, therefore, is best placed contextually, used when it brings access to appropriate resources but understood as only one of many possible ways to attribute the meaning of behaviours in a family.

## Working in the current context: drawing on knowledge stored in different generations

In my opinion, the emphasis in therapeutic work with parents who are trying to continue to meet their daily responsibilities needs to be less on the illness as a medical entity, and more on the current stress factors between family and patient that make the illness condition better or worse, which can, therefore, enhance or diminish the individual's capacity to function within the family. Looking for particularities in a situation where a parent is not able to function well enough to give appropriate thought to his or her children, is very important. The longer-term effects on the minds and emotional regulation of the children who are living alongside highly emotional and unregulated mental states, or deeply depressed states in their parent, need to be monitored openly wherever possible.

A family approach can be applied in many different ways. Members of different generations can be seen individually to talk about their own store of knowledge, wisdom, and understanding about the illness. They can also be brought together to share their ideas. Shared understandings can bring about small relational changes that improve the situation, changing the whole family equilibrium towards better emotional and practical management. Conflicts of interest and belief in relation to the progress of the illness can also be brought into the open, so they can be addressed with all the relevant family members (see the Barlow family, below). Shifts in expectation of what a father who is unwell can tolerate in his environment, and what tasks he can perform in a responsible manner, are often highly emotional. Small matters, such as whether an ill person is well enough to make his own cup of tea, whether he "deserves" to have tea made for him, or whether the children believe a sufferer as "father" is hiding behind the illness are likely to be connected with the different meanings family members and different generations assign to the illness experience. Shifts of illness and wellness can become cyclical in the context of repetitive patterns of the illness itself as behaviour moves from capability into helplessness, or new strains of ill-temper or ferocity, which might be sometimes accompanied by inexplicable and accusatory utterances.

Perceptions can also get stuck when there is no recalibration within the family in response to a change in the illness state from ill to well. The family continue to behave towards the father as though he is still in "illness mode" rather than rejoicing or toughing up their expectations of what he can undertake during a period when he is feeling better. In this way in particular, a family can maintain a father in a position of less capacity, to the detriment of both himself and the family.

Where there is no dialogue about changes in behaviours relating to changes in state, negative perceptions of the sufferer, and a failure by family members to separate the father as known before the illness took hold from the effects of the illness state on that same father, can set in. Separating the illness from the person can assist in neutralising the illness behaviour, and lead to a greater wish and capacity to support the patient and his current painful experience. However, when illness is accompanied by bad temper and disproportionate shouting at the children, they can become distanced beyond an easy return and might find it safer not be too close to their father, whether ill or well. Having a diagrammatic (or neuro–psycho–physiological) picture of the illness can then help a child in this vulnerable situation to distance himself (Cooklin, 2013).

### Paying attention to children's ideas about their father who is "unwell"

In my work, family meetings have usually been centred on concerns for the children. In this setting, I find it useful to hold more than one conversation about the possible meanings of illness behaviour in my own mind. I invite children, as well as any adult partner or relative in the family, to share their descriptions and ideas about what is causing the illness, what triggers it, what maintains it, and how the family handles it: "This is how doctors have named dad's illness ... what other ways do you see it?" and then we can sometimes move from "ill" to "grumpy, greedy, lazy, rants a lot" and include "cuddly, fun, sometimes buys me sweets, likes watching TV with me". Children also value being recognised by professionals as contributors to managing illness in a parent, as well as having their age-related needs acknowledged. How each of the family members "labels" illness is important, as these labels may be respectful and forgiving, or abusive and accusing. Illness can often include a struggle with ideas and beliefs that might not have a "normal" framework of expression in the world outside the family walls, while within the family, people often develop their own complex and subtle explanations. Discussion also allows illness phenomena to be shared by one parent or grandparent with the children, talking about "bad things that need other names".

I might encourage a family to recognise the value of a treatable diagnostic category in which medication has been shown to mitigate the effects of the illness. This enables children to take comfort from changes: "Look dad, last month you were in despair, could hardly get out of bed ... now you're back at work even though you sometimes feel shit at home." Developing an understanding of illness that is manageable to children, as well as including their descriptions and finding ways of talking about the parent's illness and the family processes associated with it, in a way that the children can enter at their own level, can be very important in freeing them: "Sometimes it just feels like ... well here he goes again ... it can follow a nice day ... just a tiny thing goes wrong and then whoosh ... so you never know when it's coming ... he's not really in his right mind when he does it" (Sam, aged nine, personal communication, 2013). This was an important starting position from which Sam could begin to understand what was happening to his father's mind and the impact on all of them as a family. It is also important to acknowledge that, at particular times, an ill father might be very closed to receiving ideas from others close to him: "We try and stroke him or cuddle him but it doesn't always work"; "You have to be careful what you say 'cos if you get it wrong you can start a massive argument, and then things are said that you don't want to say"; "It's difficult to talk about it when he's like that and sometimes it might not go as planned. Sometimes it's like he's only talking to someone inside his head and he'd rather listen to them than to me" (Nell, aged ten, and Maggie, aged eight, personal communications, 2014). A more open discussion of events that can generate troubling or persistent thoughts, like the relationship between disturbing world events seen on television and repeating concerns in the mind of the ill father, can also help children (and sometimes their father) make better sense of the concerns. Powerful alternative realities in the mind of the suffering person might filter his current constructions of life in ways that could make them temporarily or chronically closed to receiving and assimilating feedback from others in his family. This can make illness episodes, whether "psychotic" or not, dangerous for children if there is no other adult available to help validate the child's reality. Understandable sympathy for parents can also carry the risk of diluting a therapist's vigilance in ensuring the conditions of safety for the children, a bias that I have had to check in myself as a resonance from my earlier sympathy for my own father, who suffered acute depressive episodes.

## Wider lenses for considering emotionally extreme behaviour

The extremes of emotional dysregulation that often accompany episodes of illness, or that might themselves be perceived and described as "illness" by others, also pose a challenge for children. "Borderline" behaviour (behaviour associated with borderline personality disorder, but not meeting its full criteria) can be formulated differently as displaying extreme emotions, rather than keeping them in check. To proceed beyond ensuring the safety of children, so that a new framework of understanding can be developed, a clinician needs enough time to understand previous contexts in which similar behaviour has been shown. A father might not understand his own highly unregulated state, because he has not made important links between current experience and his own former experience.

Slovo, for example, lost his father in an early phase of the civil war in his country and grew up with his grandfather and the "heroic legacy" of his father. When he was in his early teens, the civil strife erupted again and he recruited himself as a boy fighter into street-by-street defence of his city. He recalled firing into the night and having no idea who he might be hitting, maiming, or killing. Subsequently, he completed a business studies degree, married, and brought his children up in a neighbouring country. He was unable to settle, always starting up businesses in new places and then moving on. His daughter, in her sixth form years, recalled him coming home "intermittently" and stirring up the peaceful household with political ideologies that her mother had moved away from. He could find no room for his turbulent feelings in the acute cultural dissonance between his adolescent experience and ideals on the one hand, and the Westernised business milieu in which he was also educating his children. As a result, he suffered severe and prolonged depressions, interspersed with terrible family rows in which he attempted to exert a patriarchal authority and demand the respect from his family that he asserted was due to him.

### Recognising the power of a mental illness when working with a couple

How do couple relationships increase or decrease mental health difficulties as well as any unregulated behaviours expressed by one of the partners? As a result of feedback from couples I have worked with, I pay particular attention to the effect of the "illness" on how a couple manage their relational world. It is common for couples who talk of their former experience of seeing counsellors to describe the difficulty of not having this extreme dimension of their living together, the mental illness itself, recognised as a difficulty: "We went to see a marriage guidance counsellor . . . and it was horrific because we were not going as a couple with marriage issues. We were going as a couple living with a demon that lived among us that no one had identified." Where one person in a couple has suffered, or is currently suffering, from mental illness, a key part of this work is considering how the illness has affected their views of, and ability to relate to, one another both in and out of the illness context. Normal questions relating to the lifespan of the couple, how long they have been together, issues to do with finance, work, and children and how these are managed, need dual examination relating to states of both wellness and illness. The work must take account of the distinctions they each make as to how they managed in either case. All couple relationship work requires exploration of how the couple negotiates over the definition of the relationship, "my relationship, your relationship", and often involves protracted fights, dragging back "my" version from the partner's version. In addition, when mental illness has to be taken into account, it is important to treat it with respect as a third factor.

## Insecure attachment and mental illness

Each partner in a couple is likely to hold a representation of formerly experienced security and insecurity within them based on earlier experiences. These can resurface when, in couple disagreements, the cumulative amplifying experience of "going to that place" in earlier rows between them has provoked a sense of despair. Mental illness adds layers of complication to former relatively reliable patterns of expressing and responding to insecurity. Recall and current management of any arousal can be threatened by the illness itself, as well as negative effects of any drug regime being used to maintain a degree of equilibrium for the patient. The latter often provoke such questions as "Am I the real me, or is this the me controlled by drugs?" and "Why can't they love me for myself, as I am?" In addition, responses from an ill person to a partner might be less related to the reality of the partner and more to his own internal state: "The preoccupation with the cognitive brain as torturer", as one father put it.

Whereas anger is often triggered by any threat of emotional distancing from a partner, a bipolar disorder can itself contribute to distancing a partner through actions "dictated" by the illness: for example, by temporary attachments to alcohol, to spending, or to other people (or combinations of these). Each temporary attachment can carry its own overwhelming accorded power in response to the emotional high. For a partner to express anger at these behaviours directly is unlikely to keep her connected, and it is more productive, in my experience, to include individual sessions alongside couple work, so that angry feelings can be acknowledged respectfully by a therapist without antagonising and arousing the other partner. Feeling used as an object by an ill partner, rather than being seen clearly as a person, is painful: "I used to feel like a teddy that a child would carry . . . when he wanted to he would hate the teddy, blame it for everything, hit it, jump on it, throw it at the walls, and sometimes he would love it and want to hug it and sit it on the pillow next to him and feel safe knowing it was there" (Sophia, 2016, personal communication).

For a child, responses to these extremes of mood in a father will depend both on her age and what has been explained to her, in addition to her own instinctive understanding of what is going on. The ways children are framed within the illness lens of a father might also vary, one child being loved and another given a hard time, or the same child taking turns in both. As in all situations when there is a distortion of relationship through parental anger or mental illness, the quality of the relationship with the father when things are going well is also of great importance in managing the relationship when things are going badly.

## Attentive listening out for resilience threads

Recent neuroscience studies have demonstrated how early traumatic experience can shape a developing brain, which can then limit pathways of the ability to think freely. As a result, developing coherent narratives about oneself and one's relationships is likely to be impaired. However, although childhood experiences can undermine a child's ability to think and reflect and can build lasting negative discourses about the self for a grown-up child who is now a father, it is important as a listener to remember that current dominant recollections might not be the whole story. In a therapeutic context, attentive listening can also unearth potential resilience threads both in a father's narrative and in the current life he might be struggling to lead. It is important to retain hope when a father has lost his. Working with positive threads in a father's story is specifically aimed at helping him to develop confidence and competence to a level that better enables him to carry out whatever tasks of fatherhood he is currently responsible for, and has to manage. Such competence has to be able to maintain itself at a level higher than the level of emotionality created when minor daily things are difficult. Sometimes, goals for living have to be broken down into smaller and more achievable pieces (mending bicycles, taking the dog for a walk, helping to check a school project). Identifying difficulties, skills, and risks and practising how to be different next time, to become someone who is seen as protective of loved ones, to find inner voices to combat those that are putting a father down, and rehearse effective responses to these voices, are all important components. I usually develop questions with a father that he is willing to try to answer before facing up to the situations occurring in life at home. For example, I might ask, "When critical voices are clamouring in your mind, how could you answer them differently next time?" or "When [these voices] are saying you are a bad, incompetent, dangerous person, what other voices can be brought into play to answer them back or defeat them?" This develops the idea of a personal capacity to be able to come back at critical voices, even if not to vanquish them entirely. Below, I give some examples of using this approach in a determined way when working with Amir and Emine over three years.

### Amir, Emine, Hafsa, and Nasrullah: traumatic childhood experience, mental illness, and being a parent

Amir, who managed a small printing company, suffered from anxiety, depression, and angry moods. He was highly critical of himself and others, and accused his wife Emine and the children Nasrullah, aged ten, and Hafsa, aged seven, of scrutinising him all the time. When he was in a low mood, he "could completely lose it, bang his head against the wall; tell us all to get out of his life". In his own narrative about his childhood, his father had suffered from obsessive–compulsive disorder and also had a violent temper. He had constantly criticised his son for not doing well enough at school. Amir had suffered from bullying from peers throughout childhood and subsequently broke down in his early teens. He was hospitalised in an adult ward, as there were no adolescent facilities available in his country at the time. He found this a terrifying experience, which subsequently coloured his view of all mental health services and deterred him from using them.

The intergenerational critical patterns were being replicated with his own son, about whom he was disproportionately negative. He had few skills to manage everyday disorderly stress created in family life with children, although he managed well in his orderly life at work. Over several months working with different family groupings, he came to the conclusion that he had no feeling of a "real" self as a parent, because the image he had of himself as a child was based on "wrongful" descriptions which had denied his own reality completely. His own parents had constantly communicated that his thoughts and feelings were unreasonable and meaningless. He found this thought useful in attempting to develop more validating responses to his own children. As a child, he had been punished or ignored when he had been upset, and, as a result, had become disconnected from his own emotions. He eventually learnt to label these more clearly through noting the responses of his children, and by giving words to the minutiae of their experience. I practised the search for the "right" descriptions and meanings in family interactions with him and Emine, studying sequences around children's homework and their behaviour of "answering back", baselines which provided opportunities for examining his beliefs associated with each sequence, and then to reposition the family participants in his usual internal story structure, making it less blaming of them. Emine showed exceptional patience in pointing out to Amir the ways he was inconsistent, and helping him note times where his own thinking became disordered and exaggerated. She encouraged him to downplay emotionally intense exchanges with the children that were out of proportion to the event. Such exchanges triggered high arousal in all the family members and made them vulnerable to irrational and redundant fears and emotions. The children described having their minds "interrupted" and taken over: "He just barges into our thoughts", and they became aware that they were not really being seen for themselves at these times, but were being reduced in their father's mind to "beings who were hostile" and whom he had to control. He would say, for example, "I can't stand it when you do this to me." He then had to learn to think more about what he was doing to them. Children being exposed to constant anxiety can develop their own anxious states, so marking positive interactions between them and their father (usually on family days out, or in the garden shed) provided a small buffer against everyone's overriding preoccupation with negative interaction and poor self-image, already manifested at times by the children.

### Obsessive thinking and being in a black hole: building a resilience ladder, however crooked, and climbing out rung by rung

While obsessive thinking is a characteristic of depression, it can also exist as a state independent of depressed mood, as the practice of critically monitoring the self becomes an ongoing habit. A series of thoughts about "Why didn't I do a better job?" can be applied in multiple contexts. When Amir used a totalising framework about himself, "I'm the depressive . . . I should have done . . .", I challenged him into sorting out areas of his life where he had done, and still did, a good job. "Give a part of each day to honouring that skill and think about it." He also taught me a trick he had learnt from his own earlier cognitive behavioural therapy—catching and dealing with negative thoughts one at a time, "Catch it, work out how you plan to deal with it, try it out, and if it works try it in a different context the next day." He labelled this "climbing out of the black hole . . . go rung by rung". On a day when he felt better, "coming out of the black hole", Amir was able to say, "I'm going to change my mental framework, I'm going to be positive. Putting myself forward and thinking of myself in a good light has been important. I am important as well." Emine pointed out to him that he had been getting great feedback from the children that month, and that they had learnt to distance themselves further from the invasive elements of their parents' emotions, conflict, and behaviour: "Look dad, you don't have to tie yourself up in knots about being ill . . . we are doing all right."

*Illness in the past can still be illness in the present: family factors that do not go away. Working with grievance around becoming a father: the Barlow family*

In some families, parental mental illness, in addition to parental alcohol misuse, experienced by children in their childhood might continue to be a factor when they become parents themselves. Making sense of former childhood experience can be acutely confusing if the family experience is continuing into adulthood, and the young adult still lives in the same house as his parents. This can be particularly hazardous in the context of three-generational family households living together. Far from such a household being a supportive environment for young parents without their own home, it can become a crucible for high expressed emotion, critical comment, and ongoing overinvolvement, as a young couple try to navigate a way to create their own distinctive family style (McFarlane & Cook, 2007; Peskin et al., 2011).

The Barlow family ran a painting and decorating business and were deeply involved with one another. They were referred by their GP following a suicidal attempt from Steve, the son of the household, in his twenties. I worked with them over two years. Steve was now also a young father making a life with his Colombian partner, Maria, whom he had met while travelling in Latin America, and their new baby, Carlos. As his mother and wife quarrelled over the right to define how Carlos should be brought up, Steve was repeatedly driven into a depressed, anxious, and highly unstable state, making a number of attempts on his own life that repeated earlier behaviour in his adolescence before he had "got away" from the family. Enmeshment in family problems, and vulnerability to women's criticism in both generations of his contemporary family drove him into personal despair at how to position himself as a father. Mabel, his mother, specialised in highly critical comments expressed about small family matters that involved her son or her grandson, while taking no responsibility for the effects of her own style of discourse. She, in turn, attributed high volatility to others. Of her new daughter-in-law, she said, "She is always making critical comments . . . if my floor's not clean enough for Carlos to crawl on then I don't know what is . . . she's not to dare question me . . .", adding to Steve, "If you want to look after your son just do it your way, I am not going to bow down to your incomer."

Steve did not want Carlos, his son, to experience the same micromanagement he had grown up with, and was unable to hear his mother's tirades without slamming out of the house, finally taking his family with him to rented accommodation down the road. He was desparate for a generational shift, for his mother to recognise his development from son to a man and a father, rather than her constant iteration of the question, "Where did the little boy who used to say he loved his mummy go to?" The family specialised in rows that escalated—phones were put down, doors were shut in faces, letters were silently stuffed through letterboxes—with liberal accusations of blame and neglect all round.

All agreed that pre-meetings with different subsystems in the family should precede family meetings, so that angry responses generated during various tellings did not re-arouse competing compulsive anger in other subsystems. The grandparental couple, Mabel and Derek, came as one couple, while Steve and Maria came as another.

Maria wanted in particular to express her sense of being disrespected because of her skin colour, and her mother-in-law's inability to accept that Carlos was her baby, not just Steve's son. Following these meetings, Steve met with his parents to outline the areas he felt they must renegotiate. "This is our first baby, we need to make our own mistakes . . . we've had a hard time. I am a father. I am not a boy any more. I am a man and I have to put my number one time into my own family now." He confronted his mother about her increasing drinking: "It's the effect on your changes of perception, mum", and (to his father), "I am not going to scramble my headspace any more trying to stop my mother drinking." To his mother he added, "If you carry on drinking it's up to you, but I want you to know it has consequences: you can't look after our son if you're having a drink", and (to me), "I don't fully feel I can get hold of her mind when she's in that state." Mabel asked him, "Am I a fundamentally different mother to the one you had five years ago? What's changed to make you feel this way?" to which Steve answered clearly, "I think you have become more dependent on alcohol, more extreme, less up for enjoying things unless you've got a drink in your hand . . . you change, mum, when you drink . . . you are not in touch with yourself [he cries]; do you think I am happy being so far away from you?" (Keller et al., 2005).

Mabel's insistence that her drinking was "situational" and triggered by specific events seemed contraindicated by the frequency with which she resorted to drink, and the hours at which she began to include alcohol in her daily routine. To address this underlying difficulty would have involved recognition of the need for a systems change at another level: her own loneliness and boredom without small children around and her husband's preoccupation with his work. At this point, Steve and his father began to recognise that this larger change was what might be necessary.

### Extended family meeting with Mabel, Derek, Steve, and Maria (scheduled for two hours)

The family had set out some rules for the meeting, which Mabel and Derek delivered at the beginning: each person to say what they want to get out of it, Derek stating "One thing to come out of it in the future is to listen to everybody else without getting highly upset and volatile

... Gill, as our family mediator, is not to leave the room ... we want a strongly facilitated meeting, an opportunity to look at issues that have caused an immense amount of hurt." Mabel was told by Steve and Maria not to be patronising or sarcastic and Derek simultaneously told by them that he must join in, not just sit there and let others fight his battles for him.

In the first half an hour, these were the main items raised for discussion.

1.  Worries about Steve's mental health, desperation, and suicidal thoughts by all in the family (including absent extended family members).
2.  Derek and Mabel's distress at being cut off from their grandson, Carlos.
3.  Worries about Mabel's mental health and increasing drinking.
4.  Worries about their own position in the family or household (on the part of both Steve and Maria).
5.  A demand that each person must say what change they are prepared to make by Derek and a suggestion by Gill that each person should ask themselves what they will give up in order to achieve the change. In response, Mabel shouted, "I don't want no change ... I have said sorry one thousand times and not got anywhere."
6.  "I would like us all to express our love for one another and move on" (Maria).
7.  "I want to follow Gill's question, 'What grievances are any of us prepared to give up?' I want to see my grandchild" (Derek).
8.  Steve: "Restructuring the family and my position in it: father and husband first, son and brother second in the hierarchy of life: establishing boundaries and a sensible interference level."

In the ensuing discussion, an attempt was made to move towards recognising positive aspects of each other's behaviour, with different members saying "Try to get moving from words alone to actions ... move from 'bad judgement' to 'let it go', if there are no agreed understandings between us and we just can't talk to each other, it's very sad ... let's move on."

I focused discussion on intergenerational change, family transitions and development, and invited each of them to think about which of them should be the decision takers in which contexts: the one Steve grew up in, and the one he is creating with Maria. I suggested that "ambiguity is part of what is doing Steve's head in".

Mabel summarised, "I can now see the move in question is about whether I am primarily to see my son as a son or as a father to his child, a parent like I am a parent. I must have overstepped a boundary. You were so angry about me having a glass of wine when I was babysitting Carlos, 'back off, our baby, our way', I felt intimidated in my own house." Steve replied, "You wouldn't accept our instructions on Carlos . . . you were patronising." Maria, feeling more recognised, became more generous: "You were good to us too . . . it was hard for us trying to make our own way. I never wanted to disrespect anyone." They all agreed they had shared a house together too long; things got stuck in old ways.

I then asked what else might need to happen for the family to get together outside this room without me, to explore how old ways could change further. Derek took out a "statement", a highly positive connotation of each person and their intentions, and proposed "Let it go. We owe it to Carlos to put him back into a secure and loving extended family."

In the fourth and final half hour of the sessions, Mabel asked for more precise details of where she herself had been out of order and was given two examples. She said cheerfully "I am a bit quirky but this is me . . . I am open to all family dialogues . . . I want you guys to be developing . . . I want to be part of your life . . . I would make a good granny if you could use me." Maria replied, "I have never deliberately tried to undermine you . . . I have never had a malevolent thought towards you." To which Mabel responded, "You are an amazing mother and Carlos is very lucky to have you." Steve added, "You need to recognise that I love Maria, we have a child together, and I am going to live with her. She has not brainwashed me into not having a relationship with my family."

## A week later

At a subsequent family meeting the following week, the positive spiral did continue to amplify, albeit hesitantly. Each person had taken a slightly modified position and was able to give a positive response to the possible position of the others "for the sake of Carlos". Maria declared again, although less dramatically, "I am completely the mother figure for my son, because I am a first-time mum." In response, Mabel now began to encourage her, "Savour every moment of it because it goes so quickly." They agreed to share knowledge and experience rather than to hang on to different preoccupations. Mabel (performing a new generational part as "elder") made a speech: "You are the mother of my grandson and partner of my son . . . the term friendship is not appropriate. I want to say how thankful I am that you had Steven's baby. I couldn't ask for a better woman."

## Reflections on the work

Over the two years that I worked with the family, the extreme mental distress that had resulted in confusion and suicidal thoughts for the young father had required particular attention to specific family inter-actions in which he would continue to be "caught" in his mind between competing generational demands. In disentangling the defi-nitions and loyalties of son, brother, husband, and father, I focused on getting individuals to speak more clearly for themselves. The family work needed to take place in subsystems, prior to whole family meet-ings, so that traumatic responses generated during various tellings did not re-arouse trauma in others. I re-established husband–wife solidar-ity in two generations in a situation where a long alliance between mother and son had developed strong negative effects for Steve's life. In Mabel's mind, Steve's primary role as a child had been to give her life emotional meaning. She had kept notes and memoirs of his child-hood well into his early twenties, using them to "throw in his face" when he made attempts to move away. To let him go, her husband, Derek, had to recognise that his own part in Mabel's life required a more active involvement. Rather than maintaining a jocular but competitive relationship with his son, he moved into a grandparental role developed more around the tasks of bringing up a little boy, and developing a three-generational alliance between the "men" in the family. He participated more in family conversations and family life. This included planning with Mabel how they might spend more time together in family life, and as a couple in retirement.

# CHAPTER TWELVE

# Reconciliation and forgiveness

Some children who have been estranged from their fathers earlier in their growing up have sought reconciliations with them once they have arrived at young adulthood and achieved some independence in their own lives. This last chapter provides a reflection on how a father's acute difficulties and separation from his children, however severe this has been at times in their lives, might remain possible to reconcile. It seems that if a father has tried to "do his best" for his children and they have sensed both love and a wish for their presence in his life, much can be forgiven, even where erratic care and irresponsible behaviour formed a large part of their childhood experience. Sometimes, fathers who feel sadness about harm they have done, or who have been absent or neglectful for periods of their children's development, also look for reparative conversations.

One of the difficulties in implementing family group processes constructed around exploring and possibly reconciling harmful processes from the past between fathers and children is that the same mental phenomena that predisposed to neglectful behaviour in the past might well remain in play in the father's makeup. Unkind aspects of his inner working model of relationships can still be triggered in the context of a family meeting, even though his children are now grown up. The holding context of a young adult group, with its own strengths, observations, and insights, is, however, different to that of childhood, so that a father's behaviour can usually be managed in a different way within it. Exploring levels of emotion, both past and present, can be valuable as long as the therapist is fully aware that anger, stored within the minds of different individuals, is not something safely relegated to childhood. Negative narratives about events where antipathy, neglect, or active unkindness have been a prominent experience in the family retain their power. The therapist needs to stay alert to manage boundaries safely if called upon to do so. In similar ways, however, the positive qualities of a father who has "offended" his children will also be present in the room, so danger co-exists side by side with warmth and hope. An optimism about the value of reconciliation has usually moved me in the direction of facilitating such meetings when the wish comes from a young person, now more mature, who wishes to make further attempts at sorting things out with a parent.

## Intergenerational conversations about shared minds

Forgiveness itself might be secondary, as an intention, to the exploration of the shared story of the past from different perspectives. Sharing a story itself opens up dialogue that contains new possibilities of naming and thinking about experience, remembering events linked to mourning about what did not go well linked to willingness to explore current understanding about these past times. As families talk around what has taken place, losses, missed opportunities, and recognition of different perspectives jointly faced co-exist in the space between them. However, where the wishes of one person, the father, have, at an earlier time, missed the needs of other people, the children, such meetings require a deep intent to understand better, so that the realities of the child's former experience do not get missed again in the present. At times, a father might be too wrapped up in his own version of his fatherhood to hear what he is being told. For example, Adam said to his daughter, "We spent most of our time together at one time in our lives . . .we had a shared mind. . . . I still have a detailed memory from long ago of how we were seen as a couple within the family, but I seem to have very little sense of self now . . . it is as though everything that happened, happened to someone else called Adam and

I really don't know who he is . . . my love for you has never diminished in any way." The idea of a shared mind has been used by a number of fathers whose children did not wish to share his view or his mind from their own perspective: "Taken over, yes, but shared, no."

Paolo said to his daughter, Rosa, that it was obvious to everyone in the family "that you and I had a special relationship . . . a twosome in a larger system of five. You were the baby of the family and [to me], while she was her mother's delight, I was the one whose mind she shared." Rosa, who had been her mother's emotional carer and assigned companion since she was six years old, wanted a different acknowledgement, of the danger to her of her mother's "madness" which she had monitored and soothed until she was old enough to leave home safely. "It's not that I wanted to *share* his mind; he was my safety. Mum was ill all day and I was sharing my mind with a person who wasn't there. He should see that now."

Habiba, whose father's disciplinarian behaviour in the context of a passionate attachment for her had led her to study away from home, concluded a marathon family session of several hours with this negative reflection (written) about her father: "Fear, cowardice, timidity, insecurity, passivity has ended the attempt that mum made to initiate a better understanding of dad. Mother wants what's best for her kids; Daddy only wants what's best for Daddy, that is peace and quiet, pandering to his delusion of dignity ('respect'), a good reflection on himself (status) and the opportunity to control and manipulate, or to 'give guidance'."

### *Forgiveness and family courage—Kit, Paul, and their family: "the shit and the love"*

How important is it for both children and parents that forgiveness for the hurts of the past takes place? And how important is it for this to be openly shared, rather than something that might slowly happen inside one individual? Is recognition of the context in which wrong-doing took place more possible in adult life, and does it also enable shifts in perspective around childhood victimisation at different generational levels? A father who has been seen as neglectful, or even cruel, in one generational context can additionally and alternatively be reconstructed as having once been a victim in a former generational context (the bully as a victim in his own childhood). This allows a different framing of subsequent life events that can be jointly explored. The fact that exploration is interactional pushes the conversation between past and present, so that at one moment a mother can say, "I was only sixteen at the time I had you", a daughter (now many years older than her mother was then) can explore that perspective, "You could only do what you knew at the time, you were desperate to keep daddy", and another daughter can think about the different experience of her over-disciplined brother, "We kept our childhoods at the expense of his." The interplay between the past, present, and future of the participants on behalf of one another can soften rigidities of view because the associated strong emotion that is present is accepted by all in the room. However, this very freedom can also lead to the expression of strong views about the right to have had a different relationship with a different father.

Kit and his father, Paul, had a relationship that dated back to his birth, although his father had never lived with his mother, Bella. Over time, there were many variations on neglect and instability in Kit's life. His parents' relationship was marked by binges of alcohol and drug use from which Bella had died young. Paul's memory remained impaired for details and dates of the early relationship he had with Bella, but he knew that, although erratic, he had hung in there with his son in imperfect ways. During the same period, he had a second family in which he had another son and a daughter. Kit had been in and out of care a number of times and, early in our work together, we decided to reconstruct as detailed a history of the care Kit had received as was possible, with the use of contemporary records from the local authority children's department of the time. The work which Kit and his father undertook, both individually and jointly, going through files in addition to diaries kept by Paul, was both painful and hopeful, Kit saying to his father, "Well, I can see you tried at least." The atmosphere in the room was often charged with what neither of them felt ready to speak out loud, and childhood memory would occasionally burst through in painful ways. As Paul said about himself, "I have a cruel streak . . . you were such a little runt, I couldn't hold back from bullying you." This made Kit pull back from him in the work together, so that the process between them stopped for a few weeks until he felt more balanced in his adult self.

Kit was tormented by the question of whether his father had known that he was being badly treated by one of his foster mothers, Paul's "other partner", Dervla, where he was later placed by Paul, while he, Paul, was away working. Kit felt sufficiently secure in the work he had done with his father to request the larger family to gather for a whole family meeting. Paul and Kit met with Dervla and her son and daughter, Paul's other family. "I was caught up in my job, and I didn't recognise Kit's signs that he was distressed, and needing protection. It's like I was aware at one level but at another I didn't want to act on the knowledge. A moment came when I had to face it and I decided to take him away and look after him myself. I could see he wasn't happy . . . the vibes finally reached me . . . unhappy like I was unhappy as a child at boarding school." As a child, Paul himself had been bullied and beaten by his father (Kit's grandfather) to "make a man" of him. As with other fathers whose guilt has threatened to overwhelm them during a family meeting, we focused on the intrinsic goodness in his intentions: "You attempted to be both mother and father to Kit at different times." The stable base of a mother had not existed for Kit since he was four years old, and had been very patchy prior to that, and Paul had to accept that he could not make it all up to Kit by talking through it in adult life. For Kit, seeing the evidence that his father had put in time and finance towards his care over the early years, as well as looking after him directly, if raggedly, in his later childhood, gave him a new sense that his dad had thought about him.

Kit's half-sister and his half-brother had also been fostered for a six month period while their own mother, Paul's partner Dervla, was unwell. They had all wished for a time when Kit and Dervla (their mother and, for a period, his foster mother) could "sit down in a room together comfortably", and for "everyone to share the truth so that people could heal". Dervla said she was also very scared that what might "come out of this meeting could affect us all in the present". She reminded everyone that she had not felt like a parent at the time she had been asked to look after Kit, more like an older sister, an overwhelmed young woman with two children of her own, in her early twenties and drinking heavily to manage her stress. "I never thought of myself as a mother to Kit, but more of a minder while his father was away."

Early in his life, Kit had been admitted to care, due to lack of safety in the home with his own mother Bella, who had worked full-time and was also a heavy drinker. His care throughout his pre-school years, involving a number of child-minders, had been erratic, and, following his mother's death, he had also been placed with foster parents prior to living with Dervla. There was a lot of emotion in the reliving of a tempestuous year in Dervla's household, where each person's memories of neglect of Kit, as the youngest member of the household, were shared. "We decided to keep quiet about a lot of things to keep the family together." Dervla spoke of her own helplessness, the sense that she could not manage three children and should not have been put in that position, as well as her identification with how Kit was suffering, as she herself had suffered in her childhood as a child abandoned by her own mother. "Was I neglecting Kit like my mother neglected me?" she mused. The last straw for her was when Paul left to work on a series in Ireland, and she believed he would not come back. "I had no reserves left, and thought I just couldn't make it with Kit because he was the child of another relationship . . . not a blood tie, though he was Paul's child . . . but he sent money and he did come back in the end."

The younger generation all contributed. Dervla's daughter Bridie said forcibly, "You had two children of your own and then a third child to look after . . . a person who can be so unkind to a child is like an abuser . . . child abuse is a terrible taboo and we haven't been able to talk about it in this family until now; I feel pity for all of us." Kit brought a further dimension into the room: the cruelty that he had experienced from his father in one of the sessions we had together and his outrage about this experience. "I experienced a lot of energy in a cruel way . . . not just helplessness and being overwhelmed. I don't know if I will ever understand that, as it must have been part of what happened." His half-brother, Ryan, spoke of his own fears that he might not become a good enough father because of the experiences he had lived through. Bridie told her parents, "You both have little people inside you who have been abused and we can't trust what you will come out with." Dervla asked bravely, "If we go to that place, will you go with willingness? We can just do 'passing' or we can go into the depths of it." Kit spoke of his fear of this: "Bringing it into the room to have it witnessed, speaking it out, I found myself wanting to keep things hidden after our first meeting, the idea that I was treated with shame and neglect." In looking into the detail of "shame and neglect", it was also important to recognise Dervla's generosity in the attempt to take a third child into her life at a time when she herself felt uncertain whether Paul would stand by her. The discussion recalled the huge pressure on her to make a home for a child who had had so many changes already (at least six) and who had been born within the time when she was herself having children with Paul. "Seeing someone's profound neediness put me in touch with my own . . . my own terror and the tragedy was that no stability followed because Paul had removed himself from the family at that time. The end point is that we have to accept the shit and the love."

Paul was bemused at the generosity of his children. They were "inspiring" young people. "Once they had spoken out, I felt better . . . the room felt like an even playing field when we finished and it hadn't when we started." He mourned his damaged father self, "I had been waiting for three children to shout at me about abandonment: my inner damaged father was yelling at me saying I was a damaged father in my turn. Instead, I felt held by their justice, represented by them fairly, 'oh yes here we are'." While facing losses for which there were no compensations, the conversations and the work done dissolved the power of the dominant story of antipathy and neglect. History did not have to repeat itself through a third generation of abusive fathering, as Kit had feared and Ryan had expressed.

Qualities of adult conversations that allow children to reconcile with their fathers might not include forgiveness as much as the recognition of new dimensions in him which they had not previously been open to experiencing. These seem to include recognising a father's passionate feelings about them (frequently a depth of emotion not formerly recognised) without feeling overtaken by these, hearing what a father has learnt about himself and his relationships over the years, witnessing his courage to sit through pain and show responsibility, as well as being able to express and acknowledge where he failed in his responsibility to them earlier in their lives and his regrets about this. For a father to share with children how he has changed within his own lifetime can also expand understanding at a common human level. His children will also have different ideas of what a father is and what being a father involves to those he might have had himself, leading to the idea of fatherhood and responsibility being later expanded (Denborough, 2016).

### Final remarks: elasticity in fatherhood–work in progress

This book has addressed work with men on the margins of their families, or in disorganised relationship to them, as well as to their relationships with their children through troubled times in their lives. Within the book, a number of ways of seeking and doing fatherhood have been described, with my admiration for many fathers' persistence, with anger about violence as a medium for expressing emotion, and with a sense of shame that society does so badly by many young men. It seems fatherhood now is moving in different ways, most of which could offer hope for men because they address attachment and connection, rather than distance and dissociation. We are moving steadily towards more nurturing and caring models of involved hands-on fathering. Socially accepted and legitimised models of parenting that include multiple ways of including and doing "dad" are now on the increase.

There is also ongoing development of reliable systems for bringing up children in which men may play more optional parts among a variety of family forms: lone women-led families, gay women partner families, families for whom matrilineal descent remains the logical way to do the bringing up of children. In many communities, of different cultural heritage, each construction of family and the performances of fatherhood or social fatherhood is also subject to negotiation in the twenty-first century, rather than there being common agreements about naming and performing these roles. However, for fathers on the margins of emotional family warmth, such as "looked after" boys, unaccompanied refugee children, sons of mothers or fathers with mental illness, society's responsibility will be to raise men who can still retain more sense of being cared for themselves. This involves offering men childhoods with a range of emotional warmth and expression, teaching them to communicate without recourse to violent actions, and to regard women as friends and equals. The substance of Bateson's warning sixty years ago, about the overarching principle of the dominator culture in Britain, has become less valid, although it is still there, waiting in the wings. The trappings of patriarchy are no longer the basis for most family culture. Giving up attachment to older models of fatherhood requires letting go forever of some aspects of the post-war male identity described in Chapter One, although during periods of change individual men might lack the confidence to relinquish these, and will need wider support from women in both private and public discourses.

Looking at the current generation of younger fathers offers a much more optimistic picture of future fatherhood than imagining that the future will be determined by the past. Watching younger fathers joining more passionately in bringing up their children highlights this change, as do the multiple conversations with other fathers, online as well as in daily life, that were not previously available to aspiring nurturing men.

Perhaps the single greatest piece of learning for me in the course of working alongside fathers, as well as in writing this book, has been the importance for men of finding their own words to give authentic voices to their own experiences in relation to their children, as well as developing appropriate actions to back these up. Words are needed to locate and differentiate between emotions, and to negotiate relationships. When words are more accessible and language more elaborated, then the need for inappropriate physical outbursts is diminished. The development of emotional language needs to grow in addition to ongoing recognition and respect for the mothers of their children, despite whatever ruptures have occurred in the sexual and intimate relations between men and partners. The capacity to express passion, tenderness, protectiveness, and responsibility for the children of the present and the future needs to be nourished and continually translated into fitting actions of fathering, love, and responsibility that endure independently through family rupture and change.

# NOTES

1. This can be thought of, in older systems language, as a second order change within the family itself: in first order change, corrective changes occur within a system that itself remains unchanged; in second order change, the system itself changes, and there is a change in its own internal structure. Second order change is based on feedback that augments deviations, and, thus, initiates the development of new structures of self-organisation.

2. In both American and English studies, factors that bring non-married fathers involvement to an end include an inability to contribute to children's wellbeing financially, lack of employment, feelings of parental incompetence, and strained relationships with mothers who act as gatekeepers. However, no research findings should be viewed as binding. Over the past fifteen years, in men who are active and primary fathers, the capacity to retain fathering as a central task seems to connect to many variables: economic choices about lifestyle, abandoning some ambitions and accepting part-time job opportunities, as well as an ability to accept responsibility for their own children as simply part of the job. "I know it is my way through life . . . whether it be a thread that runs through a lot of my life, and whether it be fatherhood, career, education, and criminality, sexuality, race, all sorts of diverse things . . . they have all in their different ways impacted

upon me deciding to bring up my daughter . . . I was really lucky that I grew up in a time when there was beginning to be discussion about we didn't have to be this restricted nation and I didn't have to go and do that job thing" (Jim, 2000, personal communication).

3. There are longer term implications of leaving a child in the first year of life. Bradshaw and colleagues (1999), pointed out that one tangible form of staking a claim to a child is for a father to provide for them economically. In none of the families described above had the biological father done this. Where a mother perceives or frames a separation as an unjust abandonment, and it happens early in a child's life, the wound of being "left to manage" as a lone parent might not be healed by either adequate maintenance or the provision of a home, but provision soothes rather than amplifies loss. By the act of leaving, a father, unless he shows strong determination to play an equal part in his child's life, becomes a "secondary" parent, and a child's mother who objects to his participation in his child's life can undermine this goal in a number of ways, fuelled by her own sense of injustice.

# REFERENCES

Adie, K. (2013). *Fighting on the Home Front: The Legacy of Women in World War One*. London: Hodder & Stoughton.

Arnold, E. (2012). *Working with Families of African Caribbean Origin: Understanding Issues around Immigration and Attachment*. London: Jessica Kingsley.

Ayres, G. (2014). Recognising and working with parental alienation (PowerPoint presentation shared by the presenter at the Association of Family Therapy, Jersey).

Barnes, J., Belsky, J., Broomfield, K. A., Dave, S., Frost, M., Melhuish, E., & The National Evaluation of Sure Start Research Team: Harper, G., Leyland, A., & McLeod, A. (2005). Disadvantaged but different: variations among deprived communities in relation to child and family well-being. *Journal of Child Psychology and Psychiatry*, 46(9): 952–962.

Bateson, G. (1973a). Morale and national character. In: *Steps to an Ecology of Mind* (pp. 62–88). St Albans: Paladin.

Bateson, G. (1973b). Style, grace and information in primitive art. In: *Steps to an Ecology of Mind* (pp. 101–125). St Albans: Paladin.

Bateson, G. (1973c). The effects of human purpose on conscious adaptation. In: *Steps to Ecology of Mind* (pp. 415–422). St Albans: Paladin.

Bateson, P. P. G. (1976). Rules and reciprocity in behavioural development. In: P. P. G. Bateson & R. Hinde (Eds.), *Growing Points in Ethology*. Cambridge: Cambridge University Press.

BBC (2015). *Debate on International Women's Day, 'Can Porn Empower Women'*, 8 March.

Beauchaine, T. P., Neuhaus, E., Zalewski, M., Crowell, S. E., & Potapova, N. (2011). The effects of allostatic load on neural systems subserving motivation, mood regulation, and social affiliation. In: *Development and Psychopathology, 23*: 975–999. Cambridge University Press.

Bifulco, A., & Thomas, G. (2013). *Understanding Adult Attachment in Family Relationships*. London: Routledge.

Blow, K., & Daniel, G. (2002). Post-divorce processes and contact disputes. *Journal of Family Therapy, 24*(1): 85–103.

Bowlby, J. (1951). *Maternal Care and Mental Health*. Geneva: World Health Organisation, Series 2.

Bowlby, J. (1953). *Child Care and the Growth of Maternal Love*. London: Penguin.

Bowlby, J. (1969). *Attachment and Loss* (Vol. 1: Attachment). Harmondsworth: Penguin.

Bowlby, J. (1973). *Attachment and Loss* (Vol. 2: Separation anxiety and Anger). London: Hogarth Press.

Bowlby, J. (1981). *Attachment and Loss* (Vol. 3: Loss, Sadness and Depression). London: Hogarth Press.

Bowlby, J. (1984). Violence in the family as a disorder of the attachment and caregiving systems. *American Journal of Psychoanalysis, 44*: 9–27.

Bradshaw, J. (1999). *Absent Fathers*. London: Routledge.

Brannen, J., & O'Brien, M. (1996). *Children in Families: Research and Policy*. London: Falmer Press.

Brannen, J., Moss, P., Owen, C., & Skinner, C. (1997). *Mothers, Fathers and Employment: Parents and the Labour Market in Britain 1984–1994*. London: Department for Education & Employment.

Bream, V., & Buchanan, A. (2003). Distress among children whose separated or divorced parents cannot agree arrangements for them. *British Journal of Social Work, 33*: 227–238.

Bugental, D. B. (2000). Acquisition of the algorithms of social life: a domain based approach. *Psychological Bulletin, 126*: 187–219.

Burck, C., & Daniel, G. (1995). *Gender and Family Therapy*. London: Karnac.

Burghes, L., Clarke, L., & Cronin, N. (1997). Fathers and fatherhood in Britain. *Occasional Paper, 23*: 1–93.

Byrne, J. G., O'Connor, T. G., Marvin, R. S., & Whelan, W. F. (2005). Practitioner review: the contribution of attachment theory to child custody assessments. *Journal of Child Psychology and Psychiatry, 46*(2): 115–127.

Cabrera, N. J., Tamis-LeMonda, C. S., Bradley, R. H., Hofferth, S., & Lamb, M. E. (2000). Fatherhood in the twenty-first century. *Child Development*, 71: 127–136.

CAP (Child Arrangements Programme) (2014). *Guiding Legislation for Private Law*. London: Child and Family Court Advisory Service.

Carlson, M. J., McLanahan, S. S., & Brooks Gunn, J. (2008). Co-parenting and non-resident fathers' involvement with young children after a non-marital birth. *Demography*, 45: 461–488.

Child, N. (2016). *Climbing the Mountain*. http:thealienationexperience.org. United Kingdom.

Children Act (1989). Welfare checklist and 16A of the act—duty to risk assess. Practice Direction—Domestic Violence and Harm. London: Child and Family Court Advisory Service.

Cicchetti, D. (2011). Allostatic Load. In: *Development and Psychopathology*, 23: 723–724. Cambridge University Press.

Collier, R., & Sheldon, S. (2008). *Fragmenting Fatherhood: A Socio-legal Study*. Oxford: Hart.

Cooke, R., (2013). *Her Brilliant Career: Ten Extraordinary Women of the Fifties*. London: Virago.

Cooklin, A. (2004). *Being Seen and Heard. The Needs of Children of Parents with Mental Health Illness*. DVD and Training Pack. London: Royal College of Psychiatrists.

Cooklin, A. (2006). Children as carers of parents with mental illness. *Psychiatry*, 5(1): 32–35.

Cooklin, A. (2010). Living upside down: being a young carer of a parent with mental illness. *Advances in Psychiatric Treatment*, 16(2): 141–146.

Cooklin, A. (2013). Children's resilience to parental mental illness: engaging the child's thinking. *Advances in Psychiatric Treatment*, 19: 229–240.

Cooklin, A., & Njoku, C. (2009). *When a Parent Has a Mental Illness*. London: Royal College of Psychiatrists.

Cooklin, A., Bishop, P., Francis, D., Fagin, L., & Asen, E. (2012). *The Kidstime Workshops: A Multi-Family Social Intervention for the Effects of Parental Mental Illness*. London: CAMHS Press.

Cooklin, C., & Hyde, A. (2014). *Developing Private Law Skills*. London: Children and Family Court Advisory and Support Service.

Cox, M. J., Mills-Koonce, R., Propper, C., & Gariépy, J. L. (2010). Systems theory and cascades in developmental psychology. *Development and Psychopathology*, 22: 497–506.

Cummings, E. M., & Davies, P. (2002). Effects of marital conflict on children: recent advances and emerging themes in process oriented research. *Journal of Child Psychology and Psychiatry*, 243: 31–63.

Cummings, E. M., Merrilees, C. E., & George, M. W. (2010). Fathers, marriages and families: re-visiting and updating the framework for fathering. In: M. Lamb (Ed.), *The Role of the Father in Child Development* (5th edn) (pp. 154–176). Cambridge: John Wiley.

Cummings, E. M., Simpson, K. S., & Wilson, A. (1993). Children's responses to inter-adult anger as a function of information about resolution. *Developmental Psychology, 29*(6): 978–985.

Davis, K., & Andra, M. (2000). Stalking perpetrators and psychological maltreatment on partners, anger jealousy, attachment insecurity, need of control and break up context. *Violence and Victims, 15*: 407–425.

Denborough, D. (2016). Coming to reasonable terms with our histories. In: S. McNab & K. Partridge (Eds.), *Creative Positions in Adult Mental Health* (pp. 67–86). London: Karnac.

Dermott, E. (2008). *Intimate Fatherhood: A Sociological Analysis*. London: Routledge.

Doucet, A. (2006). *Do Men Mother? Fathering, Care, and Domestic Responsibility*. Toronto: University of Toronto Press.

Dowling, E., & Gorell Barnes, G. (1999). *Working with Children and Parents through Separation and Divorce*. London: Palgrave Macmillan.

Duffell, N. (2000). *The Making of Them: The British Attitude to Children and the Boarding School System*. London: Lone Arrow Press.

Dunn, J. (2002). The adjustment of children in step-families: lessons from community studies. *Child and Adolescent Mental Health, 7*(4): 154–161.

Dunn, J. (2004). Understanding children's family worlds: family transitions and children's outcome. *Merrill-Palmer Quarterly, 50*(3): 224–235.

Dunn, J., & Deater Deckard, K. (2001). *Children's Views of Their Changing Families*. York: Joseph Rowntree Foundation.

Dunn, J., Brown, J. R., & Beardsall, L. (1991). Family talk about feeling states and children's later understanding of other emotions. *Developmental Psychology, 27*: 448–453.

Dunn, J., Cheng, H., O'Connor, T. G., & Bridges, L. (2004). Children's perspectives on their relationships with their non-resident fathers: influences, outcomes and implications. *Journal of Child Psychology and Psychiatry, 45*(3): 553–566.

Dunn, J., Davies, L. C., & O'Connor, T. (2000). Parents and partners life course and family experiences: links with parent–child relationship in different family settings. *Journal of Child Psychology and Psychiatry, 41*(8): 955–968.

Emde, R. N. (1988). The effect of relationships on relationships: developmental approach to clinical intervention. In: R. A. Hinde & J. Stevenson-

Hinde (Eds.), *Relationships Within Families: Mutual Influences* (pp. 354–367). Oxford: Oxford Scientific.

Fabricius, W. V., Braver, S. L., Diaz, P., & Velez, C. E. (2010). Custody and parenting time: links to family relationships and well-being after divorce. In: M. E. Lamb (Ed.), *The Role of the Father in Child Development* (pp. 201–240). Hoboken, NJ: John Wiley & Sons.

Fakhry Davids, M. (2002). Fathers in the internal world: from boy to man to father. In: J. Trowell & A. Etchegoyen (Eds), *The Importance of Fathers: A Psychoanalytic Re-evaluation* (pp. 67–92). London: New Library of Psychoanalysis, Kakhry Davids.

Fatherhood Institute (2012). The United Kingdom's fatherhood think and do tank. www.fatherhoodinstitute.

Fearon, P., Schmueli-Goetz, Y., Viding, E., Fonagy, P., & Plomin, R. (2014a). Genetic and environmental influences on adolescent attachment. *Journal of Child Psychology and Psychiatry, 55*(9): 1033–1041.

Fearon, P., Schmueli-Goetz, Y., Viding, E., Fonagy, P. & Plomin, R. (2014b). Genetic and influences on adolescent attachment security: an empirical reminder of biology and the complexities of development – a reply to Rutter. *Journal of Child Psychology and Psychiatry 55*(9): 1043–1046.

Featherstone, B. (2009). *Contemporary Fathering: Theory, Policy and Practice.* Bristol: Policy Press.

Feldman, R. (2007). Parent–infant synchrony and the construction of shared timing: physiological precursors, developmental outcomes and risk conditions. *Journal of Child Psychology and Psychiatry, 48*(3–4): 329–354.

Fletcher, R. (1962). *The Family and Marriage.* London: Penguin Special.

Flouri, E. (2005). *Fathering and Child Outcomes.* Chichester: John Wiley.

Flouri, E. (2008). Fathering and adolescents' adjustment: the role of father's involvement; residence and biology status. *Childcare, Health and Development, 34*: 152–161.

Flouri, E., & Buchanan, A. (2004). Early father's and mother's involvement and children's later educational outcomes. *British Journal of Educational Psychology, 74*: 14–153.

Fonagy, P. (1999). Male perpetrators of violence against women: an attachment theory perspective. *Journal of Applied Psychoanalytic Studies, 1*(1): 7–27.

Fonagy, P., Gergely, G., Jurist, E. L., & Target, M. (2004). *Affect Regulation, Mentalization and the Development of the Self.* New York: Analytic Press.

Fonagy, P., Moran, G. S., & Target, M. (1993). Aggression and the psychological self. *International Journal of Psychoanalysis, 74*: 471–485.

Frosh, S. (1997). Fathers' ambivalence (too). In: B. Featherstone & W. Hollway (Eds.), *Mothering and Ambivalence* (pp. 37–53). London: Routledge.

Gabb, J. (2010). *Researching Intimacy in Families*. Basingstoke, London: Palgrave Macmillan.

Gallese, V. (2009). Motor abstraction: a neuroscientific account of how actions, goals and intentions are mapped and understood. *Psychological Research PRPF*, 73(4): 486–498.

Ganzel, B. L., & Morris, P. A. (2011). Allostasis and the developing human brain: explicit consideration of implicit models. *Development and Psychopathology*, 23: 955–974.

Gavron, H. (1966). *The Captive Wife: Conflicts of Housebound Mothers*. London: Routledge & Kegan Paul.

Gavron, J. (2015). A *Woman on the Edge of Time*. London: Scribe.

Geertz, C. (1983). *Local Knowledge: Further Essays in Interpretive Anthropology*. New York: Basic Books.

George, J., & Stith, S. M. (2014). An updated feminist view of intimate partner violence. *Family Process*, 53: 179–193.

Goldman, R. N., & Greenberg, L. (2013). Working with identity and self-soothing in emotion focused therapy for couples. *Family Process*, 52: 62–82.

Goldner, V. (1991). Feminism and systemic practice: two critical traditions in transition. *Journal of Family Therapy*, 13: 95–115.

Goldner, V. (1998). The treatment of violence and victimisation in intimate relationships. *Family Process*, 37(3): 263–286.

Goldner, V., Penn, P., Sheinberg, M., & Walker, G. (1990). Love and violence: gender paradoxes in volatile attachments. *Family Process*, 29: 343–364.

Golombok, S., & Tasker, F. (2010). Gay fathers. In: M. E. Lamb (Ed.), *The Role of the Father in Child Development* (pp. 319–340). Hoboken, NJ: John Wiley & Sons.

Golombok, S., & Tasker, F. (2015). Socio-emotional development in changing family contexts. In: R. M. Lerner & M. E. Lamb (Eds.), *Handbook of Child Psychology and Developmental Science, Vol. 3* (7th edn) (pp. 419–463). Hoboken, NJ: Wiley.

Gorell Barnes, G. (1985). Systems theory and family theory. In: M. Rutter & L. Hersov (Eds.), *Child and Adolescent Psychiatry: Modern Approaches* (2nd edn) (pp. 216–232). Oxford: Blackwell Scientific.

Gorell Barnes, G. (1990). The "little woman" and the world of work. In: A. Miller & R. Perelberg (Eds.), *Gender and Power* (pp. 221–244). London: Routledge.

Gorell Barnes, G. (1995). The intersubjective mind. In: M. Yelloly (Ed.), *Learning and Teaching in Social Work: Towards Reflective Practice* (pp. 85–102). London: Jessica Kingsley.

Gorell Barnes, G. (2002). Getting it right and getting it wrong (confronting racism in personal experience). In: B. Mason, & A. Sawyer (Eds.), *Exploring the Unsaid, Creativity, Risks, and Dilemmas in Working Cross-culturally* (pp. 133–147). London: Karnac.

Gorell Barnes, G. (2005). Narratives of attachment in post-divorce contact disputes: developing an intersubjective understanding. In: A. Vetere & E. Dowling (Eds.), *Narrative Therapies with Children and Their Families* (pp. 188–204). London: Routledge.

Gorell Barnes, G. (2011). Early family therapy in London in the 1960s: the Welfare State, Woodberry Down and Robin Skynner. *Context, 115*: 21–24.

Gorell Barnes, G. (2015). Narratives of attachment and processes of alienation in post divorce parenting disputes. In: A. Vetere & E. Dowling (Eds.), *Narrative Therapies with Children and Their Families: a Practitioners Guide to Concepts and Approaches* (pp. 182–198). London: Routledge.

Gorell Barnes, G., & Bratley, M. (2000). Fathers and their children: what holds them together? Unpublished manuscript, Tavistock Clinic, London.

Gorell Barnes, G., Thompson, P., Daniel, G., & Burchardt, N. (1998). *Growing Up in Step-families*. Oxford: Clarendon Press.

Greenberg, M., & Morris, N. (1974). Engrossment: the new-born's impact on the new father. *American Journal of Orthopsychiatry, 44*: 520–531.

Grossman, K., Grossman, K. E., Fremmer Bombik, E., Kindler, H., Sheurere Englisch, H., & Zimmerman, P. (2002). The uniqueness of the child father attachment relationship: Fathers sensitive and challenging play: a 16 year-long study. Social *Development, 11*: 307–331.

Harold, G. T., Leve, L. D., Elam, K., Thapar, A., Neiderhiser, J., Natsuaki, M., Shaw, D., & Reiss, D. (2013). The nature of nurture: disentangling passive genotype-envionment correlation from family relationship influences on children's externalising problems. *Journal of Family Psychology, 27*(1): 12–21.

Hawkins, A. L., & Haskett, M. E. (2014). Internal working models and adjustment of physically abused children: the mediating role of self-regulatory abilities. *Journal of Child Psychology and Psychiatry*, 135–143.

Hendrick Harris, J., Black, D., & Kaplan, T. (2000). *Father Kills Mother: Guiding Children through Trauma and Grief*. London: Routledge.

Hetherington, E. M. (1989). Coping with family transitions: winners, losers and survivors. *Child Development, 60*: 1–7.

Hill, J. (2002). Parental psychiatric disorder and the attachment relationship. In: M. Göpfert, J. Webster, & M. V. Seeman (Eds.), *Parental Psychiatric Disorder: Distressed Parents and Their Families* (pp. 50–61). Cambridge: Cambridge University Press.

Hill, J., Fonagy, P., Safier, E., & Sargent, J. (2003). The ecology of attachment in the family. *Family Process, 42*(2): 205–221.

Hill, J., Wren, B., Alderton, J., Burck, C., Kennedy, E., Senior, R., Aslam, N., & Browden, N. (2014). The applications of a domains based analysis to family processes: implications for assessment and therapy. *Journal of Family Therapy, 36*: 62–80.

Hinde, R. A. (1979). *Towards Understanding Relationships*. London: Academic Press.

Hinde, R. A., & Stevenson-Hinde, J. (Eds.) (1988). *Relationships Within Families: Mutual Influences*. Oxford: Oxford Scientific.

Hofstadter, D. R. (1979). *Godel, Escher, Bach: An Eternal Golden Braid*. New York: Basic Books.

Howell, B. R., & Sanchez, M. M. (2011). Understanding behavioural effects of early life stress using the reactive scope and allostatic load models, *Development and Psychopathology, 23*: 1001–1016.

Hrdy, S. B. (2009). *Mothers and Others*. Cambridge, MA: Harvard University Press.

Humphreys, C. (2006). Thinking the unthinkable: the implications of research on women and children in relation to domestic violence. In: The Rt Hon Lord Justice Thorpe & R. Budden (Eds.), *Durable Solutions* (pp. 159–169). Bristol: Family Law/Jordans.

Imperial War Museum London Blitz Archives (accessed at: www.iwm. org.United Kingdom/history/the-blitz).

Jacobs, E. (2016). Shared parental leave: the fathers bringing up baby. *Financial Times*, 13 March.

Jenkins, J. M. (2003). Mechanisms in the development of emotional organisation. In: J. Davies (Ed.), *Child Emotional Security and Interpersonal Conflict. Monographs of the Society for Research No. 270. Child Development, 67*: 116–127.

Jenkins, J. M., & Curwen, T. (2008). The longitudinal impact of child gender, maternal depression, and parental hostility on child emotional difficulties. *Journal of American Academy of Child and Adolescent Psychiatry, 47*: 399–405.

Jenkins, J. M., Dunn, J., Rasbash, J., O'Connor, T. G., & Simpson, A. (2005). Mutual influence of marital conflict and children's behaviour problems: shared and non-shared family risks. *Child Development, 76*: 24–39.

Joyce, A. (2014). Maternal perinatal mental illness: the baby's unexperienced breakdown. In: M. Boyle & F. Thomson Salo (Eds.), *The Winnicott Tradition: Lines of Development* (pp. 221–236). London: Karnac.

Keaveny, F., Midgely, N., Asen, E., Beavington, D., Fonagy, P., Jenning-Hobbs, R. (2012). Minding the family mind: the development and initial evaluation of mentalisation based treatment. In: N. Midgely & F. Vrouva (Eds.), *Minding the Child* (pp. 90–113). Hove: Routledge.

Keller, P. S., Cummings, E. M., & Davies, P. (2005). The role of marital discord and parenting in relations between parental problem drinking and child adjustment. *Journal of Child Psychology and Psychiatry, 46*(9): 943–951.

Kiernan, K., & Smith, K. (2003). Unmarried parenthood: new insights from the Millennium Cohort Study 114. *Population Trends, 26*: 26–33.

Kraemer, S. (2000). The fragile male. *British Medical Journal, 32*(321): 1609–1612.

Kraemer, S. (2017). Narratives of fathers and sons: 'There is no such thing as a father'. In: A. Vetere & E. Dowling (Eds.), *Narrative Therapies with Children and Their Families: A Practitioners Guide to Concepts and Approaches* (2nd edn) (pp. 115–132). London: Brunner-Routledge.

Krause, B. (1998). *Therapy Across Cultures*. London: Sage.

Laing, R. D. (1960). *The Divided Self*. London: Tavistock.

Laing, R. D., & Esterson, A. (1964). *Sanity, Madness and the Family*. London: Tavistock.

Lamb, M. E. (Ed.) (1999). *Parenting and Child Development in "Non-traditional" Families*. Mahwah, NJ: Lawrence Erlbaum.

Lamb, M. E. (2013). The changing faces of fatherhood and father child relationships: from fatherhood as status to father as dad. In: M. Fine & F. D. Fincham (Eds.), *Handbook of Family Theories* (pp. 87–104). London: Routledge.

LeDoux, J. (1996). *The Emotional Brain: The Mysterious Underpinnings of Emotional Life*. New York: Touchstone.

Lenzenweger, M. F. (2010). A source, a cascade, a schizoid: a heuristic proposal from the Longitudinal Study of Personality Disorders. *Development and Psychopathology, 22*: 867–881.

Lewis, C., & Lamb, M. E. (2005). Father–child relationships and children's development: a key to durable solutions? The Rt. Hon Lord Justice Thorpe and R. Budden President's Interdisciplinary Conference, Dartington Hall, 30 September–2 October.

Lewis, C., & O'Brien, M. (1987). *Re-Assessing Fatherhood: New Observations on Fathers and the Modern Family*. London: Sage.

Lewis, C., Papacosta, A., & Warin, J. (2002). *Cohabitation Separation and Fatherhood*. York: Joseph Rowntree Foundation.

Lewis, J. M., Beavers, R., Gossett, J. T., & Phillips, V. A. (1976). *No Single Thread: Psychological Health in Family Systems*. New York: Brunner Mazel.

Lieberman, A. F., Chu, A., Van Horn, P., & Harris, W. W. (2011). Trauma in early childhood: empirical evidence and clinical implications. *Development and Psychopathology, 23*: 397–410.

Lieberman, A. F., Van Horn, P. J., & Ghosh Ippen, C. (2005). Towards evidence based treatment: child parent psychotherapy with pre-schoolers exposed to marital violence. *Journal of the American Academy of Child and Adolescent Psychiatry, 44*: 1241–1248.

Lorenz, K. (1952). *King Solomon's Ring* (reprinted 1973). London: Routledge.

Luijk, M. P. C. M., Roisman, G. I., Haltigan, J. D., Tiemeier, H., Booth-LaForce, C., Van IJzendoorn, M. H., Belsky, J., Uitterlinden, A. G., Jaddoe, V. W. V., Hofman, A., Verhulst, F. C., Tharner, A., & Bakermanns-Kranenburg, M. J. (2011). Dopaminergic, serotonergic, and oxytonergic candidate genes associated with infant attachment security and disorganization? In search of main and interaction effect. *Journal of Child Psychology and Psychiatry, 52*(12): 1295–1307.

Lummis, T. (1982). The historical dimension of fatherhood: a case study 890–1914. In: L. McGee & M. O'Brien (Eds.), *The Father Figure* (pp. 43–56). London: Tavistock.

Main, M., & Hesse, E. D. (1990). Parents' unresolved traumatic experiences are related to infant disorganized attachment status: is frightened and/or frightening parental behaviour the linking mechanism? In: M. Greenberg, D. Cicchetti, & M. Cummings (Eds.), *Attachment in the Preschool Years* (pp. 161–182). Chicago, IL: University of Chicago Press.

Main, M., Kaplan, N., & Cassidy, J. (1985). Security in infancy, childhood and adulthood: a move to the level of representation. In: I. Bretherton & E. Waters (Eds.), *Growing Points in Attachment Theory and Research. Monographs of the Society for Research in Child Development, Serial No. 209, 50*(1–2): 66–104.

Maitra, B., & Krause, I. B. (2015). *Culture and Madness*. London: Jessica Kingsley.

Masten, A. S., & Cicchetti, D. (2012). Risk and resilience in development and psychopathology: the legacy of Norman Garmzy. *Development and Psychopathology, 24*: 333–334.

Matta, D. S., & Knudson-Martin, C. (2006). Father responsivity: couple processes and the coconstruction of fatherhood. *Family Process, 45*: 19–37.

McCrory, E., De Brito, S. A., & Viding, E. (2011). The impact of childhood maltreatment: a review of neurobiological and genetic factors. *Frontiers in Psychiatry/Child & Neurodevelopmental Psychiatry*, 2(48): 1–14.

McFarlane, W. R., & Cook, W. L. (2007). Family expressed emotion prior to onset of psychosis. *Family Process*, 47: 185–197.

McHale, J., Waller, M. R., & Pearson, J. (2012). Co-parenting interventions for fragile families: what do we know and where do we need to go next? *Family Process*, 51: 284–306.

McIntosh, J. E. (2001). Thought in the face of violence: a child's need. *Child Abuse & Neglect*, 26: 229–241.

McLean, D., Hearle, J., & McGrath, J. (2002). Are services for families with a mentally ill parent adequate? In: M. Göpfert, J. Webster, & M. V. Seeman (Eds.), *Parental Psychiatric Disorder: Distressed Parents and their Families* (pp. 333–344). Cambridge: Cambridge University Press.

Minuchin, P. (1988). Relationships within the family: a systems perspective on development. In: R. A. Hinde, & J. Stevenson-Hinde (Eds.), *Relationships within Families: Mutual Influences* (pp. 7–27). Oxford: Oxford Scientific.

Minuchin, S. (1974). *Families and Family Therapy*. London: Tavistock.

Mogey, J. M. (1956). *Family and Neighbourhood*. Oxford: Oxford University Press.

Montagu, R. (2014). *A Humour of Loving*. London: Quartet.

Moutsiana, C., Johnstone, T., Murray, L., Fearon, P., Cooper, P., Pliatsikas, C., Goodyer, I., & Music, G. (2011). *Nurturing Natures: Attachment and Children's Emotional, Sociocultural, and Brain Development*. Hove: Psychology Press.

Music, G. (2014). *The Good Life: Wellbeing and the New Science of Altruism, Selfishness and Immorality*. London: Routledge.

Newson, J., & Newson, E. (1963). *Patterns of Infant Care in An Urban Community*. London: Allen & Unwin.

Ngu, L., & Florsheim, P. (2011). The development of relational competence among young high risk fathers across the transition to parenthood. *Family Process*, 50(2): 184–202.

Oakley, A. (2014). *Father and Daughter Patriarchy: Gender and Social Science*. London: Policy Press.

Ochs, E., & Taylor, C. (1992). Family narrative as political activity. *Discourse and Society*, 3: 301–340.

Orwell, G. (1941). The art of Donald McGill. In: S. Orwell, & I. Angus (Eds.), *The Collected Essays, Journalism and Letters of George Orwell, Vol. 2: My Country Right or Left 1940–1943* (pp. 155–165). London: Secker and Warburg.

Panter Brick, C., & Leckman, J. F. (2013). Editorial commentary: resilience in child development—interconnected pathways to wellbeing. *Journal of Child Psychology and Psychiatry, 54*(4): 333–336.

Parsons, T., Bales, R. F., Olds, J., Zelditch, M., & Slater, P. E. (1955). *Families Socialisation and Interaction Process*. Glencoe, IL: Free Press.

Paternity Leave Policy United Kingdom (2015). Pay and leave (available at: www.gov.United Kingdom/paternityleave).

Patterson, G. R. (1982). *Coercive Family Process*. Eugene, OR: Castalia.

Patterson, G. R., & Dishion, T. J. (1988). Multilevel family process models: traits, interactions and relationships. In: R. A. Hinde & J. Stevenson-Hinde (Eds.), *Relationships Within Families: Mutual Influences* (pp. 283–310). Oxford: Oxford Scientific.

Patterson, J. E., & Vakili, S. (2014). Relationships, environment, and the brain: how emerging research is changing what we know about the impact of families on human development. *Family Process, 53*: 22–32.

Pedersen, F. A., Anderson, B., & Cain, R. (1980). Parent–infant and husband wife interactions observed at 5 months. In: F. A. Pedersen (Ed.), *The Father–Infant Relationship: Observational Studies in a Family Setting* (pp. 71–86). New York: Praeger.

Perry, A. R., & Langley, C. (2013). Even with the best of intentions: paternal involvement and the theory of planned behavior. *Family Process, 52*: 179–192.

Peskin, M., Raine, A., Gao, Y., Venables, P. H., & Mednick, S. A. (2011). A developmental increase in allostatic load from ages 3 to 11 years is associated with increased schizotypal personality at age 23 years. *Development and Psychopathology, 23*: 1059–1068.

Place, M., Reynolds, J., Cousins, A., & O'Neill, S. (2002). Developing a resilience package for vulnerable children. *Child and Adolescent Mental Health, 7*(4): 162–167.

Portch, C. (2011). Becoming queer and what I did afterwards. *Context, 111*: 8–11.

Priest, P. (2013). Working with men who have experienced childhood family violence. *Context Association of Family Therapy Newsletter, October*: 12–16.

Prior, V., & Glaser, D. (2006). *Understanding Attachment and Attachment Disorders: Theory, Evidence and Practice*. London: Jessica Kingsley.

Propper, C., & Moore, G. A. (2006). The influence of parenting on infant emotionality: a multi-level perspective. *Developmental Review, 26*: 427–460.

Pruett, K. D. (1993). The paternal presence. *Journal of Contemporary Human Services, 74*(1): 46–50.

Ramchandani, P., Domoney, J., Sethna, V., Psychogiou, L., Vlachos, H., & Murray, L. (2013). Do early father–infant interactions predict the onset of externalising behaviours in young children? Findings from a longitudinal cohort study. *Journal of Child Psychology and Psychiatry, 54*(1): 56–64.

Ramchandani, P., Stein, A., & Murray, L. (2009). Effects of parental psychiatric and physical illness on child development. In: M. Gelder, J. J. Lopez-Ibor, N. Andreasen, & J. Geddes (Eds.), *New Oxford Textbook of Psychiatry* (2nd edn) (pp. 1752–1758). Oxford: Oxford University Press.

Raphael-Leff, J. (2008). Paternal orientations in the 21st century. *Psychoanalytic Psychotherapy in South Africa, 16*(1): 61–85.

Renn, P. (2012). *The Silent Past and the Invisible Present: Memory, Trauma and Representation in Psychotherapy*. London: Relational Perspectives Book Series.

Reynolds, V. (2010). Fluid and imperfect ally positioning: some gifts of queer theory. *Context 2011, 111*: 3–17.

Rose, S. (2003). *The Making of Memory from Molecules to Mind*. London: Vintage.

Rutter, M. (1966). *Children of Sick Parents: An Environmental and Psychiatric Study, Maudsley Monograph 16*. London: Open University Press.

Rutter, M. (2015). Attachment is a biological concept: a reflection on Fearon et al 2014. *Journal of Child Psychology and Psychiatry, 55*(9): 1042–1043.

Sandler, J., & Sandler, A.-M. (1978). On the development of object relationships and affects. *International Journal of Psychoanalysis, 59*: 285–296.

Scheff, T. J. (1999). *Being Mentally Ill: A Sociological Theory* (3rd edn). Piscataway, NJ: Aldine Transaction.

Schoppe-Sullivan, S. J., Brown, G. L., Cannon, E. A., Mangelsdorf, S. C., & Sokolowski, M. S. (2008). Maternal gatekeeping, co-parenting quality, and fathering behaviour in families with infants. *Journal of Family Psychology, 22*(3): 389–398.

Schore, A. N. (2001). The effects of early relational trauma on right brain development: affect regulation and infant mental health. *Infant Mental Health Journal, 22*: 201–269.

Scourfield, J. (2006). Gender and child protection. In: B. Featherstone, M. Rivett, & J. Scourfield (Eds.), *Working with Men in Health and Social Care* (pp. 132–148). London: Sage.

Shaw, D. S. (2013). Intervening with challenging families in challenging contexts: making parenting work for children's mental health. *Pittsburgh Early Steps Project and Early Steps Multi Site Study* (accessed at: www.pitt.edu/rppcc).

Sheldon, S. (2005). Reproductive technologies and the legal determination of fatherhood. *Feminist Legal Studies*, *13*(3): 349–362.

Shonkoff, J. P., & Garner, A. S. (2012). The lifelong effects of early childhood adversity and toxic stress. *Paediatrics*, *129*(1): 232–246.

Siegel, J. P. (2013). Breaking the links in intergenerational violence: an emotional regulation perspective. *Family Process*, *52*(2): 163–168.

Skynner, R. (1968). Conjoint family therapy. *Journal of Child Psychology and Psychiatry*, *10*: 81–106.

Skynner, R. (1976). *One Flesh: Separate Persons: Principles of Family and Marital Psychotherapy*. London: Constable.

Sluzki, C. E. (2007). Lyman C Wynne and the transformation of the field of family and schizophrenia. *Family Process*, *46*(2): 143–149.

Smith, G. (2011). How family therapists encounter and respond to hegemonic masculinity in family therapy. Unpublished Doctoral dissertation. London: Birkbeck College.

Snarey, J. P. (1993). *How Fathers Care for the Next Generation; A Four Decade Study*. London: Harvard University Press.

Solomon, J., & George, C. (1999). The development of attachment in separated and divorced families: effects of overnight visitation, parent and couple variables. *Attachment and Human Development*, *1*(1): 2–33.

Sroufe, L. A. (2005). Attachment and development: a prospective, longitudinal study from birth to adulthood. *Attachment and Human Development*, *10*: 349–367.

Sroufe, L. A., & Fleeson, J. (1995). The coherence of family relationships. In: R. A. Hinde & J. Stevenson-Hinde (Eds.), *Relationships Within Families: Mutual Influence* (pp. 27–47). Oxford: Oxford Scientific.

St Aubyn, E. (1992). *Bad News* (in the *Some Hope* trilogy). London: Heinemann.

Steele, H., & Steele, M. (2005). Understanding and resolving emotional conflict: findings from the London Parent–Child Project. In: K. E. Grossman, K. Grossman, & E. Waters (Eds.), *Attachment from Infancy to Adulthood: The Major Longitudinal Studies* (pp. 137–164). New York: Guilford Press.

Stern, D. (1977). *The First Relationship: The Interpersonal World of the Infant*. New York: Basic Books.

Storey, A. E., Walsh, C. J., Quinton, R. L., & Wynne Edwards, R. E. (2000). Hormonal correlates of paternal responsiveness in new and expectant fathers. *Evolution and Human Behaviour*, *21*: 79–95.

Straus, M. A., Gelles, R. J., & Steinmetz, S. K. (1980). *Behind Closed Doors: Violence in the American Family*. Garden City, NY: Anchor Press.

Streeting, J. (2015). Who cares? We do. *Journal of School Health, March*: 24–26.

Sturge, C., & Glaser, D. (2000). Contact and domestic violence – the expert's Court Report. *Family Law, September*: 615–629.

Szasz, T. (1984). *The Myth of Mental Illness* (revised edn). New York: Harper Perennial.

Target, M., & Fonagy, P. (2002). Fathers in modern psychoanalysis and in society: the role of the father in child development. In: J. Trowell, & A. Etchegoyen (Eds.), *The Importance of Fathers: A Psychoanalytic Re-evaluation* (pp. 45–66). London: Brunner-Routledge.

Tomm, K. (1993). The courage to protest: a commentary on Michael White's work. In: S. Gilligan & R. Price (Eds.), *Therapeutic Conversations* (pp. 62–80). New York: W. W. Norton.

Trevarthen, C. (1979). Communication and co-operation in early infancy. A description of primary intersubjectivity. In: A. Bulow (Ed.), *Before Speech: the Beginning of Human Communication* (pp. 321–347). London: Cambridge University Press.

Trinder, L., Kellet, J., & Swift, L. (2008). The relationship between contact and child adjustment in high conflict cases after divorce or separation. *Child & Adolescent Mental Health, 13*(4): 181–187.

Trowell, J., & Etchegoyen, A. (Eds.) (2002). *The Importance of Fathers: A Psychoanalytic Re-evaluation*. London: New Library of Psychoanalysis, Institute of Psychoanalysis Trowel and Etchegoyen.

Van der Kolk, B. (1994). The body keeps the score: memory and the evolving psychobiology of post-traumatic stress. *Harvard Review of Psychiatry, 1*: 253–265.

Van der Kolk, B., & Fisler, R. (1994). Childhood abuse and neglect and loss of self-regulation. *Bulletin of the Menninger Clinic, 58*: 145–168.

Van der Kolk, B., & Fisler, R. (1995). Dissociation and the fragmentary nature of traumatic memories: overview and exploratory study. *Journal of Traumatic Stress, 8*(4): 505–521.

Vik, K., & Hafting, M. (2009). The outside view as facilitator of self-reflection and vitality: a phenomenological approach. *Journal of Reproductive and Infant Psychology, 27*(3): 287–298.

von Bertalanffy, L. (1950). The theory of open systems in physics and biology. *Science, 3*: 25–29.

Walters, A. (2016). Fatherhood is always a work in progress. *Guardian*, 12 November.

Walters, J. (2011). *Working with Fathers*. Basingstoke: Palgrave Macmillan.

Wetherell, M., & Potter, J. (1990). Narrative characters and accounting for violence. In: J. Shotter & K. J. Gergen (Eds.), *Texts of Identity: Inquiries in Social Construction* (pp. 207–219). London: Sage.

Wilkinson, P. O., & Goodyer, I. M. (2011). Childhood adversity and allostatic overload of the hypothalamic–pituitary–adrenal axis: a vulnerability model for depressive disorders. *Development and Psychopathology*, 23: 1017–1037.

Woolgar, M., & Murray, L. (2010). The representation of fathers by children of depressed mothers: refining the meaning of parentification in high-risk samples. *Journal of Child Psychology and Psychiatry*, 51(5): 621–629.

Wynne, L. (1984). The epigenesist of relational systems. A model for understanding family development. *Family Process*, 23: 297–318.

Yoshikawa, H., Aber, J. L., & Beardslee, W. R. (2012). The effects of poverty on the mental emotional and behavioral health of children and youth. *American Psychologist*, 67(4): 272–284.

Young, M., & Willmot, P. (1957). *Family and Kinship in East London*. London: Routledge & Kegan Paul.

Zeanah, C. H., Berlin, L. J., & Boris, N. W. (2011). Practitioner review: clinical applications of attachment theory and research for infants and young children. *Journal of Child Psychology & Psychiatry*, 52(8): 819–833. Oxford: Blackwell.

# INDEX

isolation, 168
level, 2
life, 230
media, 5, 16, 47–48, 78, 94, 110
narratives, xxi, 48
needs, xxiii
networks, 48
norms, 4, 97, 182
orbit, 84
partner, 158
policy, xxvi
position, 5
power, 98
recognition, 3
regulation, 40
relationship, 72
resources, 71
science, xxvi
services, 5, 174
settings, xxviii, 30
situations, 167
status, 232
strata, 179
stress, xxvii
support, 169
systems, 7, 165, 169, 202, 214
underclass, 97
upheaval, 195
values, 19, 98, 155
withdrawal, 102
workers, xv, 214
world, 78
socio-political, 167
Sokolowski, M. S., 104
Solomon, J., 59
sperm donor, 18–19, 47–48, 61–62
Sroufe, L. A., 166
Steele, H., 187
Steele, M., 187
Stein, A., 63, 232
Steinmetz, S. K., 168
Stern, D., 33
Stevenson-Hinde, J., xxvii
Stith, S. M., 173
Storey, A. E., 51
Straus, M. A., 168
Streeting, J., 41, 230
Sturge, C., 216
Swift, L., 96
systemic
    approach, xvii, xxvi, xxvii, 20–21, 30,
        104, 187

change, 8
discourse, xviii
factors, 228
field, 27
framework, xxvi–xxviii, 172
implications, 172
influences, 52
lenses, 172
nature, 181
pattern, 149
psychotherapies, 232
social work, xvi
theory, 21
therapy, xxvi
    family, xxiii
thinking, xii, 21, 225
un-, xxx
understanding, 92
systems thinking, 18, 21
Szasz, T., 225

Tamis-LeMonda, C. S., 7
Target, M., 18, 33–34, 38, 170
Tasker, F., 46, 156–157
Tavistock Clinic, xxv–xxvi
Taylor, C., 120
Thapar, A., 168
Tharner, A., 42
Thomas, G., 36
Thompson, P., 23, 141, 148, 230
Tiemeier, H., 42
Tomm, K., 172
trauma(tic), 190, 212, 219
    childhood, 182
    cumulative relational, 38
    early life events, 213
    existence, 51
    experience, 38, 173, 190, 213, 219, 240
    -influenced difficulties, 212–213
    internal, 38, 190
    memory, 190
    migration, 142
    ongoing, 40
    original, 178
    relationship, 194
    responses, 248
    stress, 40
    transmission of, 190
Trevarthen, C., 34
Trinder, L., 96
Trowell, J., 18